CW00740690

PEMBROKESHIRE'S PAST

Effigy of Sir John Carew who died on 21st February 1637,
St. Mary's Church, Carew Cheriton village.

PEMROKESHIRE'S PAST

JOHN ROOBOL

Pembrokeshire's Past

Published by The Conrad Press Ltd. in the United Kingdom 2024

Tel: +44(0)1227 472 874
www.theconradpress.com
info@theconradpress.com

ISBN 978-1-915494-52-8

Copyright © John Roobol, 2024

Typesetting and Cover Design by:
Charlotte Mouncey, www.bookstyle.co.uk

The Conrad Press logo was designed by Maria Priestley.

Printed and bound in Great Britain by Clays Ltd, Elcograf S.p.A.

Each summer families drive long distances along the motorways to reach the clean air, coastal scenery and green countryside of Pembrokeshire. This volume is written for them and also for anybody who will love reading about one of the most spectacular parts of Britain and seeing images of it, not as a formal history book, but a selection of interesting events and people that have shaped the land found today. It is hoped they will provide the visitor with ideas of places to visit in Pembrokeshire. The stories might also be of interest to local people, for those of us who were in Pembrokeshire schools in the 1950s were not taught local history.

John Roobol January 2024

A NOTE ON RADIOCARBON DATING.

The ages of archaeological sites and artifacts are given in years BP and BC. The understanding of the history and archaeology of Pembrokeshire has recently been much improved by a great wealth of new accurate radiocarbon dates obtained by Professor Mike Parker Pearson and his colleagues with 'The Stones of Stonehenge' and 'The Stonehenge Riverside Project'. Sampled materials have been wood, charcoal fragments and hazenut shells as well as bone and antler. The ages are expressed in years BP meaning 'Before Present' which is 1950, determined from the measured decay of the radioactive isotope of carbon (Carbon 14). 2000 BC would be expressed as 3950 BP. Years BP are then corrected to give a better age expressed as 'years cal BC' or 'AD' and a certain % probability. This means 'Calibrated age in years Before Christ' or 'AD' 'Anno Domini' (counted since the birth of Jesus Christ). So for example two bone samples dated at 4103 +-38 BP and 4105+-35 BP yield a calibrated age of 2870-2490 cal BC at 95% probability. The calibration curves used are based on tree ring growth which corrects for variations in global radiocarbon with time. The religiously neutral terms CE and BCE for 'Common Era' and 'Before Common Era' have not been utilised.

Contents

PLATE CAPTIONS

Plate 1. The entrance to Hoyle's Mouth Cave where Upper Paleolithic hunters sheltered thousands of years ago. The author is sitting where the hunters gathered around their fire.

Plate 2. Tusk of woolly mammoth found when digging foundations for Hakin Bridge, now in Milford Haven Museum. The tusk is approximately one meter long.

Plate 3. Pentre Ifan Neolithic burial chamber. The author's wife Anne gives the scale of the structure.

Plate 4. A large fallen oak tree 5,000 years old, sunken forest, Marros.

Plate 5. The lookout on Foel Eryr, looking south over Llys-y-Fran reservoir.

Plate 6. The Bronze Age stone circle of Gors Fawr.

Plate 7. The Bronze Age stone circle of Dyffryn Syfynwy.

Plate 8. The Iron Age fortified settlement of Foel Drygarn in light snow showing the defensive walls, the three Bronze Age cairns and numerous depressions marking the sites of round huts (Toby Driver, 02/02/2022).

Plate 9. Iron Age round houses at the reconstructed fortified settlement of Castell Henllys.

Plate 10. Carew Celtic Cross.

Plate 11. Nevern Celtic Cross.

Plate 12. Hubba and his Vikings remembered in a Milford Haven carnival.

Plate 13. Pembroke Castle viewed from the north.

Plate 14. Carew Castle viewed from the east.

Plate 15. Pembroke Castle and the adjacent part of the town to the east (right) with a single street and long narrow gardens surrounded by the city wall.

Plate 16. Effigies of Sir John Carew and his wife Dame Elizabeth on their tomb in St. Mary's Church, Carew Cheriton village.

Plate 17. The three sons of Sir John and Dame Elizabeth on their parents' tomb in St. Mary's Church, Carew Cheriton village.

Plate 18. Effigy of unknown knight with crossed legs in a recess at St Mary's Church, Carew Cheriton village.

Plate 19. Effigy of Sir William Malefant on his recessed tomb in Upton Church.

Plate 20. Effigy of a lady on her recessed tomb in Upton Church, possibly Margaret Malefant.

Plate 21. The ruins of Haverfordwest priory with its raised garden beds.

Plate 22. The chancel arch of Pill Priory showing the roofline of the choir and on the right the flight of night steps leading from the monks sleeping quarters into the choir.

Plate 23. Stack Rock Fort – a Palmerston Folly.

Plate 24. Five-meter long palm tree trunk with a heavy coating of goose barnacles on Newgale beach in January 2023.

Plate 25. Two sea beans or tropical drift seeds from Pembrokeshire beaches. Lower left is a snuffbox sea bean (*Entada rheedii*) common on Caribbean beaches, found on Freshwater West beach. Upper right is a bull's eye seed (*Dioclea sp.*) from the Amazon River, found on Lindsway Bay.

Plate 26. Five 'floating stones' collected from Sandy Haven beach. Black scoria of basaltic andesite composition and cream-coloured pumice of dacite composition have travelled 5,000 miles from the Caribbean volcanoes. A fifty pence coin is shown for scale.

FIGURE CAPTIONS

Figure 1. Map of Pembrokeshire showing roads, towns, castles and some historic sites

Figure 2. Map showing the limits of the Devensian Irish Sea and Welsh glaciers (after John, 2018)

Figure 3. Flint blade flake knives of Aurignacian type used by the Upper Paleolithic hunters of South Wales

Figure 4. Upper Paleolithic mammoth hunters attack their prey

Figure 5. Map the land areas around Britain at 16,000 and 8,000 years BC. The lost lands of Cantref y Gwaelod lay under the present Cardigan Bay

Figure 6. A Roman patrol marching out of Wiston Fort

Figure 7. Sketch of the three early medieval Christian inscribed stones probably alongside a Roman Road near Maenclochog village

Figure 8. Sketch of a Viking brass sword hilt guard found on the sea floor at The Smalls

Figure 9. Robert FitzStephen sets out with three ships, 390 men and horses to invade Ireland, leaving the Milford Haven Waterway in May 1169

Figure 10. The champions jousting at the Carew Tournament of August 1507

Figure 11. Currents of the North and South Atlantic Ocean

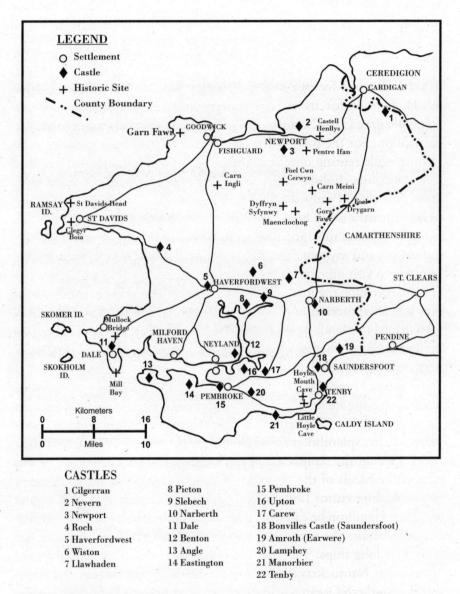

LEGEND

○ Settlement
◆ Castle
+ Historic Site
–··– County Boundary

CEREDIGION
CARDIGAN

Garn Fawr +
GOODWICK
FISHGUARD
NEWPORT
2 Castell Henllys
3
+ Pentre Ifan

Carn Ingli +

Foel Cwn Cerwyn +

+ Carn Meini

Dyffryn Syfynwy +
Maenclochog
Gors Fawr +
Foel Drygarn

RAMSAY ID.
+ St Davids Head
ST DAVIDS
Clegyr Boia

CAMARTHENSHIRE

4 ◆

6 ◆

5 ◆ HAVERFORDWEST
7 ◆

ST. CLEARS

SKOMER ID.
Mullock Bridge ○

8 ◆ 9 ◆

NARBERTH
10 ◆

11 ◆ DALE
SKOKHOLM ID.

MILFORD HAVEN ○
NEYLAND ○
12 ◆
19 ◆
PENDINE
18 ◆
SAUNDERSFOOT

Mill Bay +

13 ◆

16 ◆ 17 ◆
14 ◆ PEMBROKE
15 ◆ 20 ◆

Hoyles Mouth Cave +
TENBY
22 ◆

21 ◆
Little Hoyle Cave

CALDY ISLAND

Kilometers
0   8   16
0   Miles   10

CASTLES

1 Cilgerran	8 Picton	15 Pembroke
2 Nevern	9 Slebech	16 Upton
3 Newport	10 Narberth	17 Carew
4 Roch	11 Dale	18 Bonvilles Castle (Saundersfoot)
5 Haverfordwest	12 Benton	19 Amroth (Earwere)
6 Wiston	13 Angle	20 Lamphey
7 Llawhaden	14 Eastington	21 Manorbier
		22 Tenby

Figure 1. Map of Pembrokeshire showing roads, towns, castles and some historic sites

1. INTRODUCTION.

Pembrokeshire forms a peninsula jutting out into the Irish Sea (Figure 1), famous for its coastal scenery and sandy beaches (now the Pembrokeshire Coast National Park). Today it is a popular summer holiday destination. For the past twelve years I have enjoyed busy summers with visitors while renting out 'The Anchorage' at Sandy Haven for holidays (www.anchorageholidaycottage.com). Surprisingly many of the visitors know little about Pembrokeshire's long history. This volume is not intended to be a formal history book but rather is a series of interesting highlights from Pembrokeshire's long history. These are the things that I would like the visitors and my grandchildren to know and they will give some ideas of places to visit other than the beaches.

After travelling the motorways to Pembrokeshire, these histories should promote an appreciation of some of the people and passions of the past who shaped this land. Be surprised to learn of the vast areas of land during the last Ice Age, when sea levels were much lower and woolly mammoth migrated across these lands.

These past histories tell of the anger of big Sir John Perrot who modelled himself on King Henry VIII and was imprisoned in the tower of London for calling Queen Elizabeth 1st 'a base bastard piskitchin woman'. Gaze in awe at the splendid attire of the effigies of former knights and their ladies. Lament the slaugher of the brave Princess Gwenllian and her two sons at the hands of the Normans. Groan in despair at the injustice to Pembrokeshire visitor Lord Nelson, whose last request that his daughter and Lady Hamilton be cared for if he died for his country at Trafalgar, was ignored. Admire the courage of Robert FitzStephen who in 1169 set out with three long ships, 390 men and horses to invade Ireland. Admire the more recent Nantuckett whalers who came to Milford Haven and established a Southern Ocean whaling industry to supply the lamps and candles for London. Also ponder the execution of John Poyer, former mayor of Tenby, and parliamentrary leader during the Civil War, who refused to surrender his men until their wages had been paid.

Pembrokeshire, jutting out into the vast green Irish Sea is at the receiving end of predominant south-westerly winds, where the seas have eroded high cliffs in the ancient Palaeozoic rocks. The area has gained world recognition for outstanding natural beauty. The creation of the Pembrokeshire Coast National Park in 1952 resulted in the opening up of the coast path over the next twenty years. The National Park has done a great deal to publicise what is there with organised activities, and has an informative website: www.pembrokeshirecoast.org.uk.

The coastline is a major visitor attraction with water sports, sailing, surfing, boating, kayaking, paddle boarding, coasteering, bird watching and fishing being popular in summer. The islands of Skomer and Skokholm off the Dale peninsula are world famous nature reserves. From the coast path especially along the north-west coast from Ramsay Island to Strumble Head, it is possible to watch seals, porpoises, and common dolphins, rarely Riso's dolphins. In recent years whale sightings are increasingly common as they pass the northwest coast to enter Cardigan Bay, especially from the Fishguard to Ireland ferry. Sightings are reported at: http//whaleswales. blogspot.com

Boat trips take visitors to see the coast and its islands with their vast variety of birds including auk, gull, tern, shearwater; gannet, puffin, oystercatcher, white throat, curlew, pigeon, woodpecker, chough, pipit, fulmar, linnet, house martin, black bird, jackdaw, whimbrel, ducks, wren, flycatcher, chaffinch, sand piper, Canada goose, swan, dunlin, swift, pheasant, crow, tit, and guillemot. Skomer Island is popular with its puffins, seals and spring carpets of blue bells. Isolated Grassholm Island has the second biggest gannet colony in the world. Rare visitors in 2021 were a walrus ('Wally') and a hoopoe bird.

Sea and freshwater fishing are both popular tourist activities with boats for hire for fishing trips as well as wildlife cruises. Sea angling produces summer mackerel, bass, cod, pollack, wrasse, flounder, huss, garfish, conger eel, shark, dog fish, salmon, mullet, herring, sole, and gurnard. There are also well-stocked freshwater fishing sites with carp, tench, roach, rudd, perch, pike, eel, bream and gudgeon.

Fishguard in north Pembrokeshire (Figure 1) has a latitude 52 degrees north. On the opposite side of the Atlantic the same latitude corresponds to the coast of Labrador, north of Newfoundland in Canada. There today there are six months of winter snow and ice and the sea freezes in winter. In spring the baby seals are born with white fur on the ice sheets. In contrast Pembrokeshire, jutting out into the Irish Sea, sits in a conveyor belt of warm water that crosses the Atlantic from the Caribbean (the Gulf Stream or North Atlantic Drift). A lot of the flotsam and jetsam on the

Pembrokeshire beaches is carried across the Atlantic from the Caribbean. Turtles, sharks, trigger fish, crayfish and other tropical fauna also arrive in the waters around Pembrokeshire in the same manner. Water-rounded fragments of orange-coloured mahogany bark from the Caribbean are common. But large tree trunks, seeds including coconuts, fish floats and even bottles cross the Atlantic on their long journey, when they grow large goose barnacles. Water rounded blocks of pumice from the Caribbean volcanoes are not uncommon on Pembrokeshire beaches.

So if after a storm you find a tree trunk covered in writhing goose barnacles you know from where it has freshly arrived. Gerald the Welshman who was born in Manorbier Castle in Pembrokeshire recorded in the thirteenth century that monks in Lent had to fast. But certain items classified as not being food could be eaten. The goose barnacles arriving on Pembrokeshire's shores were one of these non-foods. Today not many people eat them but they report that if steamed they are delicious.

In summer the coast path and hedges of Pembrokeshire abound with colourful wild flowers that have been captured by a number of painters and photographers. Honeysuckle is particularly fragrant. In spring the islands and the coast path show snowdrops and primroses, to be followed by bluebells and then pink campion. Blackberries and elderberries abound around the coasts. On the Preseli Mountains in late summer it is possible to see both the purple heather and the yellow gorse in flower together.

The many sea cliffs of Pembrokeshire show a wide variety of ancient rocks in which fossils are common. One very noticeable feature of the Pembrokeshire beaches is that the rocks of the cliffs are of very different types and colors. In the south of the county, the Milford Haven, Gelliswick, Sandy Haven, Lindsway Bay, Dale and Watwick areas are made of the red sandstones and shales of the Devonian Period (416 to 359 million years ago) containing rare fossil fish. The cliffs between Little Haven and Newgale are different with khaki-coloured sedimentary rocks of the Coal Measures of the Carboniferous Period (359 to 299 million years ago). They contain fossil plants and old coal mines and are an extension of the South Wales Coal Field.

The cliffs at Marloes Bay are mainly grey-coloured sediments of the Silurian period (443 to 416 million years ago) where extensive beds of fossil ripple marks can be seen and fossil shells and corals can be found. The south coast of the county around Stackpole, Bosherton and Broad Haven South, show cliffs made of hard grey limestone of the Carboniferous period with large white fossil shells and fossil corals. A splendid block of grey limestone filled with white fossil corals lies on the foreshore at Lydstep (south Pembrokeshire) immediately west of the concrete ramp for boat launching.

In the north of the county the rocks are quite different. They are somber black shales of the Ordovician Period (488 to 443 million years ago) containing graptolite fossils These can be seen in the sea cliffs at Musselwick, Abereiddy and the Blue Lagoon. Within them is an ancient volcanic complex that can be seen in Trefgarne Gorge and at Haycastle.

Some of the rocks of Pembrokeshire have caused considerable interest. There is a huge variety of beach pebbles - many brought from outside Pembrokeshire carried by the ice sheets of the Ice Age. Some of these exotic rocks helped British geologists to piece together the story and trace the paths of the ice sheets of the Great Ice Age from two million to ten thousand years ago. Pieces of the very distinctive Ailsa Craig granite traced the ice path, as do pieces of vesicular basalt and flint from northern Ireland, where there are extensive young basalt lava flows and cliffs of white chalk with flints. Today the bluestones of the inner ring of Stonehenge are causing much controversy. Geologists have matched them with several different outcrops in the Preseli Mountains. But how did they get to Salisbury Plain? A controversy exists today. Many geologists believe the stones were carried there by the ice sheets of the Great Ice Age. But many archaeologists favour their being transported by dragging them or using boats. One well-organised but unsuccessful attempt was made to move a stone from the Preselies by dragging and by raft.

In north Pembrokeshire the rounded hills of the Preseli Mountains were smoothed by over-riding ice sheets during the Great Ice Age. From them looking northward on a clear day, one can see the frost shattered peaks of Snowdonia, where the rocks protruded through the great ice sheets. On clear days the ice smoothed hills of the Wicklow Mountains of Ireland can also be seen.

At the end of the Great Ice Age, much water was locked up in the ice caps and sea level was much lower. The North Sea and English Channel did not exist. Great herds of woolly mammoths migrated north each summer across the site of the future English Channel to their summer grazing site on what is now the floor of the North Sea. Fishermen in Lowestoft and others in Holland regularly find mammoth tusks, teeth and bones in their nets. These are today sold in rock-hound shops in the UK. A single mammoth tusk was dug up in the foundations of the bridge connecting Milford Haven with Hakin and Hubberston and is on display in the Milford Museum.

The surrounding sea and the presence of a large sheltered waterway in the middle of Pembrokeshire have attracted countless generations of seagoing peoples. A brief outline is presented next followed by thirty-five selected topics.

In the limestone caves of south Pembrokeshire and the nearby Gower Peninsula, about 30,000 years ago, Upper Paleolithic remains of early mankind and the cold-weather fauna that he hunted can be found. These people were cave dwellers and hunted amongst other things the woolly mammoth. About 11,000 years ago they were followed by Mesolithic people who lived in a warmer climate and hunted in forests. As the climate warmed, the ice sheets continued to melt and sea level to rise. Around the coasts of Pembrokeshire sunken forests dating back to 7/ 8000 years BC can be seen at very low tides.

Neolithic people arrived around 5 or 6,000 years ago. They were the first farmers and left a rich legacy of megalithic monuments in Pembrokeshire. They were followed by the Bronze Age people who arrived around 4,300 years ago. Sea level had risen by then, so that they probably travelled in boats without ribs made by sewing planks together with yew saplings. Excellent examples of their boats about 4,000 years old have been found and excavated at Dover and on the Humber at East Ferriby in Yorkshire.

The war-like Celts - horsemen and fierce warriors - expanded out of Central Europe. They brought the skill of iron smelting with them around 800 to 600 BC. They crossed the sea in iron-clenched boats. They built fortified farms and villages on the hilltops. Their fortified settlements with stone walls, trenches and earth banks are still very visible today in large numbers on headlands around the coast, inland on hilltops and on the Preseli Mountains in the north of the county. Metal detectorists have found gold torques from the Bronze and Iron Ages in Pembrokeshire.

Next the bays and rivers of Pembrokeshire were used by the Romans who operated a fleet in the Bristol Channel and charted St. David's Head which they named as the Octapitarum Promontorium. The Roman senator and historian Tacitus around the year AD 98 wrote a book about his father-in-law General Julius Agricola in which he recorded 'the swarthy faces of the Silures (the Celtic tribe then occupying south-east Wales), the tendency of their hair to curl and the fact that Spain lies opposite, all lead one to believe that Spaniards crossed in the ancient times and occupied the land.' Two major legionary bases with up to 5,000 troops each, were at Chester and Caerleon. The nearest Roman town to Pembrokeshire was Moridunum – site of today's Carmarthen. Archaeologists have recently discovered a Roman Road extending west from it into Pembrokeshire almost as far as Haverfordwest. A Roman fort for 5,000 auxiliar troops was recently discovered on this road near Wiston.

The Romans were followed by Irish settlers who crossed the 80 mile wide channel to Pembrokeshire. They were the Deisi Tribe of south-east Ireland. The Irish settlers may have been encouraged by the Romans who used them as auxilliary troops. After the Roman withdrawl, larger numbers of Irish tribal groups came to Pembrokeshire and expanded eastwards into Breconshire. The Irish presence in Pembrokeshire is in strong evidence with the Ogham script on burial marker stones. From early Irish chieftains, it has been asserted that the later Welsh princes had Irish roots. One Irish chieftain was called Boia who settled on the St. David's Peninsula. He considerably bothered St. David by sending out naked women to test his monks celibacy. When the northern prince Cunedda (progenitor of the dynasty of Gwynedd) and his successors moved into north Wales (around AD 450 to 460), he forcibly removed the Irish settlers. His son Ceredig did the same in what is now Ceredigeon. Anglesea was also cleared of Irish settlers.

From AD 460 onwards warfare took place along the Saxon (English) frontier. The British people were led by Ambrosius and followed around AD 480 by Arthur. These two leaders established their frontier from Wiltshire to the Cambridge area. London remained British but the Saxons penetrated up to the River Trent boundary. Arthur was victorious in a major battle at Badon around AD 500 possibly in the present day Bath area. Until his death in 515 Arthur's kingdom covered a large area. From 500 to 510 Authur and his generals campaigned against the Irish settlers and the Demetae of south Wales. This resulted in the conquest and expulsion of the Irish from south and west Wales. The result is that today there are many Arthurian place names in south Wales as well as Powys and north Wales. In the oldest book in Wales – the Mabinogion – the legends of King Arthur are recorded including two visits to Pembrokeshire. The Mabinogion also records that King Arthur was a cousin to St. David's mother (Saint Non).

The next wave of invaders were the Vikings. A rather nasty fellow called Hubba or Ubbe Ragnarsson– one of three brothers who conquered much of Britain - wintered in the Milford Haven Wateray in AD 877. Hubba brought twenty-three ships with 2000 men. After wintering he sailed off to be killed in battle in Cornwall when attacking one of King Alfred the Great's strongholds. The Viking legacy in Pembrokeshire is widely scattered with many Norse names such as the islands at the approach to the Milford Haven waterway of Skomer, Skolkholm, Gateholm and place names such as Hasgard Cross (Asgaard) on the Dale peninsula.

Next the Norman war machine took over. They conquered for the land and then built earth and wood castles and finally the great stone castles. The policy of King William I and his son William Rufus was to give the marcher lords (Chester, Shrewsbury, Hereford and Gloucester) a free hand to conquer Wales. All four lords made incursions into Wales. The Montgomery family advanced along the Severn Valley. An expedition under Arnulf Montgomery crossed into Ceredigion and built a fort near Cardigan, near the present Old Castle on the north bank of the Teifi estuary. They then crossed the Preseli Mountains and captured the Pembroke area with a fort where the castle now stands. This fort was attacked by Welsh forces but was defended for Arnulf Montgomery by Gerald of Windsor, whose father was castellian of Windsor Castle. By 1102 Robert Montgomery (Belleme) the Third Earl of Shrewsbury rose against King Henry I. He and his brother Arnulf were banished to France. So Pembroke became king's property.

The Normans tired of the warring Welsh defending their lands and replaced most of the Welsh population of south Pembrokeshire with large numbers of Flemish settlers. The Flemish settlers provided auxiliary troops for the Norman lords. They penetrated Pembrokshire up to a boundary line with the lands of the Bishop of St. Davids (by 1115 the Norman Bishop Bernard). A military line of demarcation ran from the Preseli Mountains to Newgale (before the Landsker Line). The Flemish settlers were mainly in Rhoose (north-west of the Milford Haven waterway) and the Daugleddau area of Wiston, Letterston, and New Moat, but were also strongly settled west of the Cleddau in the Llangwm and adjoining areas.

The Norman invaders built over fifty earth and timber motte and bailey castles to hold their newly seized lands in Pembrokeshire. South Pembrokeshire evolved into a Norman stronghold and great stone castles replaced some of the earlier motte and bailey castles. At this stage there had been intermarrying of the Norman invaders with the daughters of the Welsh princes, so that a new Anglo-Norman hierarchy evolved. The most famous was Welsh Princess Nest who started life as a hostage and concubine to the future king and who eventually gave rise to three great Anglo-Norman families.

King William The First (William the Conqueror) made a pilgrimage to St Davids in 1081 bringing an army (just in case it was needed). But he found many Norse settlers in Pembrokeshire who welcomed their Norman relations from Normandy and there was no fighting. He met and made peace with Rhys ap Tewdwr, the prince of Deheubarth. South Pembrokeshire eventually became a Norman stronghold and stone castles were built on the banks of the Milford Haven Waterway. Princess Nest raised several

Anglo-Norman families. Some of her sons and grandsons were involved in the Norman invasion and conquest of Ireland. The Norman invasion fleets were assembled at Pembroke Castle on the Milford Haven Waterway, and were partly led by Earl Strongbow of Pembroke and later followed by King Henry II with a bigger army. In the twelfth century Princess Nest's grandson Geraldus Cambrensis (Gerald the Welshman), born at Manorbier castle in south Pembrokeshire, wrote extensively about life in Wales and Ireland. The many Norman lords, earls and knights of Pembrokeshire and their ladies left their images in the form of effigies on their tombs.

In 1348 and 1349 about a third of the British population died of the 'Black Death' or bubonic plague. Pembrokeshire was not spared and today there is a house in Dale that is haunted and believed to be built over a plague burial pit.

In 1405, Owain Glyndwr with his army met and joined an invading French army in the Milford Haven Waterway. The French arrived in 140 ships with 800 men at arms, 600 cross bowmen and 1200 lightly armoured troops. The combined armies fought their way across south Wales to unsuccessfully invade England.

In 1435 Henry Tudor landed near Dale in the Milford Haven Waterway and marched against King Richard III. He defeated him at the Battle of Bosworth Field, to establish the Tudor Royal dynasty.

From 1528 to 1531 Roger Barlow of Pembrokeshire, in company with Sebastian Cabot, explored much of South America including Peru for the King of Spain.

In the eighteenth century, Sir William Hamilton married into the Barlow family of Slebech with much land for dowry, before marrying Emma Hamilton. He, with his nephew Charles Greville, established the town and docks at Milford Haven. Greville brought the first settlers from Nantuckett with their whaling ships away from a blockade during the American Civil War, to Milford Haven. They set up a whaling industry in the southern ocean and provided whale oil for the lamps and candles of London. There followed the famous visit of the Hamiltons and Lord Nelson to the new town. Admiral Lord Nelson and the Hamiltons dined at the New Inn, that was renamed the Lord Nelson Hotel in Milford Haven.

In the nineteenth century Lord Palmerston fortified the Milford Haven Waterway and south Pembrokeshire against a French invasion. Vast forts were built of huge shaped blocks of local limestone. With technological advances, they soon became obsolete, but are still prominent around the Milford Haven Waterway.

A great Naval dockyard operated at Pembroke Dock from 1814 to 1926 and 250 warships, as well as five Royal yachts, were built there. At its peak the dockyard employed 3,000 men. In 1930 the former Naval Dockyard was transferred from the Admiralty to the Air Ministry and became an air station. This lasted for twenty-three years until 31st March 1959 when the station closed. The air station expanded steadily until the Second World War. Aircraft hangers and slipways to bring the seaplanes out of the sea were constructed. Flying boats moored off the former dockyard were a daily sight. It became the largest flying boat station in the world and was operational throughout the six years of the war. Its wartime role was to protect convoys in the Battle of the Atlantic. The post-war era was one of a peacetime role for the Sunderland aircraft that continued to fly until the station was closed.

The Milford Haven waterway played a prominent role in both world wars. Convoys were assembled there and many old fortifications are dotted around its entrance. The waterway has brought prosperity to south Pembrokeshire first with the whaling industry (c.1791 to 1821), the fishing industry (1888 to 1959), the oil industry (1960 to present) and now the liquid natural gas (LNG) industry. Today the waterway is one of the main UK ports and one of the main energy centres for Europe. Ship watching is popular from the grassy slopes of 'The Rath' seafront of Milford Haven.

A chronological list of Pembrokeshire's historic events is given as Appendix 1 and a list of historic places to visit in Appendix 2. Some informative websites are listed in Appendix 3.

2. NORTH AND SOUTH PEMBROKESHIRE

Geographically there are two very different parts to Pembrokeshire with the peoples of each being physically different and speaking different languages. The geography, geology, climate and histories of each half are very different. North Pembrokeshire is mountainous with moorland and sheep farming and has a Welsh speaking population with dark eyes and dark hair. It is sometimes referred to as 'The Welshry'. These are the descendants of the ancient British tribes who remarkably have survived many invasions, first by the Romans, then Irish settlers, followed by the Vikings from Denmark and finally came the Normans who invaded England in 1066 and arrived in Pembrokeshire in 1093. These ancient British people of south Wales have many legends about King Arthur and the wizard Merlin, although there is no proof of their presences in the area.

In contrast south Pembrokeshire is a plateau of rich farm land, forests and an Anglo Saxon-Flemish-Norman people who speak English and is sometimes referred to as 'The Englishry'. It was a great Norman stronghold protected by a ring of Norman castles and has long been known as 'Little England beyond Wales'. Because the Welsh people resisted the Norman invasion, the Normans drove the Welsh people out of the south to the cold windswept Preseli Mountains of north Pembrokeshire with their poorer soils. It must have caused considerable hardship in the north as the lands are poorer and could not support a large increase of population.

The Normans replaced the Welsh people with Flemish immigrants (William the Conqueror's wife Matilda was Flemish and the daughter of King Baldwin of Flanders) who came in great numbers and who were loyal to their Norman Lords and would join them in battle as armed foot soldiers. Access throughout the south was via the flooded river valley or ria of the Milford Haven Waterway with its two great branches the Eastern and Western Cleddau rivers. The waterway was vital to the Normans for their later preparations for the departure of their invasion fleets to Ireland from their stronghold of Pembroke castle.

An early desription of the two halves of Pembrokeshire, written in 1603 in Elizabethen times, is given by George Owen of Henllys (Owen,1994).

He reports that at that time there were large numbers of Irish refugees in Pembrokeshire escaping war in Ieland. Owen's account is today well know for his detailed description of the sport of cnapan that was practiced in the Welshry of the north. This sport then evolved into todays rugby. However at that time it was played by several thousand men, some on horseback.

The cnapan was a wooden ball that could be held in the hand, but had been well boiled in grease. The sport was believed to have evolved in ancient times as training for battle. At certain times of the year or when one gentleman challenged another a game would be planned. The annual games were played between the men of the parishes of Emlyn and Cemaes, Newport and Nevern, Eglwyswrw and Meline, and Penrhydd and Llanfihangel Penbedw. As many men as possible were recruited. The players were naked and barefoot except for a pair of breeches. The objective was to get the ball back to the land on one of the two sides. There were no goals to be had and the purpose was to demonstate a good show. Up to 2,000 men would follow the ball for several miles across country jumping over hurdles. A good player might run for several miles with the ball hotly persued by 600 or more players.The game could become rough as the horsemen carried cudgels and it was customary for the footmen to throw stones at them to keep them away. It was normal for fighing to break out between players. After the game the players would return home some with broken heads, black faces, bruised bodies and lame legs yet riotously happy with the stories of the highlights of the game.

There is a sharp line separating the two parts of Pembrokeshire known as the Landsker – a word of Norse origin meaning 'boundary'. The Landsker follows a line of Norman stone castles through the centre of the county from west to east from Roch on the west coast, through Haverfordwest, Picton, Wiston, Llawhaden, and Narbeth to the site of Amroth castle. These castles defended the Norman-held south of the county and separated it from the Welsh of the north. Geographically the landsker passes from Newgale through Treffgarne, to Clarbeston and Narberth and on to the mouth of the River Taf.

On either side of the Landsker Line there are two different cultures. This is seen in the place names that are English in the south and Welsh in the north. It can also be seen in the churches. In the Norman area the churches have battlemented high towers that were used as lookouts over the captured Welsh lands. Some of these towers are remarkably high, for example Carew Cheriton Church built on flat lands near Carew Castle has a tower one hundred feet tall. In the north, the churches are simple affairs with only bellcotes. The Norman churches of south Pembrokeshire are mostly dedicated to Biblical saints such as Peter, Paul, etc. In contrast the welsh churches of the north are mostly dedicated to Welsh saints. Excellent descriptions of the characters of the Englishry, the Welshry and the Landsker are given by John (1976, 1995).

The two parts of Pembrokeshire are refreshingly different. The division started with the Iron Age tribes of Wales – the Celts or Cymri and the mountainous nature of the land. In the far south west from Carmarthen westwards was the land of the Demetae tribe. North Wales was dominated by the Ordovices and the south west by the Silures with a smaller tribe the Deceangli in what is now Flintshire (the latter being the first tribe in Wales defeated by the invading Roman armies). Across what is now the border of Wales and England were the Cornovii in the north and the Dobunni of the south.

The Celts were fierce warrior people who lived in fortified settlements and hill forts and fought competitively on horseback with each other for women, cattle and horses. They collected the heads of their rivals. These fierce warrior people provided a strong resistance against the Roman and later invaders. However after four centuries of Roman occupation, the Celtic citizens of Britain had become Christianised Roman citizens and it seems ironic that they were driven westwards by the pagan Saxon invaders who brought their Germanic gods and goddesses with them to Britain. The Welsh tribes were later assisted in their resistance by Norse settlers and Irish settlers from the east coast of Ireland. The Celts survived sufficiently intact to resist the Norman Invasion, although it was not until around 1100 that most of Wales had been brought under Norman control.

The invasion of Celtic Wales heralded the invasion of Celtic Ireland. The invading Normans were descendants of Norsemen who had settled on the banks of the River Seine in northern France in the tenth century. Their territory became known as Normandy and the people there as North Men or Normans. Duke William of Normandy brought a male army of mercenaries with around 2000 knights and 3,000 bowmen. After the defeat of the Anglo-Saxon British Army in 1066, Britain was subdivided between the Norman barons who built first smaller earth and wood motte and bailey castles and later, on the more important sites, large stone castles to protect themselves and their new holdings (See Figure1).

Pembrokeshire abounds in old mounds of former motte and bailey castles (most Norman but some Welsh) and there are many large stone castles marking the main Norman centres. Many of the Norman fortifications were manned by Flemish mercenaries and the land, its peoples and animals became the property of the invaders, who soon proved to be very effective farmers.

The invasion of Wales was delayed some years because the Welsh prince Rhys ap Tewdwr retained control of the medieval principality of Deheubarth (south Wales) despite Norman raids. When William the Conqueror as King William 1st in 1081 made a pilgrimage through west Wales to St. Davids, he met Prince Rhys ap Tewdwr and according to the Domesday Book, Tewdwr paid him an annual tribute. After the death of King William 1st, Rhys ap Tewdwr was captured and executed in 1093.

Next the Norman Lord William FitzBaldwin advanced from Devon to establish a castle at Carmarthen and the Norman Lord Roger de Montgomery advanced from mid-Wales to establish castles at Cardigan and Pembroke. In 1109 King Henry I granted to Gilbert de Clare 'all the land of Cardigan if he could win it from the Welsh'. What areas they could not subdue by the sword, the Normans went a long way towards controlling by intermarriage with the Welsh. The Norman Walter FitzOther married Gladys, daughter of the Prince of North Wales. His son Gerald married the famous Nest, daughter of Rhys ap Tewdwr, Prince of South Wales. This pattern was repeated with the Norman Invasion of Ireland. Although the Celtic peoples were driven westwards and survive in Cornwall, Wales, Ireland and Scotland, the number of invading Normans was not great enough to destroy the language and culture and their rapid intermarrying resulted in the merging and formation of the hybrid culture that is modern Britain today.

The speed and efficiency of the Norman takeover of Britain is recorded in the Domesday Book of 1086, only twenty years after the invasion. It was ordered by William the Conqueror as a record of what existed in his new kingdom and to provide the basis for the taxes to be collected. The somber name is after the Day of Judgement as the results shown in the book were final.

The Norman lords who took the lands of Britain were ambitious fighting men and must be regarded as considerable adversaries. This applies to their Anglo-Norman, Welsh-Norman and Irish–Norman descendants of today when they stand out in our modern society in times of crisis. Field Marshall Bernard Montgomery was Britain's great field commander in World War II. His ancestor Roger de Montgomery commanded the right wing of the Norman army at Hastings in 1066. The Welsh-Norman descendants of Princes Nest, daughter of Prince Rhys ap Tewdwr, produced several Norman family lines who become the leading Irish Norman families in Ireland.

William the Conqueror and his succeeding sons deliberately installed strong Norman knights at Chester, Shrewsbury, Hereford and Gloucester. They had license to take what land of Wales they could. So over the past 1,000 years, South Pembrokeshire with its ring of Norman castles centring on the Milford Haven Waterway, became the English speaking south of 'Little England beyond Wales'. The Norman invasion of Ireland from Pembroke is told in a later chapter. Prominent in it was Richard de Clare (Earl Strongbow) who went to Ireland in 1168. He was assisting Irish leader Dermot against other Irish leaders. There he married Demot's daughter Aoife. Earl Strongbow died in 1176 leaving a daughter Isabel - a child of three. She was an heiress to vast estates in Wales and Ireland. In 1189 under King Richard I she was married to William Marshall who became Earl of Pembroke. He was responsible for building a large part of the stone Pembroke castle including the great keep. Henry II went to Ireland from Pembrokeshire in 1170 with a large army to prevent Ireland becoming an independent Norman state.

Suggested Further Reading

John, B., 1976, *Pembrokeshire*: David and Charles (Publishers) Ltd., 206 p., ISBN 0 905559 54 1.Reprinted 1984, Greencroft Books, Cilgwyn, Newport, 208 p.

John, B., 1995, *Pembrokeshire – Past and Present*: Greencroft Books, Cilgwyn, Newport, 256 p.

Lockley,R.M., 1957, *Pembrokeshire*: Robert Hale Ltd., London, 1957, 163 p.

Owen, G., 1603, Reprinted 1994, *The Description of Pembrokeshire*: Miles, D., (Ed.), Gomer Press, Llandysul, Dyfed, 319 p.

3. THE GLACIATION OF PEMBROKESHIRE AND THE BLUESTONE CONTROVERSY

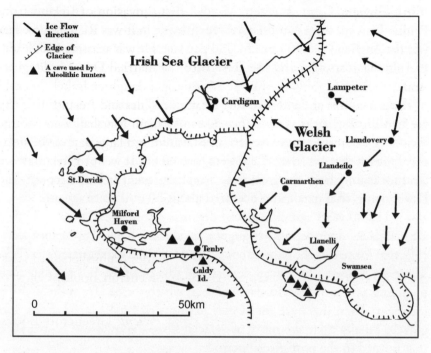

Figure 2. Map showing the limits of the Devensian Irish Sea and Welsh glaciers (after John, 2018)

Ice Ages are times when the northern and southern ends of our planet are coated in ice. Vast amounts of water become tied up in the ice caps, resulting in world sea levels being much lower than they are today. There have been at least five major Ice Ages throughout our planet Earth's long history. Oldest is the Huronian (from 2.4 to 2.1 billion years ago). Next was the Cryogenian (from 720 to 630 million years). This may have been the greatest of all glaciations and produced 'snowball earth', when the glaciers reached the equator. This was followed by the Andean-Saharan glaciation (from 460 to 420 million years) corresponding to the late Ordovician and Silurian periods. Then came the Late Paleozoic glaciation from around 360 to 260 million years. The last one – the Great Ice Age or Quaternary glaciation – started only about two million years ago in the Quaternary period and continues today. It rather looks as if the present time is just one of several interglacial warm periods and there may yet be millions of years more of ice age ahead of us.

The present ice age is divided into two epochs. The Pleistocene runs from 2.588 million years ago to 11,700 years ago. The Holocene runs from 11,700 years ago to the present day and is probably a warm interglacial episode. In the Alps, the Quaternary glacial stages or advances were named Biber, Danube, Gunz, Haslach, Mindel, Riss and Wurm. In Britain, the British-Irish Ice sheet comprised three different stages or advances. Oldest was the Anglian (478,000 to 424,000 years ago), the Wolstonian (300,000 to 130,000 years ago) and the Devensian (about 27,000 to 11,300 years ago).

The glaciations of Pembrokeshire are recorded in surface deposits. There are two distinct areas. The higher parts of Pembrokeshire in the north, including the northern and western coastal areas, have glacial and fluvioglacial deposits that are fresh. They were formed in the last or Devensian Ice advance mainly from the great Irish Sea glacier and the Welsh icecap. The Devensian glacial maximum occurred about 20,000 years ago and ended about 11,700 years ago. The glacial deposits record a glacial cycle. Oldest are periglacial slope deposits of angular rock debris banked up against steep cliffs that formed as the climate cooled and frost and ice shattered the cliffs. These are followed by glacial deposits of tills composed of angular rock fragments of many types in clay matrices, which formed from the melting ice sheet. Then there are meltwater deposits of fluvioglacial sands and gravels. Finally there are more periglacial slope deposits and blown sand that formed in the post-glacial period.

In the lower lands of central and southern Pembrokeshire the glacial remains are not well preserved and are much older and rotten with weathering. This indicates that these areas escaped the Devensian Ice advance and preserved the deposits of earlier glacial advances. The two great ice sheets of the Devensian glaciation are shown for South Wales in Figure 2 (after John, 2018).

When the British Geological Survey first mapped the geology of Pembrokeshire in the nineteenth century, they were able to trace the route of the Irish Sea glacier because of large blocks of 'erratic' rock or 'glacial erratics' scattered in Pembrokeshire. Erratic rocks are blocks of rock not found in Pembrokeshire that were transported here by the ice sheets. The most famous of these are blocks of Ailsa Craig granite. The small island of Ailsa Craig lies off the west coast of Scotland. The granite has a distinctive 'salt and pepper' speckled appearance and is easily recognised. Today the distinctive Ailsa Craig granite is used to make curling stones. Blocks of this granite have been ice rafted into Pembrokeshire from Scotland along the length of the Irish Sea – a distance of up to 600 miles (1,000 km). Other common erratics found in Pembrokeshire (and particularly well seen on the stony beaches of the county), are flint nodules and less commonly cobbles of black fresh vesicular basalt lava. Both of these originate in Antrim in Northern Ireland where relatively young basalt lavas overlie chalk cliffs with lines of flints similar to those of Kent.

There are other indicators of the passage of an ice sheet as it advanced over rock. Blocks of rock carried by the ice can gouge out long linear grooves in the underlying rock. These are called 'glacial striations' and they record the direction of flow of the ice sheet. Rock surfaces polished flat by the passage of ice are called 'glacial pavements'.

Another indicator of ice flow direction is a structure known as a 'roche moutonnee' or a 'sheep like' rock. This forms when the ice flows over a small hill of rock. On the upflow side the rock is ground smooth by the advancing ice. On the downflow side, the ice as it flows away plucks away blocks of rock so the hillside becomes steep and broken. The Preseli Mountains show this structure on a grand scale with smooth northern sides and steep somewhat irregular southern sides particularly well seen on Foel Drygarn, Carningli and Carn Alw. The smooth tops of the Preseli Ridge rise to 536 meters (1759 feet) on Foel Cwm Cerwyn and the smooth top of this ridge as well as directional indicators show that the Devensian ice sheet flowed NW to SE and N to S over them. Dr. Brian John who has made a Ph.D. study of the glaciation of North Pembrokeshire has estimated that in order for the Irish Sea Ice Sheet to be able to flow over the Preseli Mountains, it must have had a minimum thickness of at least 1,600m.

During the Devensian glaciation between about 24,000 and 59,000 years ago conditions were stable, cold and dry, but not as cold as the times immediately before and after it. This was the time of the mammoth steppe because extensive grassland with herbs and scrub existed over a vast area extending from Eurasia to Canada and from the Arctic Islands to China. Over these grasslands numerous herds of woolly mammoth, bison and horses roamed.

When the Devensian ice sheet melted, many meltwater channels formed. Deeply incised narrow valleys form a belt paralleling the north coast of Pembrokeshire. They extend from Mathry in the west, are particularly prominent inland of Fishguard, and extend to Newport and Cardigan – a distance of forty-two kilometers (twenty-six miles). The most prominent of these is the narrow steep-sided Gwaun Valley along the northern foothills of the Preseli Mountains. The significance of these deeply incised narrow valleys as being glacial meltwater channels was recognised by J.K. Charlesworth in 1929. However he interpreted the associated Pleistocene deposits to have formed in large meltwater lakes trapped between the mountains and the retreating Irish Sea glacier. More modern work has reinterpreted the sediments. No such lakes existed. Instead the deep melt-water channels have been shown to have fed into subglacial tunnels in the ice sheet in the Fishguard area. This new model requires much more ice to be present in the area than the earlier model of Charlesworth.

The evidence for the glaciation of Pembrokeshire is clear and accepted today. However what is not well known is the story of the erratic rocks carried by the ice. The stony beaches of Pembrokeshire commonly show water-rounded pebbles of rocks that do not occur in the county. A few of these are ballast rocks brought by ships in the past, but most are erratics brought in by the Irish Sea glacier and deposited when the ice melted. This brings us to an aspect of the glacial story that is causing considerable debate and controvery in the press, on the television and causing disagreement between archaeologists and geologists. This is the interpretation of the so called 'Bluestones' of Stonehenge on Salisbury Plain.

Stonehenge is one of the most impressive and puzzling ancient monuments on Earth. It started being built in the Bronze Age, continued with changes through the Neolithic and was still in use in the Iron Age. The latest radiocarbon dating indicates that the work started around 3000 BC on what is now the surrounding ditch. The Aubrey holes were dug about 2,900 BC. Most of the monument is built of large shaped slabs of sarsen rock – a silicified sandstone found in slabs and boulders scattered about the Chalk dry valleys and may be remnants of a 'duricrust' layer. These were erected by men from 2450 to 2300 BP. However inside the ring of sarsen stones at Stonehenge there is another ring of smaller stones, mainly 'bluestone', weighing up to four tons each. The 'Bluestone' oval was built around 3000 BC.

The 'bluestone' is a dolerite, most commonly 'spotted'. In 1923 geologist Herbert Thomas published a famous paper on the rocks of Stonehenge. He identified 'foreign stones'. These were twenty-nine 'bluestones', four of rhyolite and one (the Altar Stone) of sandstone derived from the Senni Beds possibly near the mouth of the River Taf. Thomas identified the source of these stones as rock outcrops at the eastern end of the Preseli Mountains of Pembrokeshire - in particular to Carn Meini, Carn Alw and Foel Drygarn. He went on to speculate how these foreign stones got to Salisbury Plain and settled for an interpretation that they were taken there by tribes of Neolithic men. This caused great interest worldwide that has not abated today. The cause has been taken up by many archaeologists and numerous books and scientific papers have appeared discussing the logistical problems of moving such large and heavy rocks so far by manpower. An attempt was made to drag a large block of 'bluestone' to Salisbury Plain, but without success. It was not until many years later that several geologists made the counter proposal that the 'bluestones' of Stonehenge could be glacial erratics carried there by the Irish Sea glacier after it crossed the Preseli Mountains and turned east to flow up the Bristol Channel. The controversy rages on today.

The glacial theory is strongly supported by Dr. Brian John through a series of books. He lives in north Pembrokeshire and made his Ph.D. study of the glaciation of the area. Most geologists led by Brian John believe that the 'bluestones' are glacial erratics torn by the ice from the Preseli Mountains and ice rafted to Salisbury Plain by the great Irish Sea Ice stream. The latter advanced south down the Irish Sea to Pembrokeshire where it abutted the Preseli Mountains and then turned east into the mouth of the Bristol Channel. The Devensian ice sheets did not advance far enough to reach Salisbury Plain or transport Pembrokeshire rocks eastwards. However the previous two glaciations did. Dr. Brian John has in 2018 published a most excellent summary of the debate with many color photographs and made an excellent case for the transportation by ice rafting.

The other side of the arguement is presented by Professor Mike Parker Pearson – a popular archaeologist, professer and television personality who has excavated and written much about Stonehenge and the megaliths of north Pembrokeshire. Many people led by Mike Parker Pearson believe that large stones were quarried in the Preseli Mountains by the Neolithic people and then transported 230 kilometers by them to Salisbury Plain. Professor Parker-Pearson and his colleages have produced large numbers of excellent radiocarbon ages from ancient sites and fire places that have shown a surprisingly long history associated with the sites that ranges from Mesolithic, through Neolithic to Bronze and Iron Age.

Professor Parker Pearson and others have now dated the formation of Stage I of Stonehenge – a bluestone circle to between 3,080 to 2,755 years BC. The surrounding ditch and bank is dated to 2,995 to 2,900 years BC. The trilithons were put in place between 2,600 and 2,400 B.P; He has described what he thinks are three quarry sites for the Neolithic mining of 'bluestone' in the Preseli Mountains. Two of these sites are on the north side of the Preseli Ridge. At Craig Rhos-y-felin beside the Afon, Bryn Berrian rhyolite has been quarried but is not identified in any of the standing stones at Stonehenge. At Carn Goedog a spotted dolerite was worked some two centuries before the bluestones of Stonehenge were set up. The site shows evidence of quarrying that has been radiocarbon dated to 7,000 and 5,000 BP. But were the quarries for making hand axes or for large stones to take to Stonehenge?

Professor Parker-Pearson and his team also carried out much radiocarbon dating at the Waun Mawn stone ring of unspotted dolerite in north Pembrokeshire. They found many Mesolithic ages showing ancient man was living in the area well before Stonehenge was built. There was no evidence of Mesolithic quarrying of megaliths. The numbers of earlier age dates from the different millennia were: ninth millennium BC – one sample; eighth millennium – three samples; seventh millennium - nine samples; sixth millennium – four samples, fifth millennium – ten samples; fourth millennium - six samples. There were eleven samples younger than the fourth millennium. The professor and his team came to a surprising conclusion. This was that the Waun Mawn ring was built between 3,600 and 3,000 BC. This makes the ring older than the early bluestone ring at Stonehenge. As most of the stones are missing at Waun Mawn, the team concluded that many of the bluestones of Stonehenge were originally from the Waun Mawn ring and were transported to Stonehege by Neolithic people, either by boat and overland or just overland.

So the controversy continues. One interesting problem is whether the British Ice sheets reached Salisbury Plain and the Stonehenge area. The Devensian Ice sheet at 27 to 20,000 thousand years ago did not. However the earlier Anglian Ice sheet at 450,000 years ago either just reached Salisbury Plain or stopped just short of it. This would have transported Preseli Bluestones across south Wales and just into England. For the ice transporation people it suggests that the Pembrokeshire bluestones could have been ice transported almost all the way there and an 'eratic trail' has been found acoss the south coastal area of Wales including Flat Holm island in the Bristol Channel, south of Cardiff.

Dr John in particular has drawn attention to erratic trails. These are trails of erratic boulders dropped by the melting ice that lead back to the source rock. For example in the USA and Canada rare diamonds were known from glacial till. But it was not until quite recently that geologists traced them to their source pipes by following, not the diamonds but the far more common red pyrope garnets that occur in the kimberlite pipe with the diamonds. Erratic trails of pyrope garnets have now resulted in diamond mining taking place in the USA and Canada. The Devensian, Walstonian and Anglian glaciations all tansported glacial erratics. Many came to Pembrokeshire from the Scottish Islands and north-west Ireland.

Rocks from Pembrokeshire were picked up particularly by the earlier glaciations, and transported eastwards along the south coast of Wales towards the Salisbury Plain area.

Recent work on the stones of Stonehenge and the tors of the Preseli Mountains has concentrated on the microscopic and geochemical composition of the rocks and a pretty strong case has emerged for an erratic/ice transportation origin. The argument is as follows. The British Geological Survey map of north Pembrokeshire shows that the 450 million year old black Ordovician shales that make up most of the area have been intruded by about sixty thick sheets (elongate sills and dikes) of 'bluestone'. These are dark coloured dolerites some of which have white feldspar clusters. Of the forty-three identified Welsh bluestones at Stonehenge only thirty are of dolerite and most have the feldspar clusters.

Three lithological rock types have been matched with north Preseli tors. These are: a) Spotted dolerite on Carn Goedog; b) Unspotted dolerite of Cerrigmarchogion and Craig Talfynydd; c) Spotted dolerite from Carn Breseb and Carn Gyfrwy both of the Carn Alw area. The spotted dolerite of Carn Meini was previously thought to be a source but later studies have eliminated this. The remaining 'blue stones' are rhyolites, sandstone and argillaceous tuffs. These tough rocks form rocky outcrops or 'tors' all over north Pembrokeshire. For example around the Golden Road across the Preseli Ridge they outcrop on Carns Meini, Goedog, Rica, Breseb Gwr, Ddafad-Ias, Gyfrwy, Goi, Gaseg and Sarn. On Carn Alw the rock is rhyolite and on Foel Drygarn it is several igneous rocks. These are the source tors first identified by geologist Herbert Thomas that have given rise to a trail of 'bluestone' erratics.

The latest studies of the 'bluestones' at Stonehenge including chippings of worked 'bluestone' in the ground there, reveal that in addition to the thirty-four visible 'spotted dolerite bluestones' first studied by Herbert Thomas, there are others. Five are composed of altered volcanic ashes or tuffs, five of different rhyolites, two dacites, two micaceous sandstones and a greenish sandstone of the Altar Stone. The detailed work shows that the 'spotted dolerite bluestones' have come from three distinct sources. The most spotted of these rocks matches, not with Carn Meini, but with Carn Goedog. The four rhyolite stones were all different coming from four locations. Three appear to come from Carn Alw on the Preseli Ridge, Carn Clust-y-Ci near Dinas and Carn Llwyd near Newport. The fourth sample did not match the Preseli rhyolites and may have come from near Strumble Head or even North Wales.

In addition fragments of rhyolite from Stonehenge indicate different sources. Altogether including the sandstones, the stones at Stonehenge come from at least fifteen different sources. This conclusion does not support their origin in a few quarries but rather fits with the idea of the ice sheet plucking rocks from the many tors. Interestingly some of the rhyolites show microscopic textures that suggest they were produced by volcanic eruptions as ignimbrites (pyroclastic flows) or sheets of hot ash and gas.

A considerable amount of work is in progress with the 'Stone of Stonehenge' project and more will be learned about Stonehenge and its environment. In particular the site has a thick deposit made up of rock fragments – the debris of millennia of rock chipping. Amongst the chippings 'bluestone' fragments are common, although the number of 'bluestone' boulders present in the monument is small. This has suggested that Stonehenge might have been the site of a factory making 'bluestone' hand axes for a long time.

Suggested Further Reading

John, B., 2013, *The Bluestone Mystery - Stonehenge, Preseli and the Ice Age*: Greencroft Books,, Newport, 160 p.

John, B, 2018, *The Stonehenge Bluestones*: Greencroft Publications, Newport, 47 p.

Parker Pearson, M., Cleal, R., Pollard, J., Richards, C., Thomas, J., Tille, C.,Welham, K., Chamberlain, A., Chener, C., Evans, J., Montgomert, J., and Richards, M., 2007, *The Age of Stonehenge*: Antiquity, v. 81, Issue 313, p.617-639. doi.10.1017/50003598X 00095624

Parker Pearson, M., Bevins, R., Ixer, R., Pollard, J., Richards, C., Welham, K., Chan, B., Edinborough, K., Hamilton, D., and Macphail, R., 2015, Craig Rhos-y-felin: *a Welsh bluestone megalith quarry for Stonehenge*: Antiquity, v. 89, Issue 348, p. 1331-1352. https.//doi.org/10.15184/aqy.2015.177

Parker Pearson, M., Pollard, J., Richards, C., Welham, K., Kinnaird, T., Shaw, S., Simmons, E., Standord, A., Bevins, R., Ixer, R., Ruggles, C., Rylatt, J., and Edinborough, K., 2021, *The original Stonehenge? A dismantled stone circle in the Preseli Hills of west Wales*: Antiquity, v. 95, Issue 379, p. 85-103. https://doi/org/10.15184/aqy.2020.23

4. THE PEOPLING OF WALES

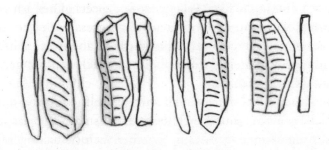

Figure 3. Flint blade flake knives of Aurignacian type used by the
Upper Paleolithic hunters of South Wales

During the Great Ice Age for a period of about 2 million years the polar icecaps of earth expanded and contracted. They advanced several times and then in warmer intervals called interglacials they melted and retreated. Over the past 500,000 years there have been five major ice advances. At their greatest extents, the ice sheets covered much of Britain, so that only a strip of land south of London was free of ice. Around two million years ago three different hominid ancestors coexisted in the Drimolan Cave Complex of South Africa. They were Australopithecus, Paranthropus and Homo erectus. The latter was a direct ancestor of Homo sapiens. In Europe in areas free of ice a species known as Homo neaderthalensis was identified from remains in the Neader Valley in the Rhineland of West Germany in 1856 and existed from 400,000 to 40,000 years ago. Between 60,000 and 40,000 years ago Neanderthal Man coexisted with modern man (Homo sapiens).

The oldest human remains found in Wales to date are an early Neanderthal jaw dated to 230,000 years found in Pontnewydd Cave in Denbighshire. Late Neanderthal hand axes have been found in Coygan Cave in Carmarthenshire. The prehistory of Wales is very well represented in the collections of the National Museum of Wales. The evolution from the crude chipped stone tools of the Paleolithic, to the polished stone axes of the Neolithic with fine flint arrowheads to the wide variety of Bronze Age tools and finally to the early Iron Age is well represented and has been catalogued by Grimes (1951).

Paleolithic or Old Stone Age (500,000 to 30,000 BC).

The oldest stone tools found in Britain occur on the Norfolk coast in sediments dating between 950,000 and 780,000 BC. The sediments were deposited in a long interglacial interval preceding a glacial advance. Two Acheulian handaxes found at two locations in Pembrokeshire suggest a lower Paleolithic presence in Pembrokeshire. The oldest human remains found in Wales were in a cave in the Elwy Valley near St. Asaph in Denbighshire. The human remains appear to have belonged to a forerunner of Neanderthal Man. Stone axes and scrapers date from about 225,000 BC, corresponding to the interglacial interval (from about 245,000 to 30,000 years ago) between two glacial advances.

The early Neanderthal men hunted animals while making use of caves and rock shelters. Bones found with their remains are hippopotamus and rhinoceros, long extinct in Britain, together with bones of bear, wolf, leopard, horse, bison and lion. Large numbers of their early stone tools were also found – handaxes, scrapers, sharp flakes and blades made using the 'Levallois' technique. Burnt stones were also found. Fully developed Neanderthal Man lived from 70,000 to 30,000 years ago before becoming extinct and leaving only the one human species of Homo sapiens. However modern genetic studies show that today most of us carry about 10 to 15 % of the genes of Neanderthal man who evidently interbred with our species.

Another important record of late Neanderthal man was obtained from Coygan Cave between Pendine and Laugharne in Carmarthenshire. The cave has since been quarried away. The cave had been used by spotted hyenas as a den and contained the bones of mammoth, woolly rhinoceros, bison, and cave lion. A small collection of stone tools was also recovered including three 'bout coupe' handaxes. These are a part of the Mousterian industry which is exclusively produced by the late Neanderthals. The latter must have occupied the cave, probably about 50,000 years ago.

Early Upper Paleolithic (EUP) People c.38,000 to 27,000 years BP.

During the upper Paleolithic much of Wales was covered in ice sheets of the last glacial advance – the Devensian. But the ice sheets stopped short of parts of south Wales (Figure 2). Modern people – Homo sapiens sapiens – evolved around 160,000 years ago and migrated into Europe about 54,000 years ago. These hunters were more advanced than their predecessors, and used stone tools made from thin flakes of flint (Figure 3). Vital to their survival at the time were a series of caves in the belt of Carboniferous limestone of south Pembrokeshire and the Gower (Figure 2). Here in the caves of Paviland at Rhossili on the Gower and in south Pembrokeshire such as Hoyle's Mouth Cave near Tenby (Plate 1), and the Wogan Cave under Pembroke Castle, Upper Paleolithic people found shelter.

They were hunters moving in small groups across the land in search of game, insects and plants. They would shelter in caves and make their tools from stone, especially flint. There were two distinct periods of hunting in south Wales. An Early Upper Paleolithic (EUP) people had characteristic Aurignacian culture flint tools. These were long thin-bladed flint knives (Figure 3) with hand axes, spearheads, scrapers, borers and fish hooks. Towards the end of this period the people discovered how to make and use fire. The fauna at this time would have been herds of woolly mammoth, horse, bison and reindeer. Spotted hyenas were common

The story of a spectacular burial with a partial (EUP) skeleton known as 'The Red Lady' was found in Goat's Hole Cave - one of the Paviland caves of Rhossili on the Gower Peninsula. This story is presented in the next chapter.

During and since World War II, prehistoric cave paintings have been found in caves in France, Portugal and northern Spain. The paintings were drawn by both Neanderthal and modern man. They show the ancient fauna of the areas.

Late Upper Paleolithic (LUP) People. 14,000 to 10,000 years BP.

Between about 25,000 and 14,500 years BP the climate in Britain became extremely cold and there are no human remains from this period suggesting the people migrated south. The second period of hunting was by the Late Upper Paleolithic (LUP) peoples with characteristic Cresswellian culture flint tools, not unlike those of the EUP people. At this time the fauna had changed and they hunted red deer, reindeer, antelope, arctic hare, pika (a small hare) and rabbits. In France their cave paintings include bison, woolly mammoth, deer, bulls, lions, fish and birds. These exquisite works of art are attributed to the Upper Paleolithic.

Mesolithic or Middle Stone Age People (10,000 to 6,000 years BP).

As the ice sheets retreated, the climate improved and ice-free land areas increased. Post-glacial forests of birch and pine became widespread over the land. Into this migrated wild cattle, deer and wild pig. Ancient man followed them northwards hunting in small bands. But his stone tools had much improved. In particular microliths - small sharp flint flakes - were used to arm arrow heads and make barbs on spears. There was also a big increase in the use of bone and antler tools. A new form of stone axe was introduced, used mainly for felling the forest before settlement.

Between 8,000 and 7,500 BC, sea level rose and cut off Britain from Europe. By 7,500 years BC much of the North Sea had formed. Around 6,200 BC a 180 mile (290 km) section of the submarine continental shelf off Norway collapsed. It is called the Storegga Slide. It caused a vast tsunami or tidal wave that destroyed coastal areas in Scotland and Denmark and overwhelmed Doggerland. Around the entire coastline of Wales and around the coast of Pembrokeshire sunken forests of trees are often revealed after storms and at low tide today. The sunken trees are pine, oak, alder, and birch and in the peat deposits with them the remains of auroch, red deer, brown bear and pig have been found in Pembrokeshire. Radiocarbon dating has shown that these sunken forests grew between 7,000 and 4,500 years BP. They show that global warming after the ice sheets melted, continued as sea level rose. The Mesolithic people were more skilled at food gathering and managed red deer and hunted a wide variety of smaller animals, sea birds and wild fowl. They spent time fishing, collecting shellfish as well as edible plants and nuts. They were still nomadic but probably followed a pattern of migration revisiting places at certain times according to the expected hunt and wild food gathering. There is evidence of the use of skin tents. Trading also began as the population increased.

Wales is quite rich in Mesolithic sites. Several with human remains have been identified in Pembrokeshire. They have been found in three caves on Caldy Island - Ogof-yr-Ychen, Nana's and Daylight Rock caves. Here human remains have been radiocarbon dated at around 7000 years BC, as have associated hazel nut shells from a midden. Assemblages of stone tools–microliths, scrapers, awls or drill bits were found. Animal bones represented woolly rhinoceros, hyena, brown bear, wild cat, wolf, reindeer, bison and aurochs (wild cattle). A rhinoceros bone was dated at 21 to 20,000 years BC. In another Caldy cave –Potter's Cave – part of the jaw of a Mesolithic dog was found suggesting that Mesolithic Man may have domesticated the dog to assist him in hunting. Sea shells in the middens indicate that seafood was a part of the diet, although the sea was then some six kilometres away.

A famous Mesolithic site occurs on Nab Head on the Dale Peninsula of Pembrokeshire - a promontory jutting out into St. Brides Bay - near the hamlet of St. Brides. Here there are two sites. Nab Head Site I is Early Mesolithic and has yielded 40,000 stone artefacts plus sixty-four perforated beads of blue-grey shale. Nab Head II is Late Mesolithic and has yielded around 30,000 stone artefacts. The most common stone used on both sites is flint which is available on the local beaches where it has washed out of glacial till. Nab Head II has also yielded three ground and pecked stone axes and three perforated stone discs that are probably mace heads. The shale beads are associated with drill bits and 'blank' beads indicating that Nab Head was once a Mesolithic bead factory. Also found was a carved shale object resembling either a female form or a phallus which may be a modern forgery. Charcoal from cooking fires has been dated at around 6000 and 5,300 years BC.

Other Mesolithic sites occur in the south of the county – Priory Farm Cave above the Pembroke River, Hoyle's Mouth and Little Hoyle Caves near Tenby, Daylight Rock Cave and Valley Field both on Caldy Island. The Hoyle's caves have yielded assemblages of stone tools of both Late Upper Paleolithic and Mesolithic types. Little Hoyle Cave has also yielded a bone needle used in making clothes. This cave was also later used for the burial of around ten people associated with Roman and later artefacts.

Surprisingly Mesolithic footprints are not uncommon, preserved in old muddy surfaces. In 2010 on the beach at Lydstep in south Pembrokeshire a peat deposit was exposed with both adult and children's footprints deeply embedded and nearby the imprints of red deer. They are thought to be Late Mesozoic, about 6000 years old. Unfortunately they were shortly eroded away by the sea waves.

Large numbers of Mesolithic footprints have also been found at three locations in the Severn Estuary, also on peat surfaces. Peat overlying the footprints at one site has been radiocarbon dated at 5500 to 5000 years BC, and at another site the overlying peat was dated to around 4,000 years BP.

The Mesolithic people were hunter gathers and probably had a vigorous lifestyle not unlike the North American Indians of the Great Plains. Their religious beliefs are unknown but must have played a major role in such a precarious lifestyle.

A surprise find at Stonehenge when the carpark and visitor centre were being constructed in the 1960s, was the presence of four pits that once held huge pine posts that were each about three feet in diameter. Radiocarbon dating showed them to be Mesolithic and built between 10,500 and 9,600 years BP. This was about 5000 years before the Neolithic people started to build the famous stone monument that we know today. Could these giant pine poles have been carved totem poles to the Mesolithic Gods? Was Stonehenge built on a site that had been in use as a sacred area for thousands of years before the stone monument was started there?

Neolithic People (6,000 to 4,000 BP).

New groups of people arrived by boat in Britain and brought with them the new skills of farming. They brought with them the seed corn, flocks and herds that would change man's lifestyle for ever. They would clear the forest and then sow crops of wheat and barley. Their animals were cattle, sheep and goats. Their plants and animals before domestication had originated in the Middle East. When the ground became exhausted they would move to another area and repeat the process. They continued to use stone for their tools, but now heavy highly-polished stones axes were made that were capable of cutting down trees. A major advance was the discovery of how to make pottery. These changes evidently led to an organised tribal life with barter. Their social organisation also produced large Megalithic tombs that required much cooperative effort to build. Some of the capstones in the tombs weigh many tons. The capstone at Pentre Ifan weighs around sixteen tons.

The Neolithic way of life required a calendar to give the times for crop sowing and animal breeding. Their farming methods produced a surplus of food, so that an astronomer priesthood could be supported. The positions of the sun, moon and stars were studied and the seasons defined. The cardinal days of the year were identified – longest and shortest days and equinoxes - so that appropriate ceremonies could be carried out. Their traditions and histories were preserved in folk memory and long stories repeated around fires in the evenings. Some ancient tales may still survive today in the stories of the flood or the continued rise in sea level and the loss of vast tracts of land.

The religion of the Neolithic people was centred on the Mother Earth Goddess. From the womb of earth sprang life, crops, food and drink. It was from the earth that we came and to the earth we would return. The Earth Goddess was carved in wood and stone and built as earth mounds showing her form. The dead were placed back into her womb in cromlechs, dolmens or chambered tombs. In Pembrokshire, Pentre Ifan is the best known but there are dozens of others. The tombs were for individual families and burials were accompanied by food and drink for the journey to the next world. After 2,500 BC the megalithic tombs were no longer built. They were replaced by round barrows and cairns for individuals. A number of man-made earth mounds up to 30 meters high exist in Wales. They resemble Silbury Hill in Wiltshire (not far from the Avebury stone circle), where recent study has convincingly shown that the 4,500 year old mound is the womb of the Earth Goddess whose form the mound takes.

The Neolithic people were short and dark haired and for 1,500 years lived peacefully in harmony with their world. They did not need to possess the weapons of war.

Iberian People (c. 2,000 BC).

At around this time in Wales there as an influx of Iberian people who arrived by boat. These were a dark-haired tempestuous people with a swarthy skin who were seafarers. The Roman senator and historian Tacitus around the year AD 98 wrote a book about his father-in-law General Julius Agricola in which he recorded

'the swarthy faces of the Silures (the Celtic tribe then occupying southeast Wales), the tendency of their hair to curl and the fact that Spain lies opposite, all lead one to believe that Spaniards crossed in the ancient times and occupied the land.'

Modern Wales is peopled by their descendants mixed with later Bronze Age, Celtic and Irish invaders. DNA studies of the modern population of west Wales indicates a strong Italo-Celtic signature confirming a northern Iberian connection.

The Bronze Age and the Beaker People (4,500 to 2,700 BP).

Around 4,500 BP new settlers from Europe brought new skills to Britain, in particular the working of copper. They taught the ancient Bitish people gradually how to make and work copper, bronze and gold. By 4,100 BP these metals were being mined in Britain. A new technology arrived in Wales marked by a distinctive type of highly decorated pottery drinking vessel called a 'beaker' found in burials. These Bronze Age people are known as the Beaker People, they were farmers and hunters and used bows and arrows and wore stone wrist guards. Copper daggers and ornaments accompany their remains. There was an upsurge in building small circular funerary monuments. Stone circles and stone alignments as well as many single stones or menhirs were erected.

The smelting of bronze from copper and tin ores ended the production of stone tools. Bronze weapons, tools, shields and cooking pots were manufactured. The first weaving of wool to produce capes and clothing occurred in the Bronze Age. Their major achievements were in land clearance, the introduction of new species of wheat and corn and a new burial practice for their leaders. Their burial practice was quite different to the Neolithic massive chambered tombs. They cremated their dead and the remains were placed in stone-lined cists, covered with a round mound or barrow and often rimmed by stones. The barrows were bell, disc, bowl or pond shaped.

Througout the Bronze Age the tradition of the Beaker People in setting up stone circles, alignments and standing stones, continued. They possessed boats and a fine example has been excavated near Dover.

Because most of the lowlands were covered in the Great Wild Wood, the barren uplands of Pembrokeshire above the tree line provided an important land route out of Pembrokeshire. Much Bronze Age archaeology is preserved along the Preseli Ridge which is the route of the main east-west trackway known as the 'Golden Road'. This is believed to have begun life in the Bronze Age.

Iron Age (2,700 BP to AD 43)

The Bronze Age was thought by archaeologists to have ended fairly abruptly with the invasion on horseback of new waves of Celtic people bearing iron weapons. Some were tall, fair haired with blue eyes. They originated in central and western Europe and conquered and settled vast areas north of the Alps and into Spain crossing the channel to Britain. At the height of their power in AD 400 they invaded Italy and sacked Rome. They brought new technology in wheel turned pottery, chariots, a plough and woven and dyed cloth.

The Celtic people were warriors and they believed in fighting for land, security and religious beliefs. With their new technology of iron swords, arrow heads and shields they were invincible in battle. They introduced the shadow of war – something that has remained with us to the present day. They also brought the hill fort, the promontory fort and enclosed settlements to Britain. There are about 350 of these defensive structures in Pembrokeshire and they are the most common archaeological remains in the county. They invaded right across Europe through France and Italy and crossed the Channel to Britain. They had tamed the horse and were great horsemen. Some horses were worshipped. The famous 'White Horse of Uffington' was cut into a Berkshire Downs hillside around 3,000 years ago and lies adjacent to an Iron Age fort on Dragon Hill.

These vigorous and war-like people raided for cattle and women. Their violent lives were based on the horse and the iron sword. They fought endlessly for pleasure and gain. They were head hunters and the heads of captives were sometimes displayed on their rampart walls. Their fortified sites were selected as defensible and even the highest tors of the Preseli Mountains were utilised. Natural features such as rock outcrops and cliffs were strengthened by ramparts of stones or earth and stones. Some entrances were protected against cavalry attacks by a Chevaux de Fries - a stony area to prevent a broad attack by horsemen. An excellent example can be seen on Google Earth images of Carn Alw lying close to the Bronze Age track known as the 'Golden Road' across the Preseli Mountains of Pembrokeshire. Since the 1960's archaeologists have changed their views and now regard the Iron Age as resulting not from the influx of large numbers of people but from the diffusion of new ideas and technology into a more stable population.

The Iron Age began around 1000 to 800 BC when the construction of Bronze Age barrows, standing stones and stone circles died out and was replaced by the vast and spectacular fortified settlements with their ring ditches and embankments. The people of the Iron Age had the skill of smelting iron. The replacement of bronze tools and weapons by iron ones was gradual. Rivalry between groups resulted in hilltop fortifications defended by ramparts and ditches. An elite group of warriors may have lived in the fort and the residents of small farms nearby were brought into the fort in times of attack. Inside the settlements and forts, the people lived in round houses. These were circular with low stone walls plastered with clay on which the rafters rested.

The Celts liked to decorate their whole bodies with intricate patterns drawn with blue wode. When they fought with the invading Romans, both men and women would go into battle naked to show their painted bodies. This made them vulnerable to the Romans who would link shields and then stab the Celts in their legs with their short spears or pilums. Because the Celts often wore golden torcs around their necks, these became prized treasures for the Romans conquerors.

The four largest Iron Age forts in Pembrokeshire were Carn Ingli, Garn Fawr, Foel Drygarn and St.David's Head. Each of these is likely to mark a centre of population and government at the time and were the seats of powerful leaders. It is possible that St. David's Head was mentioned by Claudius Ptolemy a Greek philosopher who lived in Alexandria in the second century AD. Ptolemy produced a book called 'Geographica' describing all the places in the Roman world. He estimated positions using his calclations that were an early form of latitude and longitude. Ptolemy's book survived to reach Constantinople. From there it was taken before the fall of Constantinople in 1452 to Bolognia in Italy.

At the end of the fifteenth centuary and early sixteenth centuary cartographers used Ptolemy's calculations to make maps of the areas described by Ptolemy. The Prima Europe Tabula of 1486 is today the oldest surviving map of the British Isles after Ptolemy. It shows Wales with the name of the St David's Peninsula as Octopitarum Promontorium meaning the promontory of the eight perils. This may refer to the offshore rocks and pinnacles today known as 'The Bishop and his Clarks'. It has also been suggested that the name might be after an Iron Age tribe – the Octapitai – who occupied the large promontory fort on St. David's Head. There are no records for the other centres.

One Pembrokeshire Iron Age fort has been excavated over several decades and partially reconstructed. It is open to visitors. This is Castell Henllys in north Pembrokeshire. There in reconstructed round houses, demonstrations of Iron Age cooking and weaving can be seen and young visitors can get their faces painted in Celtic art. The entrance to the fort is guarded by a Cheveaux de Fries.

Roman Period (AD 60 to 410)

The Romans occupied Wales in the second half of the first century AD. The occupation was completed by AD 78. Legionary forts were built such as at Chester (Deva) and Caerleon. A Roman fort possibly for up to 5000 auxiliary troops was recently found at Wiston in Pembrokeshire. Excavation suggests it was short lived and occupied from about AD 74 to 100. Administrative towns were set up such as Moredunum (present day Carmarthen). There are few remains of Roman buildings in Pembrokeshire, but clusters of Roman coins and brooches have been found on the beaches at Tenby, Amroth, Angle and Fishguard. In addition a cluster has been found at Canaston at the highest point that can be reached by boat along the eastern arm of the Cleddau River. These occurrences suggest that the Roman fleet traded with the local people at these beaches and estuaries in Pembrokeshire. For most people in Wales, their lives were not greatly affected by the Roman occupation and many of the hillforts continued to be occupied, and excavations reveal Roman pottery fragments in them.

Irish Settlers (AD 410 to 1066).

With the retreat of the Romans, the Anglo-Saxon invasion of England did not enter Wales. Rather in Pembrokeshire settlers from Ireland arrived and erected stones with their distinctive Ogham script. Throughout the Dark Ages (AD 410 to 1066) many Christian priests arrived in Wales from Ireland and established Christianity. There were three waves of these priests. The first was from the fifth to seventh centuries and established the memorial stones with Ogham script. The second from the seventh to ninth centuries and the third from ninth to eleventh centuries. It was the latter wave that carved and set up the stone Christian crosses such as those that can be seen today in Carew and Nevern.

There are written records of the Irish invaders who followed the Iron Age style of living. For example the hillfort of 'Clegyr Boi' near St. Davids is a rocky hill that has been strengthened by stone ramparts. Excavations revealed Neolithic huts, polished stone axes and flint scrapers which underlay the stone ramparts. The name of the hillfort means 'The Stronghold of Boia' who was a sixth century Irish leader (also German has been suggested). He is remembered for parading naked women in front of the priests of St. David (the sixth century Welsh bishop) to test their celibacy. 'Boia' was killed in AD 520 when his stronghold was taken by another Irish leader named 'Lisci. It is possible that the ramparts are not Iron Age but date to 'Boia', although 'Boia' could have reoccupied an Iron Age fort.

Viking Settlers. (AD 789 to AD 1066).

In AD 789 the first Viking raid on Britain occured. This was followed by three centurues (eighth to tenth) of Viking raids of the shores of Britain and Ireland. In Wales, Anglesey was raided nine times, first in 854 and finally in 987. During the latter raid a thousand defenders died and twice that number were carried off in captivity. The Gower area was invaded in 860 and the Vikings only expelled after much slaughter. The church at St Davids was attacked by Vikings eleven times between AD 907 and 1091. Bishop Morganeu was murdered in AD 999. In St. David's cathedral is a memorial stone to Hedd and Isaac – the two sons of the bishop of St. Davids who were killed by Vikings raiders in 1080. The church was ruined and rebuilt many times. The final raid was led by King Harold Hadrada in 1066 when he was defeated at Stamford Bridge by Harold Godwinson. Many Vikings settled in the areas of their raids as there were fine farms, animals and ladies for the taking according to the pagan warrior mind.

Today especially around the coast of Pembrokeshire there is a strong Viking legacy of Norse place names that can be seen on the modern maps. Not a great deal of archaeological work has been carried out in Pembrokeshire and to date there are few Viking finds, although Viking place names abound.

The Normans and Flemish People (AD 1066)

The Norman invasion of Pembrokeshire did not occur until the death in battle of the Prince of South Wales - Rhys ap Tewdwr in 1093. He had ruled with the approval of William the Conqueror. Three barons then independently and privately invaded south-west Wales. First was Martin de Turribus, who made his own private invasion by sea of north Pembrokeshire, landing at Fishguard Bay and taking Camaes for himself and building his castle at Newport. His son Robert FitzMartin inherited his estate. Second was Arnulf de Montgomery who reached Pembroke where he built a small wood and turf castle. A third baron, William FitzBaldwin, sailed from Devon and took the Carmarthen area, where he built his castle on the orders of William Rufus.

The Normans built about seventy castles in Pembrokeshire. Two thirds of these were earthworks divided equally between mottes and motte and bailey castles. Around fifteen of these early castles were later built up into major stone castles. The Welsh resisted the Normans. Most valuable to the Normans were the lower more fertile lands of central and southern Pembrokeshire and the sea access along the Milford Haven Waterway. The Normans removed the Welsh population from these areas to the colder higher lands of the north with poorer soils. They colonised parts of the area with a Flemish population as the Flemings made good foot soldiers in support of the Norman Barons. The Flemish territory ended in a military line extending from Preseli to Poinz Castle. The Flemish/Norman area became known as 'Little England Beyond Wales' and survives today and is distinct from the Welsh-speaking north. The boundary is a fairly sharp line known locally as the 'Landsker'.

Suggested Further Reading

Dames, M., 1976, *The Silbury Treasure*: Thames and Hudson, London, 192 p.

Darvill, T., and Wainwright, G., 2016, Chapter 2. Neolithic and Bronze Age Pembrokeshire: In: Darvill, T., James, H., Murphy, K., Wainwright, G., and Walker, E.A., Pembrokeshire County History, *Vol. 1. Prehistoric, Roman and Early Medieval Pembrokeshire*: Pembrokeshire County History Trust, Haverfordwest, p. 55 - 222.

Davies, D.W., and Eastham, A., 2002, *Saints and Stones. A Guide to the Pilgrim Ways of Pembrokeshire*: Gomer Press, Llandysul, Ceredigeon, 123 p.

Grimes, W.F., 1951, *The Prehistory of Wales*: The National Museum of Wales, Cardiff, 288p.

Heath, J., 2013, *Before Farming. Life in Prehistoric Wales 225,000 to 4,000 BC*: Gwasg Carreg Gwalch, Llanwst, Wales, 175 p. ISBN 978-1-84527-456-6.

Manning, W., 2001, *A Pocket Guide to Roman Wales*: The western Mail, University of Wales, Cardiff, 129 p. ISBN 0-7083-1675-1

Rees.S., 1992, *A Guide to Ancient and Historic Wales – Dyfed*: HMSO, London, 241 p.

Thompson Barker, C., 1992, *The Chambered Tombs of South-West Wales*: Oxbow Monograph 14, Oxbow Books, Oxford, 88 p.

Walker, E.A., The Paleolithic and Mesolithic Hunter Gatherers of Pembrokeshire, 2016, Chapter 1: In: Darvill, T., James, H., Murphy, K., Wainwright, G., and Walker, E.A., Pembrokeshire County History, *Vol. 1. Prehistoric, Roman and Early Medieval Pembrokeshire*: Pembrokeshire County History Trust, Haverfordwest, p. 1 – 54.

5. THE UPPER PALEOLITHIC CAVE DWELLERS OF SOUTH WALES

Figure 4. Upper Paleolithic mammoth hunters attack their prey

During the Last Great Ice Age, great sheets of ice advanced south down the Irish Sea. They turned up the Bristol Channel and advanced across south Wales. At their greatest extent the ice sheet overlying the tops of the Preseli Mountains (Foel Cwm Cerwyn rises to 536 m) was estimated by Dr. Brian John (2013, p. 128) to overtop them by 1000m. The jagged mountains of North Wales tell a different story for they stood through the Welsh ice sheet, so that their summits became frost shattered into sharp tooth-like peaks. However the last great ice advance, known as the Devensian, did not cover all parts of South Wales. A corridor of land existed along south Pembrokeshire and the Gower. This belt contains the grey Carboniferous Limestone outcrops with caves formed by solution of the limestone in past times. Before the peak of the Great Ice Age these caves were inhabited by Stone Age Man and prehistoric animals (Figure 2).

Modern man (Homo sapiens) arrived in Europe about 35,000 years ago. His remains in Wales are mainly found in caves and become more widespread (although are still uncommon) in the Upper Paleolithic. There were two distinct periods of occupation. Oldest were the Early Upper Paleolithic

(EUP) people with tools of the Aurignacian culture and are associated with the bones of woolly rhinoceas and hyena and in the case of Paviland cave woolly mammoth. Other associated animals are bear, reindeer, and fox. There followed a period of intense cold when there were no human beings in Britain. After this Late Upper Paleolithic (LUP) people returned to the caves with their Creswellian culture and are associated with the bones of reindeer, wolf, red fox, hare, and brown bear. The woolly mamoths, woolly rhinoceras and hyenas were extinct by this time.

The story of the Upper Paleolithic hunters began with a spectacular find of human remains made in the Goat's Hole Cave – one of the Paviland Caves of Rhossili on the Gower Peninsula. The cave lies in the face of a steep cliff with the sea crashing at the base. Access is not easy. It was in this cave in 1823 that the Reverend William Buckland made the remarkable discovery. He dug into the cave-floor sediments to find the bones of many animals most of which are today extinct in Wales – woolly mammoth, woolly rhinoceros, the giant Irish elk standing eight feet tall at the shoulder with a twelve foot spread of antlers, wolf, reindeer, bear, fox, hyena, horse, ox, rats and birds. The assemblage indicates a cold-temperature climate where conditions at the time were steppe like. Buried in these deposits the Reverend found a human grave with much of the skeleton surviving. Buried alongside it was the head of an 'elephant' with two tusks. The grave was unusual for the bones were stained with red ochre and present were shell beads and polished ivory decorative plates. The reverend concluded that the bones were those of a camp-following woman associated with a nearby hillfort that might have been used by the Romans who used war elephants some two thousand years ago. The skeleton (now housed in the Oxford University Museum) became known as 'The Red Lady'.

The Reverend Buckland was an eminent scientist of his time. He was Dean of Oxford and held the chair of Mineralogy there. He was a Fellow of the Geological Society and had produced geological maps. He published sixty-six papers and many books. He was a popular speaker who illustrated his talks with his finds. His findings were of great interest at a time when the origins of man were highly controversial. His contemporaries Charles Darwin (1809-82) and Thomas Huxley (1826-95) were to shake the foundations of Christianity by opposing the story of man's origin as described in the Genesis. The Reverend died at the age of seventy-two in 1856, three years before Darwin published his 'Origin of the Species'.

Modern scientific scrutiny of the remains from the cave tell a very different story to the early interpretation of the Reverend Buckland. The human bones are those of a young male adult and were radiocarbon dated in 2007 and found to be 31 to 32,000 years BC. This has recently been refined to 27,000 years BC. This age corresponds to the Late Upper Paleolithic. The species is Homo sapiens that arose in Africa around 200,000 years ago and where a skull dated to 160,000 years has recently been found. The age corresponds to the last great ice age known as the Devensian Glaciation and sea levels would have been about 120 meters (400 feet) lower than today. Goat's Hole Cave was then very far from the sea as the North Sea, Irish Sea and the English Channel were all land. At that time the Devensian ice sheets were advancing. The associated 'elephant' head is now identified as that of a woolly mammoth and the ivory plates were made from mammoth tusk. This makes the skeleton that of an EUP mammoth hunter during the last Ice Age (Figure 2).

At the time of the last Great Ice Age, South Wales was cold and rather like modern Siberia with grassland and tundra. It provided a very harsh existence and man sheltered in caves from the cold weather, but was able to keep warm and keep animals at bay with fire. However ownership of the caves would have been disputed with cave bears, cave lions and sabre toothed tigers. About 4,000 stone tools have been found in Paviland Cave and the majority are of the Aurignacian Culture, being simple tools of stone and bone for long thin blade-flake knives struck from cores (Figure 3), hand axes, spearheads, scrapers, borers and fish hooks. There is also evidence of later Neolithic use of the cave. These early Homo sapiens dressed in clothing made from animal skins as weaving and pottery had not yet been discovered. They hunted the woolly mammoth, reindeer, Irish elk, ox, horse, cave bear, birds and fish and competed with lions, hyena and wolf packs (Figure 4). They collected edible plants and berries. More EUP people lived in adjacent caves at Paviland – Bacon Hole, Cat's Hole and Long Hole. Herds of woolly mammoth would summer graze on the site of the North Sea and then for the winter migrate to the south of France and the Mediterranean area. The tusk of a woolly mammoth was found while digging the foundations of Hakin Bridge in Milford Haven and is on display in the town museum (Plate 2).

Today other 'Red Lady' internments with red ochre staining are known from across Europe. It seems that as the land was one mass and people were rather scarce, the hunters travelled over wide areas probably following the herds of mammoth and reindeer on their annual migrations (Figure 5). For young warriors killed probably in battles with large animals, the red ochre burial with objects of polished mammoth ivory together with a head of one of these revered monsters was a great honor and showed the respect of the tribe or band of EUP hunters.

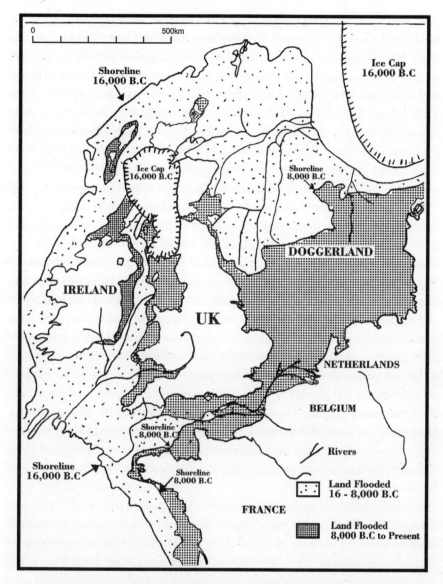

Figure 5. Map the land areas around Britain at 16,000 and 8,000 years BC. The lost lands of Cantref y Gwaelod lay under the present Cardigan Bay

Other caves occur in the limestone belt of south Pembrokeshire. Two caves have received much archaeological attention. They are Hoyle's Mouth Cave (Plate 1) and Little Hoyle cave which are near each other on Tenby Golf course at Penally. The caves are not easily found as they are not signposted and the tracks and caves are heavily overgrown in summer by nettles and blackberry and blocked by the branches of fallen trees. Permission to visit can be obtained at Tenby Golf Club.

Hoyle's Mouth cave is situated on a low ridge with an asphalt road at the base. Published latitudes and longitudes put it in a marshy field below the road. Its GPS position measured at the cave entrance is latitude 51 degrees 40.175 minutes North. Longitude -4 degrees 43.917 minutes West. Human activity began in the cave as indicated by a single Aurignacian tool of the Early Upper Paleolithic (EUP people). This would have been the time of the woolly mammoth, woolly rhinoceras and hyena, but there seems to have been little human activity at that time. However 300 Creswellian tools have been found during excavation indicating the Late Upper Paleolithic (LUP people) use of the cave. A bone from a bear has yielded an age of around 12,000 years. It seems that Hoyle's Mouth cave was mainly occupied after the time of the woolly mammoth, woolly rhinoceros and hyena. Hoyle's Mouth cave extends forty meters into the cliff as a narrow passage with two chambers named Bear and Reindeer after bones found there. The stone tools and bones extend to the back of the cave. This indicates that the people in them made use of the depths of the cave in the dark zone without daylight. This may be because the depths of the cave are at a constant year round temperature of about ten degrees and would offer protection during very cold and windy weather. In France and Spain the depths of caves have magnificent wall paintings of the animals of the time. There is no view out of the Hoyle's Mouth cave today because of the presence of tall trees and dense undergroweth. But in the Upper Paleolithic this would not have been the case. The elevated position of the cave would have made it a good lookout point for herds of animals migrating across the grasslands, especially in winter when animals would have descended to the lower levels for winter grazing.

Little Hoyle cave nearby penetrates a limestone ridge with entrances on both sides. It has also been excavated and forty-nine pieces of worked flint recovered. However study of these suggests they are all Neolithic in age, athough a single Mesolithic flint core dating around 11,000 years BP was found. The associated bones are of red deer, wolf, auroch, badger and red fox. Also found were bones of rabbits and sheep which may be post Neolithic. The remains of several human jaws were found. It has been suggested that the cave might have been are repository for human heads used in ancestor worship – a place where ancient men could go to speak with their dead ancestors asking for help with their problems.

Two puzzles for modern man is where did the Paleolithic men get the wood for their fires in the grasslands and where did they get the flint for their tools. There are no flint sources or mines in the rocks of Pembrkeshire. The nearest flint sources are in the chalk of Dorset and the south-east of England. Today good flint nodules can be seen on the beaches of Pembrokeshire where they have washed out of the glacial deposits in the cliffs. These are glacial erratics that were transported to Pembrokeshire by the Irish Sea glacier from a source in the chalk cliffs of Antrim, NE Ireland. However in the upper Paleolithic, the coast was far from Pembrokeshire because of the lower sea levels and the flints were buried in the glacial deposits. It seems the aswer to both questions lies in the fact that upper Paleolthic man travelled widely following the great animal herds. By covering a lot of ground he would find flint in the chalk and wood in sheltered places where stunted trees grew. These places would be included in his annual travels. But it would mean carrying wood and tools around.

Of interest are the details known of the 'Red Lady' skeleton. The hunter died as a young man. He was tall and slender at about five feet eight inches and died in his mid-twenties. Analysis indicates his diet included fish probably caught in the nearby paleo-River Severn (now drowned under the Bristol Channel). When he was killed he was carefully dressed in his finest shell necklace with his ivory plates of jewellery ready for the next world. His remains would stay with his family in the cave where they lived. With him was buried the head with tusks of a mammoth – possibly the one that killed him. The body was aligned with the passage of the sun suggesting a rebirth was expected and covered with red ochre possibly resembling new blood, before being covered over for the next 27,000 years. One can imagine the family crouched around the fire at night looking out of the cave mouth over the tundra covered low hills and hearing the howls of the hyenas and the wolf pack from the safety and shelter of their magical dancing fire in the cave mouth.

In the Bacon Hole and Minchin Hole caves of the Gower an older animal fauna exists but without human relics. The fauna includes the straight-tusked elephant and the slender nosed rhinoceros. These animals lived at a time when the climate was warmer than today. Some Gower caves contain many hundreds of bones and were probably hyena dens. One cave contained over a thousand shed deer antlers indicating that it was used by red deer. The caves of South Pembrokeshire have yielded a cold weather fauna of reindeer, red deer, wolf, bear, hyena, cave lion, hippopotamus, woolly mammoth, woolly rhinoceros, and Irish elk. Hoyle's Mouth and Little Hoyle Cave have yielded assemblages of stone tools of both Late Upper Paleolithic and Mesolithic types.

Upper Paleolithic bones and a few worked flint tools in the caves in the grey Carboniferous limestone of Pembrokeshire and the Gower may be rare and apparently insignificant in quantity, but the story they tell of the evolution of our ancestors in the story of mankind is immense. Let us try to explain the significance next. We are looking at our own ancestors - Homo sapiens. The geography of their world was enormously different with the great ice sheets of the Devensian glaciation advancing down the Irish Sea and over the land. In what is today Britain, ice would cover everything north of a line from London to south Pembrokeshire, leaving a small strip of South Wales ice free. The North Sea, English Channel and Irish Sea were dry land with all the water tied up in the great ice sheets as sea level was about 120 meters (400 feet) lower than today. South of the ice sheets vast steppe lands or tundra existed mainly without trees. The land was snow covered in winter but in the brief summer period vast areas of steppe grassland existed. These vast summer grasslands supported a fauna of giant mammals – animals of enormous size. Dominant were the great herds of woolly mammoth that migrated back and forth with the seasons. These vast areas of summer grassland that bordered the ice sheets to the north have been named the Mammoth Grasslands. They no longer exist for with the melting of the great ice sheet they have become once again vast forests. There were also great herds of buffalo and giant elk probably like those that survived on the North America continent until recently. Many other large mammals coexisted with them such as a giant sloth, cave bears and sabre toothed tigers. In the Ukraine, Poland and the Czech Republic huts built of mammoth bones and tusks have been found that have been dated at 21,000 to 10,000 years BC.

At times when the ice sheets melted, the area of steppe/tundra grassland shrank greatly as the warmer weather resulted in the growth of great forests. But the large cold-weather animals survived in reduced areas of grassland and were able to expand again during the next cold spell.

Early man is believed to have migrated north out of Africa around 45,000 year ago. He is believed to have discovered the grasslands of the steppes with their vast herds of huge animals not seen before. Bands of hunters formed who followed the herds and lived off them. Their settlements were large and widespread in the Czech Republic and Poland. Their camps are marked by thousands of bones in which baby mammoth predominate. They have been dated at around 30,000 years BP - a similar age to the remains found in Wales. These were the mammoth hunters of the Late Paleolithic and their descendants. Their lifestyle would have been similar to the Eskimos or Inuit of recent times. They lived in a world without much plant material for food. Instead they lived mainly off the flesh of the animals they hunted. The northern hunter bands of ancient man and his descendants were very successful and most of the fauna of giant animals eventually disappeared.

Although they hunted a wide variety of animals, top of the list was the woolly mammoth because unlike the other large mammals it carried a lot of fat. The latter provided the high energy levels required for a vigorous life in extremely cold weather. Probably like the Inuit they often ate their food raw. For the Inuit, seal is their major food because the fat is much prized as the high energy food necessity for their life in extremes of cold.

The mammoth became extinct. A major reason was loss of habitat in the warm periods between the glaciations. But for the last ice age and the present-day warm period that began about 12,000 years ago, there was a new factor against their survival. This was man the hunter. In Poland and other former steppe/tundra countries, large Upper Paleolithic hunter's camps have been found with single sites showing the bones of up to 1,000 butchered woolly mammoths. The majority were young animals as they were easier to kill and provided tender meat and fat. It seems that these small numbers of primitive hunters were enough to tip the balance and combine with the shrinking of habitat resulting from global warming, to tip the woolly mammoth and other giants into extinction.

There was another unexpected development from early man's adaptation to the life of a hunter and eater of flesh on the grasslands of the steppe. It was an evolutionary change. When teaching about the ideas of evolution proposed by Charles Darwin and Alfred Russel Wallace, it is customary to tell the story of the moths in the Midlands. Long ago there was a common white moth found in England. During the industrial revolution with the burning of many coal fires in both homes and industry, the cities and trees turned black as grime coated everything. It was only in the late 1960's and 1970's after smoke free zones had been introduced that the buildings of London were physically cleaned to reveal once again the attractive colors of the creamy Portland stone and the red bricks. In the Birmingham area a study of moths revealed that there were no more white moths left but only black ones. As explained by the Theory of Evolution, when the buildings and trees of the Birmingham area became black, the white moths stood out and were easily found and eaten by birds. Darker coloured moths were harder to see and less likely to be eaten. Over time the white moths were eliminated by natural selection and only the black variety survived.

A similar story can be told for the white polar bear. This is the same species as the northern brown bear and they are known to have interbred. But with the coming of the Ice Age, hunting on the ice-covered land and sea was more successful for the white bear than the brown-coloured variety that could easily be seen. So with time the successful bears on the ice became white.

Baby seals born on the coast around Pembrokeshire have white fur. This is a left over of an adaption to the Ice Age. On ice, the vulnerable seal pups are far less visible to predators with white fur than dark coloured fur. So again over time the pups due to natural selection became white. Today in Pembrokeshire with the Devensian ice sheets and summer sea ice lately melted and gone, the white furred seal pups remain to tell of ages past on the ice.

The hunters of the steppes lived on a diet of animal flesh because there were few edible plants available. Those Upper Paleolithic hunters with lighter coloured skins (blond hair and white faces) were less conspicuous on the snows of the tundra than those with darker skins. There was also a second advantage in that those with lighter skins were able to generate their own vitamin D in the absence of fresh fruit. People with a black skin pigment are far less able to do this. So with time the hunters of the north gradually became white people without skin pigment who had the advantage in the short summer months of better camouflage for hunting as well as having their skin generate vitamin D in sunlight.

At the time of writing the Covid-19 pandemic is in progress and it has been found that people with dark skin pigment are four times more likely to die of Covid than those with white skins. This difference is in part attributed to the white skinned people being able to generate their own vitamin D during the summer months when the sunshine is available for long hours. This is a form of natural selection operating day.

Suggested Further Reading.

Alahouse-Green, S., and Pettitt, S., 1998, Paviland Cave. *Contextualising the 'Red Lady'*: Antiquity, v. 71, Issue 278, p. 756 -772.

Rees.S., 1992, *A Guide to Ancient and Historic Wales – Dyfed*: HMSO, London, 241 p.

Stuart, A.J., 1988, *Life in the Ice Age*: Shire Publications Ltd., Aylesbury, Bucks, 64 p. ISBN 0 85263 929 5

Walker, E.A., The Paleolithic and Mesolithic Hunter Gatherers of Pembrokeshire, 2016, Chapter 1: In: Darvill, T., James, H., Murphy, K., Wainwright, G., and Walker, E.A., Pembrokeshire County History, *Vol. 1. Prehistoric, Roman and Early Medieval Pembrokeshire*: Pembrokeshire County History Trust, Haverfordwest, p. 1 – 54.

6. PENTRE IFAN – A NEOLITHIC BURIAL CHAMBER

On the north flanks of the Preseli Mountains near the north coast town of Newport is one of the most spectacular and photogenic Neolithic burial chambers in Wales. This is Pentre Ifan (meaning Ifan's homestead) where a massive wedge shaped capstone is supported on three of four tall slender support stones (Plate 3). Archaeologists call it a Portal Dolmen because at the south end between the two support stones is another which marks the entrance or portal to the tomb. Also on the south side is a forecourt. At the north end a single stone supports the slender end of the capstone that is almost seventeen feet long (5.1 meters) and weighs about sixteen tons. There are some remains of a long rectangular mound extending to the north and now marked out for visitors by a low grassed mound. The stones preserve the site of the burial chamber and the long mound of earth has largely been removed in the past probably by farmers trying to improve the local thin soil. Pentre Ifan stands in isolation on the upper slopes of a ridge with extensive views of the Nevern Valley. It has an unusual north-south orientation and the forecourt faces the mountains to the south without an impressive view. For rituals carried out there it would have been a sheltered spot warmed by the sun to the south.

Excavations in 1936-7 and 1958-9 showed that there were originally four stones at the heavy end as well as side stones. The four stones at the heavy south end of the cap stone form a curving facade to the forecourt with a central symbolic portal or doorway believed to be a symbolic gateway into the afterlife. Access to the central burial chamber beneath the capstone was probably not made by removing the vast symbolic portal slab. It was thought that the whole tomb was originally covered with a mound of soil and stones and about forty meters long. However the portal slab is so large that today it has been suggested that the top of the tomb including the capstone were not covered by the mound but remained in the open, so that the central chamber could be accessed from the sides beneath the exposed capstone. Archaeologists have ascribed the structure to the Neolithic and have radiocarbon dated it to between 5,700 and 5,400 years BP. The only building materials in the area are blocks of Pembrokeshire bluestone (doler-ite) and turf. The mound was probably built of turf and covered with dry stone walling. On the footpath to Pentre Ifan from the small car parking area (free parking) a slab of bluestone, not unlike the capstone of Pentre Ifan, can be seen exposed in the hedge. This suggests that the rock slabs used for Pentre Ifan were obtained very locally.

The Neolithic people arrived in Britain bringing seeds and flocks and herds of animals. They introduced domesticated wheat and barley, cattle, sheep and goats whose wild origins lay in the Near East. They proba-bly brought a new religion with them that required the building of the distinctive megalithic tombs. The tomb builders probably arrived by sea as the distribution of their tombs ranges from some of the Mediterranean Islands, around the coasts of Spain, Portugal and France, as well as along the west side of England and Scotland, all of Ireland and Denmark and Sweden. Tombs in the south are older than those in the north reflecting the migration of these peoples. It seems that the tombs reflect the change from simple hunter gatherer societies to fixed settlements with farming. With settled populations the tombs marked territories.

There are two types of Neolithic tombs in Pembrokeshire and along both sides of the Irish Sea. One type is the portal dolmen like Pentre Ifan which is elongate with a symbolic door or portal. The other type are passage graves that are generally circular with polygonal chambers and no obvious front. They have a stone lined passage which leads into the central chamber. The Neolithic people appear to have built another type of megalithic monu-ment in Pembrokeshire. Near the village of Llanychaer near Fishguard are four stones now standing in a hedgerow and known as Parc y Meirw or Field of the Dead. Originally the line of stones was over 130 feet long. The alignment may well have been a Neolithic calendar and was originally probably the largest of its kind in Wales.

Pentre Ifan, like the other megalithic tombs of Wales was not just a burial mound but the site of rituals involving ancestral remains. Excavations of other megalithic tombs where bones have survived show that the bones were gathered into groups that do not necessarily correspond to individual remains. Nor are the collections complete. There is some evidence that the bones have been gnawed by animals and it is possible that bodies were laid out and defleshed before the bones were gathered and interred in the tombs. There are cults surviving today where such things including ancestor worship are still practiced.

George Owen of Henllys in 1603 made a detailed drawing of Pentre Ifan. He called it 'Maen y gromlech upon Pentre Ifan land'. It became a popular site to visit and there are drawings of men on horseback riding under the capstone.

Like most of the ancient monuments in Wales there are Welsh folk tales associated with them. During the eighteenth century Pentre Ifan and two standing stones nearby (The Penlan Stones) were known to be the haunt of the Tylwyth Teg – the Welsh fairy folk. Small red coated figures with pointed caps were seen dancing around the stones. There are many of these tales of the 'wee folk' or hobgoblins in Celtic literature and today they are mainly restricted to islands off the west coast of Ireland. Interestingly the Koran of the Islamic religion describes them as 'jins'.

Many of the portal dolmens of Pembrokeshire have collapsed but during excavation of Pentre Ifan, the capstone was supported on a strong wooden frame and afterwards the structure was stabilised. Excavations revealed only charcoal and a few potsherds. Any bone remains were probably dissolved in the acid soil. Pentre Ifan is signposted and marked on the maps of Pembrokeshire.

After visiting Pentre Ifan a similar and spectacular portal dolmen can be found nearby by descending to the north Pembrokeshire coast road and proceeding west to the town of Newport. There can be found Cerreg Coetan Arthur within the eastern suburbs of Newport. Follow the road to the beach and look for the dolmen sign post. The dolmen is in its own cleared and hedged-off area within an estate of bungalows. Its similarity to Pentre Ifan is very obvious but the capstone rests on only two of the four support stones.

There are other examples of spectacular Neolithic burial chambers in Pembrokeshire but on some the huge capstones have collapsed. Others that might be of interest are:

a) Trellys, St. Nicholas – capstone with only two supports.

b) Carreg Samson, Mathry – capstone with six supports.

c) Garn Turne, near Letterston – capstone has collapsed onto fallen supports.

d) Hanging Stone, Angle – capstone with three supports.

e) Devil's Quoit, Angle – capstone with two supports on one side, other side on ground on fallen support.

f) King's Quoit, Manorbier - large capstone with two supports and one end on ground.

Because the tops of the Preseli Mountains have never been divided into fields for ploughing, the ancient stone monuments are often preserved.

However the fate of a similar Neolithic monument to Pentre Ifan is described by Fenton who visited the area in 1809 (1811 reprinted 1994). This monument existed near Maenclochog on the southern flanks of the Preseli Ridge. Originally it was part of a farm called Bwlch y Clawdd. It was purchased by a Mr. Pryce who renamed it Temple Druid after the monument then believed to have been an altar constructed by the Iron Age Druids rather than a burial chamber of the earlier Neolithic people. Unfortunately it was situated just above the house as the farm expanded, so the monument became included in the farm yard. It was then first used as a pig sty and then later as a shelter for calves. It was finally destroyed and removed. However a record of it was taken by a friend of Fenton - a Mr. Williams of Ivy Tower. The capstone was measured as over thirteen feet in diameter, eighteen inches thick at the sides and two feet thick in the centre. It stood about four feet above the ground and was supported on upright stones. Temple Druid changed hands many times and became an elegant hunting seat.

The Neolithic tombs of Pembrokeshire record part of the migration route of Neolithic peoples. The path extends from the Mediterranean, westwards through Sardinia, the Iberian coast, Brittany, the Channel Islands, Cornwall, Wales, Ireland, SW Scotland and on to Denmark and Sweden. The Neolithic peoples were the first farmers who made wooden handles for their finely ground stone axes and cultivated the soil for wheat, oats, barley and rye. They were potters and also weaved the wool from their sheep, made ropes of hair, but knew nothing about smelting metals. Their skeletal remains show long heads that differ from the later waves of immigrants.

Suggested Further Reading

Fenton, R., 1811, *A historical tour through Pembrokeshire*. Reprinted 2019, Herd Press, 818 p.

Owen, G., 1603, Reprinted 1994, *The Description of Pembrokeshire*: Miles, D., (Ed.), Gomer Press, Llandysul, Dyfed, 319 p.

Rees.S., 1992, *A Guide to Ancient and Historic Wales – Dyfed*: HMSO, London, 241 p.

7. THE SUNKEN FORESTS OF PEMBROKESHIRE

There are many traditions in Wales of inundations by the sea. Perhaps best known is the tale of the bells of Aberdovey. This coastal village disappeared beneath the sea a long time ago but the inhabitants of modern Aberdovey claim that on certain nights the church bells can be heard ringing beneath the sea. Another well known tale is of the lost land of Cantref y Gwaelod (the lowland hundred) that lies beneath Cardigan Bay. This low lying fertile land also known as the Plains of Gwyddno is reputed to have had sixteen towns and to have extended from St. David's Head in Pembrokeshire to Aberdaron at the tip of the Lleyn Peninsula. The area was defended against the sea by strong embankments and sluice gates to drain the streams at low tide. The embankments and sluice gates were the responsibility of Prince Seithennyn. The prince was a great drinker and even a drunkard who allowed the embankments and sluice gates to deteriorate. One night when Seithennyn was attending a banquet he became very intoxicated as a great storm arrived. The sea broke through the defences and inundated the land and only two people escaped together on a white horse. Today there are places where stone banks (called sarnau) on the coast of Cardigan Bay can be seen leading away to disappear under the sea. However geologists today regard these sarnau as a type of glacial moraine deposited by melting ice sheets of the Great Ice Age. In particular they are eskers formed by gravel deposited in meltwater channels usually under the ice sheet.

The last ice advance ended about 12,700 years ago (the start of the Holocene epoch) when the ice started to melt and sea-level to rise. Tales of flooded lands are known all around the world. The oldest of these is the story the ancient Sumerian King Gilgamesh of Uruk in Mesopotamia. The tale records how the king met Utnapishtim, an old man who experienced the great flood, and reported that a boat was sent to see what could be saved. Finally the boat came to rest on a mountain top and Utapishtim released birds. The Genesis version is the story of Noah and his ark.

During the glacial maximum of the last Ice Age around 20,000 years ago, sea level around the world was about 120 meters (400 feet) lower than it is today and the land area of Britain was considerable (Figure 5). Global warming began at this time and started melting the great ice sheets so that sea level has risen uniformly around the world. The great flooded valley or ria of the Milford Haven waterway is a drowned valley. The English Channel was dry land ten thousand years ago and the North Sea was a land today named Doggerland. Radiocarbon dating has shown that Britain became separated from Europe by rising sea levels between 8,000 and 7,500 years BP. French archaeologists are today excavating Queen Cleopatra's palace, which is today under thirty feet of sea water. The ancient Greek sea ports around the Mediterranean are drowned today.

As summer visitors to Pembrokeshire, it is possible to see evidence for this inundation of the sea in the form of the sunken forests of Pembrokeshire. All around the coasts of Pembrokeshire are sandy bays, where after storms have shifted sand reveal the sunken forests at low tides. These are composed of peat containing the roots in growth positions of mainly giant oak trees with some beech trees. The wood of the trees has been stained brown pink by the peat. Radiocarbon dating of the trees and dendrochronological studies (tree rings) show that most lived between 7,000 and 4,500 years BP in the Mesolithic period of the Stone Age and stone tools have been found in the peat. But some sunken forests are older, yielding ages of 7,500 years and some as young as 1,500 and 730 years BP indicating they are Neolithic. Recently at Amroth numerous footprints of these ancient people together with those of deer have been recognised in the top surface of the peat. The peat is only weakly compacted so the footprints were soon eroded by the sea.

The sunken forests can be seen all around the coasts of Wales and Pembrokeshire. In the south they can be found at very low tides at Marros Sands (Plate 4), at Amroth Sands (between Pendine and Saundersfoot) and at Lydstep near Tenby. They are also found at Newgale beach and Whitesands in the northwest. In the north they can be found at Newport and Abermawr beaches on the south coast of Cardigan Bay. The most spectacular example is that at Marros Sands where huge oak trees up to a hundred feet long and two feet wide lie as the waves have oriented them with narrow tops to the beach and dragging roots at the seaward ends

(Plate 4). Late Mesolithic stone tools have been found within the sunken forest and at Lydstep Haven a pig skeleton was found beneath a fallen tree trunk. Looking at the great tree trunks all oriented towards the land at The Marros, one wonders if some of the marine incursions were catastrophic.

The sunken forests have been known for a long time and were seen and described by Geraldus Cambrensis (a priest scholar born at Manorbier castle in 1146 in Pembrokeshire) who saw them when journeying through Wales. In 1188 he crossed Newgale Sands on his way to St. Davids, after a violent storm. He described the shore there as completely denuded so that the subsoil which had been buried was revealed. Tree trunks were visible, standing in the sea, with their tops lopped off and with the cuts of axes as clear as if they had been felled only yesterday. The soil was pitch black and the tree trunks shone like ebony. He wrote that it looked not like a shore, but a grove cut down, perhaps at the time of the Flood or perhaps a little later but certainly very long ago. The storm was so fierce that conger eels and sea fish were driven up on the high rocks and into the bushes by the force of the wind and men gathered them up.

Suggested Further Reading

Cambrensis, G., 1191 (1908 edition), *The itinerary through Wales: Description of Wales*: Dent, London.

Rees.S., 1992, *A Guide to Ancient and Historic Wales – Dyfed*: HMSO, London, 241 p.

8. FOEL ERYR - A BRONZE AGE BURIAL CAIRN IN THE PRESELI MOUNTAINS WITH VIEWS OF IRELAND, NORTH WALES AND LUNDY ISLAND

The east-west ridge of the Preseli Mountains forms the backbone of Pembrokeshire and an extension of the Welsh Mountains. The ridge has been glacially smoothed by the passage of ice sheets in the Great Ice Age. When viewing the ridge from a distance, one or more small mounds can be seen on the summits. These are Bronze Age burial tumuli composed of heaps of stones. They represent a big change in burial practice and probably religion from those Neolithic megalith builders who were replaced by the Beaker people of the Bronze Age. The skeletal remains of the latter show them to be round headed. They had bronze weapons and tools and placed the cremated remains in their graves. The cairns appear in the Early Bronze Age (about 2,500 to 1,400 BC). There are both cairns (circular mounds of stone) and barrows (circular mounds of earth). The Bronze Age people also erected standing stones. Archaeologists have found rings of post holes marking wood-henge type of monuments. It has been argued that it was easier for the Bronze Age people to fell trees using their bronze axes. This is a bit academic however as the easiest way to fell a tree is (as still used in some countries) to ring bark it and when it has died burn through the base. The latter can be easily achieved by inserting a glowing ember into the wood on a windy day.

The tops of the Preseli Mountains are fairly inaccessible to the majority of visitors especially with children. However there is one place only where one of the hilltops with a Bronze Age cairn is readily accessible and it also has magnificent views. This is where the Haverfordwest – Cardigan Road (B4329) crosses over the Preseli ridge. At the highest point (400m) there is a car park on the east side of the road well shown on the latest Google Earth images at latitude 51.954881 degrees North, longitude -4.802593 degrees West. From this the Golden Road or Ridge Way – an ancient Bronze Age track - passes both ways along the ridge. To the west is Foel Eryr (only 1000 meters from the car park and only sixty-five meters higher than the car park) with a Bronze Age cairn and a modern lookout point (Plate 5). The cairn and lookout are visible on the latest Google Earth images at latitude 51.953405 degrees north, longitude -4.816175 degrees West. To the east is Foel Cwm Cerwyn (536 m) – the highest point in Pembrokeshire. The Bronze Age cairn is not over-impressive being just a circular pile of stones with a diameter of up to thirty meters and rising a few meters.

Three similar cairns are present on top of Foel Drygarn at the eastern end of the Preseli ridge. From the air the cairns can be seen to have several pits within them indicating that they were multi-chambered. The pits are probably robber pits where the individual graves have been looted for their bronze artefacts either in antiquity of by the eighteenth century barrow diggers. What is splendid about the cairns are their sites on the tops of the Preseli Mountains. On clear days the views from the tops of these mountains are magnificent and many find the panoramic views spiritually uplifting and enervating. The sites place the dead (presumably leaders or kings) closest to their Gods and with panoramic views over the lands they once ruled. Conversely as the burial cairns are visible from great distances, the Bronze Age people could see that their old kings were still there looking over them.

The lookout on top of Foel Eryr is a modern pillar of stone with a large circular brass plaque on the top (Plate 5). On this a series of radial lines point out the most distant places visible and they are named. From here on a clear day the rounded tops of the Wicklow Mountains of SE Ireland can be seen, also the steep-sided Lundy Island. The peaks of Snowdonia are visible as is the Llyn Peninsula and also Bardsey Island. The air is bracing, the colors of the heather and gorse with the white clean wool of the mountain sheep attractive. Sometimes mountain ponies can be seen and it is a fine place for a picnic to enjoy the splendid views. However care must be taken to select a clear sunny cloudless day when sea mists and low clouds are absent. In the depths of winter with snow on the ground the mountains are very photogenic.

What the lookout does not indicate is that the Preseli Mountains sweeping away on all sides are the sites where, according to the ancient Iron Age Celtic tales of the Mabinogion (See Chapter 13), where King Arthur persued and fought the magical giant boar Ywrch Trwyth with her seven piglets. Arthur rode his mare Llamrai and had his dog Cafell, his sons and warriors with him. Three times they trapped the boar, but the animal escaped by killing eleven of Arthur's warriors and his son Gwydre.

The Bronze Age is famous for its metalwork. Most distinctive are the bronze flanged axe heads or palstaves, bronze spearheads and bronze sickles.

Several hoards of these have been found in Pembrokeshire and scattered examples collected from the peat of the sunken forests around the coasts. The Bronze Age people also worked gold into exquisite torcs worn around their necks or on their arms.

Their burial practices involved cremation and the construction of many monuments that still occur throughout Pembrokeshire. They abandoned the megalith burials of the Stone Age people and instead cremated their dead and buried the ashes in stone cysts covered by round barrows constructed of soil or round cairns constructed of stones. The various shapes have been classified as bell, disc, bowl or round barrows.

In North Pembrokeshire in the treeless Preseli Mountains, Bronze Age remains abound. On Carn Ingli near Newport there are Bronze Age circular enclosures, hut circles and field boundaries. On Foel Drygarn there are three massive stone tumuli or barrows, that have been incorporated into a later Iron Age fortified settlement. A well known pair of standing stones is that of Cerrig Meibion Arthur in the great amphitheatre of Cwm Cerwyn. These are reputed to be the grave markers of two of King Arthur's sons who fell in battle, but today interpreted by archaeologists as a Bromze Age ritual fertility site. A well known example of a single tall standing stone is Bedd Morris on the crest of a ridge near Newport. In south Pembrokeshire there is the Long Stone at Mabesgate on the Dale Peninsula.

Suggested Further Reading

Darvill, T., and Wainwright, G., 2016, Chapter 2. Neolithic and Bronze Age Pembrokeshire: In: Darvill, T., James, H., Murphy, K., Wainwright, G., and Walker, E.A., Pembrokeshire County History, *Vol. 1. Prehistoric, Roman and Early Medieval Pembrokeshire*: Pembrokeshire County History Trust, Haverfordwest, p. 55 - 222.

Rees.S., 1992, *A Guide to Ancient and Historic Wales – Dyfed*: HMSO, London, 241 p.

9. TWO BRONZE-AGE STONE CIRCLES IN THE PRESELI MOUNTAINS.

The Preseli Mountains are moorland, often boggy, without trees (except for modern fir plantations). Open moorland above the tree line was obviously attractive to ancient man, whereas the lowlands of Pembrokeshire were then covered in the great wildwood. Two stone rings occur, one on either side of Maenclochog village. The bigger ring of Gors Fawr is easily accessible by road with a small car park, prominent sign and gate though the hedge. It commands a fine vista of the Preseli Mountains rounded by the ice sheets of the Great Ice Age. It makes a fine picnic outing for the family. The slightly smaller ring of Dyffryn Syfynwy is difficult to find and is on private land, but can be seen from a farm lane leading to it.

Gors Fawr is a single ring of sixteen small stones and the location is within a magnificent vast natural amphitheatre to the north making a backdrop of the green and brown treeless ridge of the Preseli Mountains distinct against the vast open canopy of sky (Plate 6). On a sunny day the splendour of the Preseli Ridge with great white clouds in the blue sky gives this place a magic quality. The colors vary greatly depending on season and weather. On the skyline, the ridge rises to the highest point in Pembrokeshire at Foel Cwm Cerwyn (536 m) and extends to Carn Meini which has been suggested as a source of some of the blue stones at Stonehenge. The name Gors Fawr translates as 'waste land' or 'marsh'

Stone circles are rare in Pembrokeshire. Gors Fawr has a diameter of around twenty-two meters. The stones are equidimensional and the highest is only sixty centimetres. About a half of the stones appear to be composed of spotted 'bluestone'. This is a dolerite found commonly throughout the area as glacial erratics with sources in local crags such as Carn Meini. The other stones are glacial erratics found in the area. The stones increase in height towards the south-west. The Gors Fawr circle is not quite true. It is clearly visible on the latest Google Earth images at latitude 51.931421 degrees North, longitude -4.714205 West.

There is a report that at the beginning of the twentieth century, that the circle was attached by a stone avenue to two nearby standing stones located 134 meters towards the north-north-east. Both standing stones are 2m tall.

One is locally known as 'the Dreaming Stone'. Today the avenue cannot be recognised but the moor is covered in scattered boulders of local 'bluestone' rock. It has been suggested that the two standing stones mark the alignment of the midsummer sunrise over the top of Foel Drych some 2.4 kilometres away.

Dyffryn Syfynwy is an elliptical ring of eighteen stones with a diameter of about 18 meters (Plate 7). The stones range from 1.0 to 2.1 meters tall with the largest on the south-east side. Inside are the remains of an earth tumulus. The ring is clearly visible on the latest Google Earth images at latitude 51.920678 degrees North, longitude - 4.823650 degrees West.

The circles are believed to have been built in the third to second millennium BC in the Bronze Age. Their purpose is unknown, but in general stone circles are not associated with burials. Their function must therefore have been ceremonial. They often show astronomical alignments. A possible function is that as they were built by farming communities, to be used as astronomical calendars to predict the times of the year for ploughing, sowing crops, harvesting and breeding animals.

To get to Gors Fawr go to Maenclochog and drive north for 1.5 kilometres. Take the road to right and follow it across the Preselies for about 8 kilometers to the village of Mynachlog Ddu. At the village turn right (south) and follow the road for 1.1 kilometers and then park at the sign on the right hand side. Go through the gate in the hedge and follow the track to the ring.

To get to Dyffryn Syfynwy from Maenclochog, drive north out of the village for 1.1 kilometers and take the first left to Tufton. Follow the road for 2.0 kilometers. Cross a bridge with a large building on the left. Continue uphill and park in a layby by a large reservoir building. Walk back downhill to a farm gate adjacent to a barn. Take the track to the left through a gate which leads to the ring. The field may have overfriendly cattle inside. The path stops in muddy ground at the ring which is separated by a fenced hedge and gate tied shut. This is private farm land but I have never found anyone there or in the area.

Suggested Further Reading

Rees.S., 1992, *A Guide to Ancient and Historic Wales – Dyfed*: HMSO, London, 241 p.

Darvill, T., and Wainwright, G., 2016, Chapter 2. Neolithic and Bronze Age Pembrokeshire: In: Darvill, T., James, H., Murphy, K., Wainwright, G., and Walker, E.A., Pembrokeshire County History, *Vol. 1. Prehistoric, Roman and Early Medieval Pembrokeshire*: Pembrokeshire County History Trust, Haverfordwest, p. 55 - 222.

10. THE IRON AGE HILL FORT OF FOEL DRYGARN (TRIGARN)

This is one of the most spectacular Iron Age hill forts in Wales (Plate 8). It lies on a prominent mountain top at the eastern end of the Preseli Ridge on the Bronze-Age Golden Road. The very top of Foel Drygarn is occupied by three large Bronze Age stone cairns. These lie along the ridge and are visible on the skyline for many miles around. The three cairns gave rise to the name of the mountain.

The cairns lie within an elliptical Iron Age fort that is defended by a natural ridge and cliff on the south side and a man-made stone embankment and ditches that form an arc on the western, northern and eastern sides. The smallest of these is the oldest part of the hill fort. It measures 190 meters NE-SW by 120 meters NW-SE. There are three entrances to be found on the eastern, western and southern sides. This early fort was considerably enlarged at a later date by the construction of a second arcuate man-made stone rampart to the north that parallels the earlier one. The new enclosure increased the size of the hill fort to 230 meters NE-SW by 210 meters NW-SE with entrances at the east and west ends. A third extension was made at the eastern end of the hillfort with the addition of an elliptical man-made stone rampart. This brought the final dimensions to be 360 meters NE-SW with no change to the other dimension. The third extension has entrances on the north and south sides. The earliest rampart is constructed of soil and rock fragments. The rampart for the second enclosure is less substantial. The third enclosure has quite weak walls.

The fort is highly photogenic from the air especially when the sun is at low angles as up to 270 circular hut platforms represented by circular depressions can be seen (Plate 8). These show that the Iron Age huts were closely crowded together in the early fort but those present in the later two enclosures are more spaced out. It is interesting to note that when the Iron Age people were collecting the stones to build the three stages of ramparts, they did not remove anything from the Bronze age tumuli, obviously having a respect for these then-ancient graves.

Archaeological excavations at Foel Drygarn revealed few artifacts. Two stone bowls were found with rounded bottoms that might have been oil lamps. A small jet ring was found. Some Iron Age and Roman pottery fragments were found as well as spindle whorls, fine glass beads, and great numbers of sling stones. Some of the latter were still stacked in piles. The beads were all made of glass. Two were small and composed of dark blue glass. A fragment of a third bead was found composed of yellow glass containing a clear spiral. In addition seven half beads of green glass were also found. In the Iron Age these were expensive items, made mainly at Glastonbury. The beads and jet ring indicate that valuable goods were traded over wide areas.

Foel Drygarn is interpreted to have begun in the Late Bronze Age and to have continued through the Iron Age into the Roman Age. The hillfort underwent two phases of major expansion to become one of the major Iron Age settlements of Pembrokeshire. There are only three others in Pembrokeshire of similar size being Carn Ingli, Garn Fawr and St. David's Head. Each of these is likely to mark the centres of population and government at the time and the seats of powerful leaders. It is possible that St. David's Head was mentioned by Ptolemy, in his 'Geographica' (c. AD 140) who gave the name of the peninsula as Octopitarum Promontorium meaning the promontory of the eight perils, believed to refer to the offshore rocks and pinnacles today known as 'The Bishop and his Clarks'. It has also been suggested that the name might be after an Iron age tribe – the Octapitai – who occupied the large promontory fort on St. David's Head. There are no records for the other centres.

Suggested Further Reading
Rees.S., 1992. *A Guide to Ancient and Historic Wales – Dyfed*: HMSO, London, 241 p.

11. CASTELL HENLLYS - A RECONSTRUCTED IRON AGE SETTLEMENT NEAR NEWPORT

Across Pembrokeshire there are about a hundred Iron Age settlements including many small hillforts, a few major hillforts, promontory forts and defended farmsteads. The Iron Age was the age of the Celtic warrior – a time of tribal fighting and raiding for cattle and women. The Celts fought the Romans who wrote about them describing the Welsh tribes as 'war-mad and quick to battle'. The Romans liked to fight the Celts as the latter, including both men and women, fought naked to show off their bodies painted elaborately in blue woad (a blue dye extracted from the leaves of the mustard plant family). The Romans with their armour would close shields and spear the Celts in their undefended legs as they wanted the gold torques worn around their necks. The fortified settlements represent the homes of countless generations of families and tribes that occupied Pembrokeshire following the Bronze Age and often lasted into the Roman Period.

Today for a family visit there is one small hillfort that has been purchased by the Pembrokeshire Coast National Park authority that is outstanding for the excavation and reconstruction work going on there. In the summer demonstrations there show life in the Iron Age. A family visit vividly illustrates the living and working conditions of the Iron Age inhabitants and children can have their faces blue painted with intricate patterns.

Castell Henllys (Old Court) lies on a small spur overlooking a tributary of the River Nevern. The main defensive earthworks lie on the northern gentler approach and consist of a large inner bank, a ditch and a smaller outer bank. The defences curve around to a natural scarp in the east but on the west stop at the main entrance which is still used as the modern entry point.

The entrance was originally built of stone with a double ditch outside as an additional defence. Excavations of the main entrance reveal that the main gateway was begun in the fifth century BC as a long stone-walled passageway flanked by pairs of large timber posts supporting a large timber gate and probably a bridge or tower over the entrance. In the passageway were two pairs of semi-circular guard chambers, recessed into the sides. The gateway was rebuilt several times during the occupation of the fort. In its early history, stones were arranged outside as a chevaux-de-frise similar to that of nearby Carn Alw on the Preseli Mountains. This prevented attacks by bands of horsemen. Excavations uncovered several thousand sling stones stored behind the rampart. Radiocarbon dating of eleven samples of bone and charcoal from Castell Henllys gave an occupation range from 400 to 240 BC.

Inside the fort Iron Age houses have been reconstructed on the sites of original houses (Plate 9). The buildings clearly show the complex methods used in ancient times to build a round house. They had cenral fire places. Smoke leaked out through the rush roof. There were benches and sleeping places around the inner perimeter. There are guides dressed in Celtic clothing to explain the Iron Age way of life. Much is being learned about life at that time from the reconstruction. For example the largest roundhouse required thirty coppiced oak trees, ninety coppiced hazel bushes, 2000 bundles of water reeds and two miles of hemp role and twine for the construction of its posts, rafters, ring beams, wattle-and-daub walls and large conical reed roof.

The houses (or palaces as they would have been for the ruling elite) had central open hearths. They stand around an open area where excavation showed the remains of other hearths possibly used for feasting. Some were made of stone with postholes to support cauldrons over fires. Five settings each of four postholes have been found interpreted as granaries raised off the ground to protect grain and from pests. One of the houses was used by blacksmiths for iron smelting and working. The shaded interior of the house permitted the various subtle color variations of the hot metal to be seen for working. Other reconstructions are a pottery kiln, an iron smelting furnace and a short section of timber fencing on the top of the outer rampart.

Castell Henllys probably supported a wealthy ruling warrior elite of several families and a leader. The farming community of perhaps a hundred persons that they protected lived on the surrounding farmland. Crops, cereals and perhaps beans were grown nearby while livestock grazed in surrounding fields. The site gives a very good appreciation of life in Iron Age Wales before the Roman invasion.

Outside the fort to the north, a rectangular Romano-British separate settlement has been found. This was built after Castell Henllys was abandoned and its position on lower ground suggests a much lower requirement for defence.

On a first visit to Castell Henllys with a family and young children around 1983, the site was owned by Huw Foster a retired businessman from London (who had already created the London Dungeon). He was a great enthusiast of the Iron Age and of the archaeological excavations taking place there. It was he who conceived the idea of reconstructing the Iron Age village and displaying what was otherwise a fairly small ordinary Iron Age site. Huw would dress in woven robes and was very popular with the visitors and especially the children. One of his proud achievements was the Warriors Trail. This was a route for youths to follow up a muddy overgrown stream for warrior training. Our youngest son, then aged three was fascinated by Huw who wore Celtic clothing but had a fox tail attached to his belt which our son thought he had grown.

When Huw died, the site was sold by his widow to the Pembrokeshire Coast National Park who have now expanded the activities and put in a visitors center and shop. Events are held there throughout the tourist season and are proving very popular. A life-size fibreglass woolly mammoth of Huw's time has been moved to the dinosaur park near Tenby but has been replaced by a carved stone elephant in the visitors centre so there are still a few anachronisms. The Warriors Trail is no more (probably because of Health and Safety fears) but the sacred spring is still on display. The National Park organises events there which are promoted in their newspaper 'Coast to Coast'.

Suggested Further Reading
Rees.S., 1992. *A Guide to Ancient and Historic Wales – Dyfed*: HMSO, London, 241 p.

12. ROMAN PEMBROKESHIRE

Figure 6. A Roman patrol marching out of Wiston Fort

The story of Pembrokeshire in the days when Britannia was a Roman province is not well known. The old view was that there was very little evidence of Roman occupation or buildings with no ports or towns. On the other hand Roman coins and hoards are common and most interestingly are clustered around the sheltered ports, especially Tenby, Amroth, Angle, St. David's and Fishguard. Others have been found along the Eastern and Western Cleddau Rivers, especially at Canaston. For those with sailing interests this apparent enigma speaks very clearly of little Roman settlement on land, but that there was trading with the local people by sea and along the Cleddau estuaries.

It has only been since the invention of railways, asphalted or macadamised roads and motor vehicles that this practice has ceased. The many small coastal inlets and bays of Pembrokeshire were used right up into the 1920's and 1930's by small trading schooners and there is a legacy of old lime kilns and fulling mills around these sheltered ports where limestone and culm coal were landed and burned for liming the fields of rather acid soil thoroughly the area. Also the amount of archaeological work in Pembrokeshire is not great and today most finds are accidental by metal detectorists or by the construction of sites and pipelines for the new energy industry based on the Milford Haven Waterway. During the past decade this picture has been changing with some surprising discoveries, of Roman roads, villas, civilian sites and even a Roman fort.

In Roman times what today constitutes the counties of Carmarthen and Pembrokeshire was the land of the Demetae tribe. After the Roman conquest this area was administered from the Roman fort and town of Moridunum which is the Carmarthen of today. Archaeologists today regard Moridunum as the civitas capital or administrative centre for the Demetae and their lands. However this picture is beginning to change with the discovery of a Roman road leading west from Carmarthen and traced (to date) to Wiston only five miles from Haverfordwest. Also at Wiston a Roman Fort which could house up to 5,000 men has been identified with a small local settlement alongside (Figure 6). A ground penetrating radar study has confirmed a Romano-British villa near Ford at Wolfcastle on a site where a hypocaust was uncovered by a farm labourer in the nineteenth century. There is a rumour of Roman gold mining in the Treffgarne area. Gold in both the rocks and in the gravels of Treffgarne Gorge has recently been confirmed by drilling by the British Geological Survey. The Romans mined gold in the land of the Demetae and today the Roman tunnels at the Dalaucothi gold mine, situated northeast of Carmarthen south east of Lampeter are open to the public. Roman lead mines existed east of Carmarthen. The remains of a large stone Roman building (60 by 27 feet) have been excavated near Amroth.

For those who sail today, the peninsula of Pembrokeshire, jutting out into the Irish Sea with the dominant south-westerly winds, is a formidable obstacle for getting around the coast of Wales. The many headlands and outlying rocks and strong tidal currents in the boisterous and changeable weather cause boats to spend days in shelter before proceeding around the next headland. Indeed sailing today is very much a sport for the brief summer days as a look at the many marinas in winter will show. One of the most formidable headlands and peninsulas is that of St. David's where there are few sheltered bays, strong tidal races and offshore reefs. In Book 2 of the Roman writer Ptolemy's 'Geography' written in Greek in the second century AD, there is a map showing the St. David's peninsula recorded as 'Octapitarum Promontorium'. Evidently the Roman Fleet was aware of the dangers of the headland and of the Bishop and Clerks reef offshore

Richard Fenton in his 1811 book 'A historical Tour through Pembrokeshire' described Roman brick fragments from a villa at Castle Flemish and another at Ford near Wolfscastle. Both villas have been confirmed by later work. Another Roman villa was excavated at Trelissey near Amroth in the early 1950's. Yet another villa with a temple alongside has been identified in 2017 in north Pembrokeshire. The puzzle of where the Roman road traced from Carmarthen to Wiston on aerial photographs went, was advanced considerably by the recognition in 2012 of a Roman fort at Wiston. The pottery suggests it was occupied in the late first century/early second century AD and that it was reused in the mid-second to mid-third centuries. Field finds and excavation to its south side have revealed a civilian vicus settlement alongside.

Whitesands Bay on the end of the St Davids Peninsula was for a long time an important crossing point to Ireland. It was known to Pliny the Elder who in his 'Natural History' written in the first century AD, mentions that 'Hibernia lies beyond Britannia, the shortest crossing being from the lands of the Demetae, a distance of 30 miles' (Book IV, 16, 103). A Google Earth measurement shows the distance to be 130 kilometers (80 miles).

In AD 43 at Richborough in Kent the Romans invaded Britain. Led by General Aulus Plautius, about 22,000 Roman soldiers in four legions supported by an equal number of auxiliary troops landed. The well-armoured Roman troops and the Roman cavalry quickly defeated the Iron Age Celtic warriors. However the rugged terrain of Wales, other Roman priorities and strong resistance in south-east Wales by the Silures (who held out for thirty years) slowed the Roman advance.

In AD 47 the Roman General Ostorius Scapula defeated the Deceangli tribe in what is now Flintshire and then waged war against the Silures of south east Wales and the Ordovices of central Wales until almost AD 51. This resulted in the defeat of the British King Caratacus in mid Wales who had retreated there with his warriors after being defeated by the Romans in battle at the River Medway and the River Thames But it was not until AD 60 that the tribes of north and south Wales were defeated by Suetonius Paulinus. Following the Boudican revolt in AD 60-61, Governor Julius Frontinus by AD 78 moved large numbers of troops into the Welsh mountains and built a fort at Caerleon. This was followed by building a road network to link the marching camps and forts.

In retrospect today, knowing the stormy history of the Dark and Middle ages, it seems remarkable that for four centuries Brittania was a Roman province. Following the conquest, Roman rule prevailed (AD 43 to 410) and the peace and glory that was Rome, reigned. Many citizens enjoyed well-planned cities laid out on a grid plan, with temples, markets, academies. Romanised Britons joined the legions, and served with distinction across the Empire along the Rhine, the Danube and the Euphrates. The peace produced and revered craftsmen, merchants, professors of literature and rhetoric. There was law and order, respect for property and a widening culture. The Romanised Britons adopted the Roman dress and customs. It was very desirable to be a citizen of Rome as one was then a citizen of the world and had a status superior to barbarians and slaves. Travel throughout the Roman Empire was not difficult and relatively safe and a lot simpler than today as there were no frontiers and borders to cross.

The Romanised Britons grew prosperous. The most prosperous of them attained the villa way of life – possibly one of the ideals of all time. These complexes were built in places of great scenic beauty and were the heart of a farming community. The stone built villas were decorated with mosaic floors, pillars and statues. Following the departure of the Roman Legions by AD 410, raids by the Picts, Saxons and Irish increased and Britannia began to collapse into the Dark Ages. The affluent villa people in many areas saw the end of their way of life. Those at risk buried their wealth and retreated into the walled cities. Some never returned. The splendid Milden Hall silver plate was probably buried at this time and never recovered. Hoards of coins from the third and fourth centuries are being found today by metal detectorists.

Not all the villas were destroyed, many inland examples continued for a century or more. These last centres faced an interesting problem rediscovered later after the American Civil war. About a third of the population of Roman Britain were slaves. The villas ran on slave power. After the legions left it became difficult to enforce slavery and gradually the slaves left to find their own lives as freemen. So the last villas collapsed and fine stone buildings with central heating and baths disappeared to be replaced by a return to Iron Age style living in wood and thatch huts. Worse it became a nightmare of savage hordes who wrecked the Roman culture. The stone buildings were abandoned. Writing was lost. Barbarism reigned and it became a time when petty ruffians sometimes called kings savaged the land.

As Sir Winston Churchill points out in his 'History of the English Speaking Peoples', the people of these islands then remained cold and dirty for the next fifteen hundred years. It was only in the middle of the Victorian times that bath houses, bathing and heated stone houses were reattained. However in the age of darkness it was the Christian Church that became the refuge of learning, art and writing. Throughout the Dark Ages, the clerics became the civil servants of the day and they became indispensible to the proud and violent chieftains. They wore the same clothing as the Roman magistrates, as do the monks of today.

What emerged as the civitas capital of the Demetae and their lands (todays Pembrokeshire and Carmarthenshire) began as a Roman fort at Carmarthen, known as Moridunum Demetarum. It was built about AD 75 on the north side of a crossing of the River Tywi and closed soon after AD 120 when the troops were moved to Hadrian's Wall. It was never a major legionary headquarters and more likely a base for auxiliary troops. The site then became a Roman town administered by the Romanised Demetae. Archaeological excavations began only in 1970. Most of the buildings were of wood construction. A Romano-British temple has been excavated in the northwest of the town. An amphitheatre lay 200 meters to the east of the town walls, with only the arena wall and the entrance passages built of stone but possibly capable of holding 5,000 people indicating Moridunum to be a major centre. The town was defended by two ditches in the mid to late second century enclosing an area of thirty-two acres. A wall was added probably in the mid to late third century.

Although the main buildings still await excavation and study, much is known of the Roman way of life and their forts and towns were very similar. While the fort was garrisoned, the headquarters building (the Principia) was the centre of the fort with a hall open at the front where there was a courtyard with ranges of rooms on the three sides. Rooms at the back of the hall were offices for administration. The hall was the symbolic heart for the troops and the standards were displayed there. Immediately behind the hall would have been the praetorium, the residence of the commander, a Roman of high social standing with his wife and family with him plus numerous servants and slaves. Nearby on the main road through the fort (the Via Principalis) the senior officers would have their own houses. Also in the fort would have been baths, a workshop, a hospital and storerooms or granaries. Each Roman fort was supposed to store a years supply of grain as well as preserved meat, wine and olive oil. Much space was taken up by the barracks. Each barrack comprised rows of paired rooms.

The forts became the centre of growing towns which provided for the legionaries and their families when off duty. Discharged legionaries and their families often chose to live there. Before the early third century soldiers were not allowed to be married but many formed relationships with local women. From the end of the second century legionaries were allowed to live with their families. Also outside the fortress would have been the parade ground and the amphitheatre – large areas that did not need defending in time of attack. The stone facings of the arena were there to protect the spectators by stopping wild animals from climbing out. A legionary enlisted in his late teens and served for twenty-five years. By then he would have had a family and commonly chose to retire where he had worked rather than return home.

In 1989 a Roman road leading west from Carmarthen was discovered as a series of crop marks in a dry summer. The road passes just north of St. Clears and Llawhaden and just north of Wiston. Its destination has not yet been discovered but it is heading directly towards the village of Crundale (which has an Iron Age fort) situated only a mile northeast of Haverfordwest. The present known limit of the road is only five miles from Haverfordwest, which was a port (some of the Victorian warehouses are still standing) at the highest navigable part of the Western Cleddau River and also the first crossing point at which the river could be forded. However no Roman remains are yet known in the Haverfordwest area. Excavations in 1995 for a bypass near Whitland revealed a well-built Roman road founded on brushwood and timber and resurfaced several times with cobbles, slabs and gravel. It is flanked by ditches and quarry pits where gravel was dug. It will be most interesting to see if in the future an undiscovered Roman port can be found on the Western Cleddau River somewhere near Haverfordwest.

The 1843 one inch to one mile Ordinance Survey map of Pembrokeshire (Haverfordwest sheet printed several times between 1819 and 1840) show two parallel roads leading westwards across the county. They were surveyed between 1809 and 1814 and named as Roman roads by Fenton and Sir Richard Colt. The northern track-road runs along the ridge of the Preseli Mountains and continues to Abereiddy, to turn parallel to the coast and reach Whitesands Bay where a Roman settlement of Menapia is marked (today believed to be lost beneath the sand dunes there). This road was named the Via Flandrica. The southern one was named the Via Julia. It skirts the southern flanks of the Preseli Mountains and continues west through Henry's Moat to an excavated Roman fortlet or Romanised farmstead named ad Vicassium (Flemish Castle) and on to Ford where a Roman villa (first described by Fenton 1811) has recently been confirmed by ground penetrating radar. The Via Julia continues on through Brawdy to St Davids and leads perhaps to the tiny harbour of St. Justinians.

Recently the Via Julia and its settlements have been regarded as fabrications based on a forged Roman map of Britain by Charles Bertram with false names of forts and stations. Charles (1992) has found the name 'Via Flandrensica' in a thirteenth century document, 'Via Flandrenica' in a 1610 document and is named the 'fflemings waie' in 1602. Charles concludes that the track dates from the time of the Flemings arriving and settling in Pembrokeshire. However the abundance of Neolithic, Bronze Age and Iron Age burial monuments, and fortified settlements along these tracks suggests that they may be considerably older than Roman times. The trackways in the Preseli Mountains lie above the tree line and would have provided a fast route in the days when the lower lands were still heavily forested.

The Roman army was supported by the Roman Navy which comprised a number of fleets operating throughout the Roman Empire. The British fleet was known as the 'Classis Britannica' and was based in the English Channel where it operated between the ports of Boulogne and Dover, where the Roman stone lighthouses still stand. The Roman Navy was a major operation and in AD 287, Carausius the commander of the British Fleet, seized control of Britain and northern Gaul declaring himself 'Emperor of the North', but his reign lasted only seven years. During the first century the Roman Navy supported the army by carrying soldiers, horses and supplies and making speedy communications possible. The ships explored the coasts ahead of the invading armies. The named Roman fleets were reorganised in the third century and replaced by a series of smaller squadrons to tackle increased barbarian raids and piracy. A series of coastal forts were built along the coasts of south-east Britain to defend against raiding ships. Vegitius writing in the fourth century mentions a special type of light galley in the British fleet. These ships, their hulls, sails, the crews clothing and even their faces were painted sea green to be invisible and were known as 'the Painted Ones'.

It seems likely that the Romans had a fleet operating in the Bristol Channel as all the major forts of South Wales at Cardiff, Neath, Loughor and Carmarthen are all situated at the navigable heads of major river estuaries. A Roman quay has been found on the River Usk at Caerleon. It is likely that the large Roman fort at Cardiff (later built over by Cardiff castle) was the headquarters of a fleet operating on both sides of the Bristol Channel. Archaeologists have found coal from the Forest of Dean in a Roman villa at Llantwit Major near the Bristol Channel that is thought to have been shipped there by sea and probably to other parts of the welsh coast line. At Caer Gybi on Anglesey a base was built in the third or fourth century for a small Roman fleet.

Travel around the coast by Roman ships would all face the problem of rounding the Octapitarum Promontory. Roman ships rounding Pembrokeshire to reach other parts of the coastline of South Wales and Cardigan Bay in times of rapid weather changes, would need to seek shelter. The presence of the two mile wide entrance to the Milford Haven Waterway would have provided a safe haven for Roman ships. The Pembrokeshire Prospectors club has found with their metal detectors Roman coins and brooches at Angle just inside the entrance to the waterway on the south side. This would be the first sheltered bay on entering the waterway in times of the prevailing strong south-westerly winds. There is believed to be a Roman town possibly buried beneath the sand dunes of Whitesands near St. David's that might have been an anchorage for ships having difficulty rounding St. David's Head, where shelter from south-westerly storms could be found behind Ramsay Island. Did the green ships ever pass this way in persuit of Irish raiders? How well did the Roman ships know the Irish Sea or Oceanus Hivernicus?

In conclusion, Pembrokeshire was no Roman stronghold but was the outlying part of the Demetae lands administered from the Civitas Capital of the Demetae of Moridunum now Carmarthen. The coin finds and hoards around the coastal areas of Pembrokeshire suggest that the small harbours were of great use to the Roman shipping and that trading was carried out with the Celtic Iron age communities. It seems likely that many of the Celtic fortified settlements had some Roman Samian ware pottery, as shards were found during the Castell Henllys excavation. The significance of the Roman road found leading west from Carmarthen is as yet unknown but the presence of gold in the Trefgarné Gorge area (proved recently by drilling by the British Geological Survey) and rumours of a Roman gold mine there are a possible explanation. The Romans mined gold and lead at Dolau Cothi, in the lands of the Demetae in what is now the county of Carmarthen.

Suggested Further Reading

Churchill, W. S., Sir, 1956-58, *A History of the English Speaking Peoples*: Volumes 1 to VI. Casswell, London.

Fenton, R., 1911, *A Historical Tour through Pembrokeshire*: Reprinted 2019, Herd Press, 818 p.

James, H., 2006, *The Roman Empire's Wild West*: Current Archaeology, Issue 202, vol. XVII, No 10, p. 532-539.

James, H., 2016, Chapter 4. Roman Pembrokeshire AD 75 – 410: In: Darvill, T., James, H., Murphy, K., Wainwright, G., and Walker, E.A., Pembrokeshire County History, V*ol. 1. Prehistoric, Roman and Early Medieval Pembrokeshire*: Pembrokeshire County History Trust, Haverfordwest, p. 296 – 339.

Manning, W., 2001, *Roman Wales*: University of Wales Press, The western Mail, Cardiff, 129 p. ISBN 0-7083-1675-1

Pembrokeshire Prospectors, 1997. *Pembrokeshire's Past – Lost and Found 1977-1997*: T. J. International, Cornwall, 66 p. ISBN 0-09532137-0-6.

Pembrokeshire Prospectors, 2012. P*embrokeshire's Past – Lost and Found*: Volume II 1998-2012. Cleddau Press, Haverfordwest. 78 p. ISBN 978-0-9532137-1-9

Rees. S., 1992, *A Guide to Ancient and Historic Wales – Dyfed*: HMSO, London, 241 p.

Richmond, I.A., 1955, *Roman Britain*: Penguin Books, Hunt, Barnard and Co., Aylesbury, 240 p.

Symons, S., 2015, *Roman Wales*: Amberley Publications, 96 p.

Tombs, Robert, 2014, *The English and their History*: Allen Lane, 1024 p.

13. THE LEGENDS OF KING ARTHUR'S VISITS TO PEMBROKESHIRE

King Arthur led the Britons from around 480 to 515 AD against the northern European invading tribes of Angles, Saxons, Jutes and others. Today the Legends of King Arthur and his knights of the round table are known to most schoolboys. Hollywood likes to make films of knights in shining armour riding around between vast stone castles. Regrettably this is historically inaccurate for Arthur lived long before the great Noman stone castles were built. Only legends describe wars of the fifth century AD.

The Hollywood armour and large stone castles postdate the Norman conquest of Britain in 1066. This anomaly exists because a Norman - Geoffrey of Monmouth - published around AD 1136 a book known as 'Historia Regum Britannica' which promoted the Norman concept of a national hero fighting the Anglo-Saxon invaders. This created the popular Hollywood image of today. The original Arthurian legends were cherished across Celtic Britain for centuries before the time of Geoffrey of Monmouth. The Celtic bards preserved and embellished the tales as a means of defiance against the Anglo-Saxons by the Celts in Wales, southern Scotland, Cornwall and Brittany.

The time after the retreat of the Roman armies in 410 AD until the first Saxon revolt in AD 442 was the last age of Roman Britain. During this time the last king of Britannia – the Roman province of Britain - was called Vortigern. He enlisted Saxon barbarians from Germany to strengthen his defences. Things started to go wrong in 442 when the Anglo-Saxon mercenaries revolted as they had not been paid. There followed twenty years of conflict between the Celtic Romano-British population and the invading Angles, Saxons and Jutes (believed to originate in Denmark, northern Germany and a part of Holland). In the chaos of conflict, a disastrous plague occurred in AD 446. Around this time the struggling Romano-British leadership made an unsuccessful appeal for assistance to Roman General Aetius in Gaul who was himself struggling with the crumbling western Roman Empire.

The overall result was that the central government of Britain gradually collapsed. Shortly before AD 461 about 12,000 of the Celtic Romano-British aristocracy, mainly from western Britain, emigrated to Gaul and laid the foundations of Brittany. Much of the population either retreated back to the former pre-Roman hill forts or accepted defeat and became second class citizens under Saxon rule.

In Pembrokeshire there is no evidence of Roman towns and the population continued to live in the fortified settlements throughout the Roman episode. In what is now England, Celtic resistance against the invaders was generally fought more as a guerrilla campaign by light cavalry with sword and javelin from fortified bases against Anglo-Saxon fortified settlements. Perhaps surprisingly from about AD 460 to 495 the remaining Celtic warrior aristocracy rallied and organised a successful resistance. This was begun by Aurelius Ambrosius and followed around AD 480 by an hereditary prince of the Silures tribe in South Wales named Arturius (todays Arthur, sometimes written Artorius and Arturus in Latin). Between these two, the Saxon frontier was held, roughly stretching from Wiltshire to the Cambridge area. London was held by the British but there was Saxon penetration up to the River Trent boundary. Much of the fighting was centred on the Severn Valley.

Arthur's greatest victory over the Saxons was at the Battle of Badon (Mons Badonicus), sometime between AD 493 and 539, possibly in the Bath area. The resulting peace of Badon lasted for decades. King Arthur is credited with halting the westward advance of the Saxons and re-established a form of Roman imperial government. He was eventually defeated and killed at the Battle of Camlann in AD 537 or 539. A second Saxon revolt won decisive victories in the 570s but it was not until the early seventh century that most of what is now England was subdued. This is regarded as the Pagan or Early Saxon period.

Christianity was reintroduced to what is now England by St. Augustine in 597 and there followed the Christian Saxon period which was the time of the birth of England. The native British people were confined to the west. The Saxon or Old English terms 'wealh' or 'wylisc' means foreigners and this word led to the modern term 'Welsh'. Conversely the modern Welsh and Irish words for 'English' are 'Saesnaeg' and 'Sasanach'. The fifth and sixth centuries are known as 'The Age of Arthur'. The first mention of Arthur is in a manuscript of documents 'Historia Brittonum' assembled around 829-30 for King Merfyn of Gwynedd and originally attributed to Nennius but is now regarded as anonymous. The ancient British people were left with what is today Wales, southern Scotland, Cornwall and Brittany, without the support of Rome. Their tenacity is remarkable as in Pembrokeshire where they later lost the south to the Normans, yet today in north Pembrokeshire they retain their language and culture.

In the early Dark Ages people spoke Celtic or Gallic, and Latin was widespread. Many had Roman names as well as their own Celtic names. Today the successive influxes of Frisians, Jutes, Angles, Saxons, Vikings, Normans and Flemings, have evolved into the English speaking people and their language has evolved into modern English. This complicates things as ancient British people can now have a third modern anglicised name. Arthur would have spoken the Celtic language known as British (an early form of Welsh when British was in the process of dividing into separate Celtic languages. The Welsh language evolved some time after Arthur). He probably would have written in Latin and probably also understood Irish Gallic.

Today some argue as to whether a single person named Arthur existed or if the tales are embellished versions a tales of several leaders. It was the Normans who following the conquest of Britain learned of Arthur and were delighted with the stories of his triumphs against the Anglo Saxons. When his story was written down in Latin by Geoffrey of Monmouth, it began the great flood of writing that has culminated in popular television and Hollywood films. Ironically the Arthur of Hollywood riding around in shining metal armour from stone castle to stone castle is a myth based on the Norman barons in their late stone castles. The Arthur of the Dark Ages did not have large stone castles but Iron Age hillforts with earth and wooden defences, also the remains of the walled Roman towns and fortifications. His armour would have been inherited Roman armour. He was a Roman British citizen believed to be of the Silures tribe but today he has become the adopted hero of modern England and the descendants of the Anglo-Saxon ancestors that he fought.

It is not surprising at all to discover from the maps of Pembrokeshire that Arthur the defender of the ancient Britons (as distinct from the modern Hollywood version) is remembered by the descendants of his people - the Welsh-speaking Celtic people of north Pembrokeshire. Perhaps as a result of the Mabinogion legends of Arthur's persuit of the great boar and his piglets through north Pembrokeshire and the death of his son in the Preselies, that there are several sites named after him in north Pembrokeshire. At Dinas Head there is Arthurs Seat. Near Maenclochog village are the paired standing stones of Cerrig Meibion Arthur or 'The Stones of Arthur's Sons'. In the St. Davids area a Neolithic burial chamber is named Coetan Arthur which translates as 'Arthur's quoit' referring to the game of quoits said to have been played in the area by King Arthur.

The legends tell how St. David's mother Non (St. Non) was the daughter of a local chieftain in today's St. Davids area, called Cynir. In medieval genealogies she was a niece of King Arthur. The legends tell that St. David's coming was predicted by the wizard Merlin and also by St. Patrick. One of the oldest Celtic sources for legends of Arthur is the Mabinogion – a collection of eleven medieval Welsh or Ancient British tales assembled from two manuscripts – the White Book of Rhydderch dated about 1350 and the Red book of Hergest dated between 1382 and 1410. The tales give great insights into the stories circulating in Celtic Wales.

Three of the tales 'Peredur son of Efrof', 'Geriant son of Erbin' and 'The Lady of the well' center on the court of Arthur and his Queen Gwenhwyfar (English version is Guinevere) possibly at Caerleon on Usk. This was a former major Roman fortress for Wales and would be an ideal setting for the last romanised leader to make his base. Another legend 'How Culhwych won Olwen' describes two visits by Arthur and his warriors to Pembrokeshire. But these legends differ from the Normanised version of Arthur in Camelot, well known today from Hollywood films. Instead of full time rallying men and fighting the Anglo-Saxon invaders, this 'Welsh' Arthur had time for hunting of magical animals, in fact this 'Welsh' Arthur behaves much more like a leader of an Iron Age kingdom. A man not unlike the great CuChulain described in the Iron Age tales of Ireland who was a great stealer of cattle and women as the fortified Iron Age settlements raided each other.

According to the legend 'How Culhwych won Olwen', Arthur holds court in Celli Wig (widely believed to have been in Cornwall but still existing by that name in south-east Wales today on the border of Gwent and Glamorgan). In the legend, Arthur makes two visits to Pembrokeshire. On the first visit he sails there in his ship *Prydwen* (Fair Form) in search of two whelps of the magical bitch Rhymni. They arrive at Aber Daugleddy (the confluence of the two Cleddau rivers now known as the Milford Haven Waterway – also the Welsh name for the modern town of Milford Haven). The magical bitch and her two whelps were living in a cave on the shores. Arthur and his men surrounded them and the legend tells how God changed them back into their human forms and afterwards Arthur's men dispersed in ones and twos.

The second visit to Pembrokeshire is included as a legend of the hunting of a magical giant boar Twrch Trwyth who with his seven piglets is chased by Arthur and his warriors from Ireland, across south Wales to Cornwall. The part in Pembrokeshire can be summarised as:

The hunt for the magical boar and his seven piglets led Arthur and his men from Ireland across the sea to Pembrokeshire. For this second visit Arthur rode his mare Llamrei (grey or swift leaper) and had his dog Cafall with him. The boar swam across and landed at Porth Clais (near St. Davids) and Arthur and his men at the port of Mynyw (the Welsh name for Menevia which is the Roman name for a lost town near present day St. Davids). The boar and his piglets headed for the Preseli Mountains. Arthur arranged his men on the banks on either side of the Nyfer (Nevern) valley to the north east of St. Davids. The boar escaped but was held at bay in Cwm Cerwyn (the valley of Cerwyn in the Preseli Mountains) where there was a great fight and the great wild boar killed four of Arthur's warriors.

The boar was brought to bay a second time in the same valley and another battle ensued in which he killed Gwydre (Arthur's son) and three other warriors. The next morning the boar killed a further four men - three servants and Arthur's craftsman. But Arthur finally caught up with the boar in Peulinog (the land between Narbeth and Carmarthen) where the boar killed three more men and reached the coast at Laugharne where he escaped by swimming across the river Tywi. Arthur and his warriors persued him and killed the seven piglets but the boar escaped them by swimming out into the Atlantic. Today the Bronze Age pair of standing stones known as Cerrig Meibion Arthur (the Sons of Arthur) stand on the Preseli Ridge with Foel Cwm Cerwyn as a background. They are said to mark the spot where two sons of Arthur were killed in the fight with the great wild Boar Twrch Trwyth.

So according to Welsh legends, the fifth century King Arthur had family in Pembrokeshire in the form of St. Non – St. David's mother- who was his niece. The Mabinogion records two visits that Arthur made to Pembrokeshire. His lost base of Camelot was (according to the Mabinogion) situated at the old Roman fortress of Caerlon on the River Usk. There is one final link with Pembrokeshire. When Arthur was killed in his final battle in AD 539, possibly at the River Camlann in Cornwall along with his son or cousin Mordred, he was buried secretly so the Anglo-Saxons would not find his body. The grave site remained unknown for a long time but in 1191 the burial of a monk at Glastonbury revealed a stone slab with a leaden cross on it. An inscription on the cross in Latin stated 'Here lies buried the renowned King Arthur in the Isle of Avalon'. The monks continued digging and found a vast coffin hollowed out of an oak trunk. Inside were the skeletons of a large man whose head had been smashed by heavy blows as well as fragments of a smaller skeleton thought to have been Arthur's wife Guinevere.

It has been suggested that this was a fabrication by the monks to make the

Abbey of Glastonbury popular. Pembrokeshire's famous chronicler Geraldus Cambrensis (Gerald of Wales) reports seeing the bones and the cross in 1192 and reports that the inscription also mentioned Queen Wenneverla (Guinevere) but again he is a promoter of legends. Although now lost, the cross was drawn by antiquitarian William Camden in 1607 and he wrote 'Arturius' rather than Arthur. The site where the monks had dug to a depth of 16 feet to the grave was re-excavated in 1963 when the ancient report of an earlier excavation there was found to be correct.

According to Fenton (1911) one of Arthur's knights Caradog Vreichvras settled in Pembrokeshire. His descendants laid the foundation of the prominent Wogan family.

Another Arthurian legend in Pembrokeshire concerns the tiny St Goven's chapel built in a cleft in the steep limestone sea cliffs of south Pembrokeshire. The tiny building has its own holy spring, and inside is a rock cut cell with an altar and bench carved from the solid rock and dating from the fifth century, although the rest of the building dates from the eleventh century. The legend tells how it was the monastic cell of Sir Gawain, one of King Arthur's knights, who became a hermit there after the death of Arthur.

Suggested Further Reading

Fenton, R., 1911, *A Historical Tour through Pembrokeshire*: Reprinted 2018, Herd Press, 818 p.

Gantz, J., (Translator), 1976, *The Mabinogion*: Penguin Classics, 320 p.

14. DARK AGE PEMBROKESHIRE BEFORE THE NORMAN CONQUEST

Roman rule ended formally in Britain in AD 410. In the centuries following – known as the Dark Ages – there was no central authority nor national defence. There is evidence to show that present-day Pembrokeshire was influenced in the fifth and sixth centuries by Irish dynasties who exploited the power vacuum left by the Romans. There are records in both Ireland and Wales of an Irish tribe known as the Deisi who migrated into Pembrokeshire and became the rulers. They were led by Eochaid Allmuir. One of their leaders was Aircol Lawhir who held a court at Lis Castell (Lydstep). The new rulers brought with them Ogham script and the custom of erecting memorial stones with both Ogham and Latin inscriptions of prominent people with Irish names. These stones are found in Pembrokeshire and Carmarthenshire.

In the Iron Age Pembrokeshire was the land of the Demetae and their kingdom was Dyfed and the Irish settlers formed the new ruling class. Dyfed lasted from the time of the Roman departure until the male line of the royal family died out in AD 905. The land was then incorporated into a larger kingdom of Deheubarth that survived until the Norman conquest.

Archaeological evidence suggests that for the seven centuries following the collapse of Roman rule until the Norman conquest in 1066, the style of occupation in Pembrokeshire differed little from the Iron Age and the Romano-British settlements. People lived in hillforts, promontory forts and circular enclosed farmsteads. Rare U.K. archaeological finds are of fine imported pottery and ornate metalwork indicating some trade continued with the continent. There are very few written records but the main evidence is an abundance of early Christian stone monuments.

Christianity was introduced into Wales during the late Roman period but was not widely practised until the fifth and sixth centuries. During this time the whole of Wales was converted to Christianity. This was achieved by local and wandering Celtic men and women who later became known as saints and the fifth and sixth centuries became known as the Age of the Saints. There were more saints in Wales and Ireland than in all of the rest of Christendom. The Celtic saints travelled back and fore across the Irish Sea and Bristol Channel in leather and wooden framed boats similar to the Irish curraghs of today. Their sea going travels established them in the Faroes and Iceland and there is a tradition that St. Brendan reached America. The latter was successfully tested by Tim Severin in a curragh in 1976. During the Age of Saints and for the following five hundred years until the Norman conquest, the Celtic Christians left a legacy of stone monuments with over 400 recorded from all parts of Wales. Pembrokeshire has the highest concentration of these in Wales. Their brief inscriptions give a glimpse of some of the key people in Dark Age Wales.

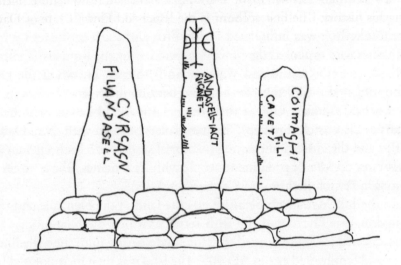

Figure 7. Sketch of the three early medieval Christian inscribed stones probably alongside a Roman Road near Maenclochog village

St. David and the Age of Saints.

The Age of Saints was a period in the fifth and six centuries when monks became Celtic Saints and travelled the western seaways spreading Christianty in Brittany, Wales, Cornwall and Ireland. Many monks preferrred to shun society and to live in isolation in prayer and personal communication with God. In Pembrokeshire the Age is dominated by the lives of St. Patrick and St. David along with the contemporaries of St. David – Saints Aidan, Ishmael, Teilo and Padarn. Probably because of their frequent use of boats and the sea with prevailing south-westerly winds, the coastline of Pembrokeshire has many places named after early Christian saints. On the south coast at Castlemartin there is St Govans chapel and well. Lamphey near Pembroke record Saints Tyfai and Teilo.

At Llanstadwell there is St. Tudwal's Church. On the Dale peninsula there is St Ishmaels village, Saint Botolph's estate and St. Bride's chapel. On the south side and end of the St. David's Peninsula there is Saint Elvis farm, Saint David's cathedral, Saint Non's chapel, Saint Justinian's chapel and Saint John Point. Inland in Pembrokeshire there is St. Leonard's well at Crundale, and St. Michael's church near St Clears. Along the north shores of Pembrokeshire there is the village of St. Nicholas, St. Hywel Church at Llanhowell and St. Brynach's church in Nevern.

Much has been written about the life of St. David, but it seems that most of it is legend and medieval propaganda to increase the importance of David and his church. His two main biographers both had reasons for embellishing his history. The first account is the 'Buchedd Dewi' ('Life of David') by Rhygyfarch written in the late eleventh century. Rhygyfarch (1056 to 1098) was the son of a bishop of St. Davids and may have become bishop himself in 1175. The second account was written by Geraldus Cambrensis (c. 1199 to c. 1223) but closely followed the earlier version. Rhygyfarch wanted St Davids to be independent of Canterbury and so strengthened his case by embellishment. Geraldus Cambrensis was nominated bishop of St. Davids in 1175 but never voted into office. The legends of St. David travelling to Rome and Jerusalem and being appointed bishop of St Davids by the patriarch there are probably not true. Similarly his reported connctions with Saint Patrick are also probably fable.

St. David and St. Patrick (the patron saint of Ireland) may both have been born in Pembrokeshire in the St. David's area – then known by the name of a nearby Roman town – Menevia (now lost). St Patrick was born around AD 373 in 'Villis Rosina' at St. Davids. Legends report that he was carried off to Ireland as a young man by pirates raiding Pembrokeshire. One day at the age of eighty-seven years he was preaching at St. Davids and he saw Non, the then pregnant mother of St. David, and he received a premonition that she was carrying the future saint who would complete the work of christianising Wales.

St. David was born around AD 462 near the site of Non's Well near St. David's. He was educated at Whitland Abbey. He joined the priesthood and finally settled in a small monastic settlement started by St. Patrick, marking the beginning of the Celtic Church in Pembrokeshire. St David and his monks led simple lives but laboured hard. They would plough their fields by hand rather than use draught animals. They would eat only bread and herbs. Meat and beer were not allowed. St. David is also known as 'The waterman' either because he would drink only water or because he followed the tradition of standing in cold river water reciting psalms.

David was a powerful preacher and founder of monasteries and churches in Wales, Brittany and south west England. He is also fabled to have performed miracles. His most famous was when he was preaching to a crowd at what is now the village of Llanddewi Brefi. The ground rose up to form a small hill so that that all might see and hear him. St. David is supposed to have presented Glastonbury Abbey with a portable shrine bearing a large apphire. A thousand years later a sapphire alter is reported confiscated from St. Davids cathedral by King Henry VIII during the Dissolution of the Monasteries.

The legends of St. David describe the time of King Arthur and the wizard Merlin in a Britain that was in turmoil with Irish invaders in the west and Saxons in the east. St. David is reported to have fought long and hard for the soul of the local pagan chieftain Boia or Voia of Irish origin who would parade naked women in front of the priests to test their religious beliefs. St. David is reported to have converted Boia's people, but Boia was killed by being struck by lightning. His name is preserved in Clegyr Boia a fortified rock ridge near St. David's.

Another Pembrokeshire saint was Teilo, born near Tenby. These early saints promoted Christianity in south Wales in the vacuum after the Romans left Britain. St. David and St. Non had strong links with Ireland, Cornwall and Britanny (where St. Non is buried). David returned to Pembrokeshire with three followers –Aidad, Ishmael and Teilo – and was advised by an angel to build his monastery in the valley where the cathedral of modern St. David's now stands. Legends say that later David with Teilo and Padarn made a pilgrimage to Jerusalem in the Holy Land, where has was consecrated Archbishop. Legends also tell that he made a pilgrimage to Rome. He is reputed to have lived for 147 years and died in 589. Today he is the Patron Saint of Wales and his life is celebrated on March 1st. He was buried at St Davids cathedral and his shrine became a popular pilgrimage in the Middle Ages.

During the tenth and eleventh centuries the cathedral was raided by the Vikings. St. Davids shrine was looted and stripped of its precious metals and jewels. In 1275 a new shrine was constructed. The relics of St. David and St. Justinian (of Ramsay Island) were placed in a casket in the shrine. During the sixteenth century Protestant Reformation, Bishop Barlow (1536 to 48), a champion of the Protestant cause stripped the shrine of its precious metal and jewels and confiscated the relics of St. David and St. Justinian. Work on the present cathedral began in 1181 on the site of St. David's monastery by the Norman Bishop Peter de Leia.

Stone Monuments of the Dark Ages.

The legacy of seven centuries of Christianity through Dark Age Wales is shown by the many stone crosses, many erected as burial markers. Archaeologists recognise three types of these stone monuments representing an evolution in style in time.

1) Standing stones with Latin and Ogham Inscriptions.

These are the oldest type and are believed to date to the fifth to seventh centuries. Ogham is an Irish form of writing used on wood and stone. The Ogham alphabet has twenty letters represented by groups of notches that were incised along the edges of a stone. Ogham script allowed only short inscriptions.

Three of these stones were recovered in the Maenclochog area of the Preseli Mountains. Two of these stones were taken from the ruined St. Teilo's church near Maenclochog. They are now in St. Mary's Church in the center of Maenclochog village (the vicar's warden has the key, ask at village shop for access). A sketch of the stones is shown in Figure 7. The tallest stone has an Ogham inscription along the left hand edge that reads from the bottom upwards as 'NDAGELLI MACU CAV' or 'The stone of Andagellus, son of Cavetus'. The Latin inscription in two lines reads from the top downwards 'ANDAGELI IACIT FILI CAVET' or 'The stone of Andagellus, son of Cavetus. He lies here.' A Christian cross on the upper part of the stone may have been added later.

The shortest stone has three lines of Latin that read 'COIMAGNI FILI CAVETI' that translates as 'The stone of Coimagnus, son of Cavetus (Figure 7). A third stone was collected from near Temple Druid near the ruins of St. Teilo's church and was placed in Cenarth churchyard in 1896. It is inscribed in Latin 'CVRCAGN FILI ANDAGELL' or 'The stone of Curcagnus son of Andagellus' (Figure 7). It seems likely that the three stones represent three generations of the same Caveti family. The stones would have been placed alongside a former Roman road through the area as memorials. Such memorial stones were not for the common people but for prominent leaders. The three Maenclochog stones appear to represent three generations of the same family and are further discussed below. It is possible that they originally stood together as a family group as in Figure 7.

The stones originated on a possible Roman road shown on the 1843 one inch to one mile Ordnance Survey map where it is named Via Julia. It runs east to west and skirts the southern flanks of the Preseli Mountains. It passes through Maenclochog and continues west through Henry's Moat to an excavated Roman fortlet or Romanised farmstead named Ad Vicassium (Flemish Castle) and on to Ford. The Via Julia continues on through Brawdy to St Davids and perhaps to the tiny harbour of St. Justinians. The road links Romano-British farms at Ford, Flemish Castle with a third farm that lay to the east of Maenclochog near Temple Druid.

Other early medieval Christian stones can be seen in the Carmarthen museum at Abergwili. The Voteporix stone has Latin and Ogham inscriptions and an incised ring cross. Voteporix was the sixth century Deisian ruler of the Demetae and was referred to as the 'tyrant of the Demetae' by the sixth century cleric Gildas, who was a contemporary of St. David. He is believed to have died in AD 540. Another stone from Cynwyl Gaeo has a Latin inscription that reads 'Preserver of the Faith, constant lover of his country, here lies Paulinus, the devoted champion of righteousness'. This is probably the grave marker of St. Paulinus who was St. David's teacher.

St. Brynach's church in Nevern has a fifth or sixth century inscribed stone in the churchyard with a latin inscription 'VITALIANI EMERETO' or 'The stone of Vitalianus Emereto'. On the left side in Ogham is written 'VITALIAN'. Inside the church, and built into the south transept window sill, is another fifth or sixth century stone with a Latin inscription 'MAGLOCVN FILI CLVTOR' or 'The stone of Maglocunus, son of Clutorius'. Along the left side in Ogham is written 'MAGLICUNAS MAQI CLUTAR'

It was the custom throughout the Roman Empire to bury the dead outside the settlements. Prominent people liked to have elaborate tombs built along the roads leading from the settlements, so that future generations might remember them. The approach roads became funereal avenues lined with tombs. Best known is the Via Appia or Appian Way leading east from Rome to Campanio and southern Italy. It was begun in 312 BC by censor Appius Claudia Caecus. Today it is a popular tourist destination to see the fine Roman tombs and catacombs that line it. One of the best preserved tombs is that of Cecilia Matella who was the daughter in law of Rome's richest man. It is a massive circular tomb built on the crest of a hill in the first century BC.

The conclusion must be drawn that the Maenclochog stones commemorate three generations of a family of the Deisi who continued to practice burial customs dating back to Roman times well into the Dark Ages. The bilingual stones provide a glimpse into life in the fifth and sixth centuries of the Dark Ages, after the Roman legions had marched out of Britain. They demonstrate that in the Maenclochog area of north Pembrokeshire a large farm complex continued to operate normally through the 5th and

6th centuries. One can imagine a stern and wise Cavetus with his two sons Andagellus and Coimagnus and also his grandson Curcagnus (son of Andagellus) holding their farm and their community together for over fifty years sometime in the days after the Roman legions left. The site is unknown today but would have been close to the place where the memorial stones were found. This is about a mile to the east of Maenclochog. The site is likely to have been overbuilt by a modern farm.

2) Medieval Stones decorated with incised crosses.

This second type of medieval stone without inscriptions but with incised Christian crosses, is thought to date from the seventh to ninth centuries. Fine examples of this type can be seen near Fishguard in the gateway of St. David's church Llanllawer. The church can be found on the B4313 Narberth to Fishguard road, 16 kilometers (10 miles) south-east of Fishguard. Enquiries should be made at the village shop.

3) Beautifully sculpted stone crosses.

This third type is believed to date from the ninth to eleventh centuries. Several are found in Pembrokeshire churches where they were moved for safe keeping. Two of the finest examples in Wales are found at Carew and Nevern in Pembrokeshire. The Carew cross (Plate 10) stands right by the side of the main road passing Carew Castle. The fine interlace art on the stone reflects the Viking influence in the county. It is a royal memorial to Maredudd who in 1033, with his brother Hywel, became joint rulers of the early medieval kingdom of Deheubarth, now south-west Wales. Two years later Maredudd was killed, so the date of the cross is known. A Latin inscription in a panel reads '(The cross of) Margiteut (or Maredudd) son of Etguin (or Edwin)'. The cross stands alongside the road in front of Carew Castle near the entrance with free car parking alongside. Join the A477 Pembroke to St Clears Road. At a distance of four miles from Pembroke turn north onto the A4075 Haverfordwest road and proceed for a half mile to the castle and cross.

Nevern churchyard has a fine Celtic cross very similar to that at Carew both being late tenth or early eleventh century (Plate 11). Nevern is a small village between Fishguard and St. David's situated on the ancient pilgrim route to St. Davids. In olden days, three pilgrimages to St. David's were considered to equal a pilgrimage to Rome because of the difficulties of travel in Wales. The church is dedicated to St. Brynach, an Irish saint of the sixth century. There are no known Roman roads in this area. Nevern

Cross is found by taking the A487 east from Newport towards Cardigan for 2.4 kilometers (1.5 miles), then turn left onto the B4582 to Nevern.

For what would become England, things started to go wrong with the first Saxon revolt of Vortegen's mercenaries in AD 442, that was followed by a plague in AD 446. However Wales was protected by the efforts of Marcus Aurelius and King Arthur who probably fought in the Severn Valley. In South Wales and in particular in the lands of the Demetae, west of Moridunum (Carmarthen), the Roman influence had not been strong. The main change was the arrival of the Deisi from Ireland who firmed the new ruling class. Cavetus and his family were not the only Romano-British citizens who upheld the Roman ways on their farm on the Via Julia. According to the Mabinogion, King Arthur based himself and his warriors in the abandoned Roman fortress of Caerleon. King Arthur is believed to have been killed in the Battle of Camlann in 537 or 539 AD. So in West Wales, the Maenclochog stones show that life continued in the fifth and sixth centuries little changed. Recent excavations in 'the Castle' at Maenclochog have shown that life continued there in a fortified Iron Age style settlement right up until the Norman invasion of Wales;

Suggested Further Reading

Barber, C., and Williams, J. G., 1989, *The ancient stones of Wales*: Blorenge Books, Abergavenny, Gwent, 192 p. ISBN 0-9510444-7-8

Dark, K.R., 1992, *The inscribed stones of Dyfed*: Gomer Press, Llandysul, Dyfed, 38 p., ISBN 0 86383 818 9

James, H., 2016, Chapter 5. Early Medieval Pembrokeshire AD 400 – 1100. In: Darvill, T., James, H., Murphy, K., Wainwright, G., and Walker, E.A., Pembrokeshire County History, *Vol. 1. Prehistoric, Roman and Early Medieval Pembrokeshire*: Pembrokeshire County History Trust, Haverfordwest, p. 340 – 532.

Rees, S., 1992, *A Guide to Ancient and Historic Wales – Dyfed*: HMSO, London, 241 p.

15. VIKING PEMBROKESHIRE.

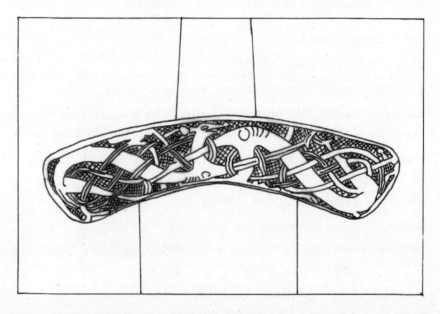

Figure 8. Sketch of a Viking brass sword hilt guard found on the sea floor at The Smalls

The sheltered sandy creeks of the Milford Haven Waterway have provided access for sea farers to Pembrokeshire for several millenia. Not least were the Vikings. For three centuries (eighth to tenth) the Vikings raided the shores of Britain and Ireland. In Wales, Anglesea was raided nine times, first in 854 and finally in 987. During the latter raid a thousand defenders died and twice that number were carried off in captivity. The Gower area was invaded in 860 and the Vikings only expelled after much slaughter. Vikings raided St. David's eleven times between AD 907 and 1091. In AD 999 Bishop Morganeu was murdered by Vikings and in either 1078 or 1080 Bishop Abraham was murdered by Viking raiders. The cathedral was repeatedly destroyed by the raiders. Overall the Vikings did not establish colonies in Wales. This was because of strong resistance by Welsh leaders such as Rhodri the Great (Rhodri Mawr who ruled Gwynedd from AD 844 to 878) and who defeated the Viking leader Gorm in 855. The Vikings were largely restricted to raiding and trading around the coasts of Wales.

Today there remains a distinct Viking legacy of Norse or Scandinavian place names that can be seen on the modern maps. A Viking map can be made by highlighting these places. There is a vast and magnificent treatise

101

on all of the place names of Pembrokeshire by Charles (1992). From this work a list of modern names with their probable Norse or Viking origins together with examples of their older uses from historic documents is listed below:

Angle – 'angel' (a hook).

Caldy – 'Kald' (cold) and 'ey' (isle).

Buckston – 'Bukki' (mans name) and 'tun' (settlement).

Dale - 'Dalr' (valley). The prominent linear valley in which Dale lies is the trace of the Ritec Fault that underlies the Milford Haven Waterway.

Fishguard was written as Fissigart in 1220 suggesting a Norse origin as 'fiskr' or 'fiski'(fish) and 'gardr'(enclosure).

Freystrop – 'Freyr' (the God of Fertility) and 'thorp'(village).

Gateholm - 'Gata' (a passage) and 'holmi'(an island).

Gelliswick was written as Gelliswyek in 1539, suggesting a Norse origin as - 'Gelli' (cold) and 'vik' (a bay)

Goodwick - 'Gud' (good) and Vik (a bay with a good anchorage).

Goulthrop – 'geul' (a bay) and 'thorp' (a village).

Grassholm was written as 'Insula Grasholm' in the fifteenth century suggesting a Norse origin in 'gras' (grass) and 'holmi' (an island).

Hasguard or Asguard was written of as 'Has-skard' – 'has' (house) and 'skard' (notch, cleft, mountain pass).

Herbrandston was written as 'Villa Herbrandi' in the thirteenth century and in a 1291 Tax return.– 'Herbrandr' (a man's name) and 'tun' (settlement).

Hubberston was written as 'Villa Huberti' in the thirteenth century and 'Villa Herbrandi' in the 1291 Tax record. It is probably not Scandinavian but 'Hubert's farm'.

Honeyborough – 'Hogni' (a man's name) and 'burgh' (burial place).

Little Haven – 'Havn' (a harbour).

Lundy – 'Lundi' (a puffin).

Marloes – 'Mar' (sea) and 'loe' (a mound).

Musselwick was written as 'Musselvick' in the thirteenth century. There is no Scandinavian word 'mussel' so the name is probably Flemish for 'moss wijck'.– 'Mos' (moss) and and 'vik' (a bay).

Newgale – 'geil' (hollow).

Ramsay – 'rammr' (a ram) and 'ey' (an island).

Sandy Haven was written as 'Sandy Havene'in the thirteenth century and 'Sandy Havyn' in 1532.– 'Sandr' or 'Sandie' (sandy) and 'havn' or 'haefen' (a harbour).

Skerryback – 'skera' (a ploughshare) and 'bakki' (a bank).

Skokholm – 'Skogar' (a corpse) and 'holmi (an island).

Stack Rock – 'stakr' (a stack).

Stackpole – 'stackr' (a stack) and 'pollr' (a pool).

Steynton – 'stein' (a stone mound) and 'tun' (settlement).

Thurston – 'Thor' (God of Thunder) and 'tun' (settlement).

Watwick – 'vik' (bay).

Whitesands – 'hvita' (white) and 'sandr' (sand).

In addition some places were named after individual Vikings:

Ambleston – Hammil

Butterhill – Budar

Hakin – Hakon

Haroldston - Harold

Herbrandston – Herbrandr

Lambston – Lambi.

The Vikings knew the Milford Haven Waterway because Hubba and his 2,000 men wintered in it in AD 877. However Viking remains are very rare. A dragon-adorned shield was found on Freshwater beach. Perhaps the most mystifying find was a delightfully engraved brass sword hilt guard (the cross piece between blade and handle that protects the hand) (Figure 8). This was picked up on the sea bed near the Smalls rocks off the west coast of the St. Davids peninsula. The guard is made of brass with inlaid silver wire and shows intertwining snake-like beasts. Was this from the wreck of a Viking ship or was the sword thrown into the sea as an offering to appease the Gods during some savage Atlantic storm? An archaeological site excavated within the Esso Oil Refinery at South Hook yielded the remains of three separate buildings and several slag-tapping furnaces for iron production. At first the site was thought to be Viking but no Viking artifacts were found. Radiocarbon dating revealed that the site was occupied for three hundred years and that it predated the Viking visits. The technology used on the site was typically Irish.

In 877 Hubba Ragnarsson (also spelled 'Ubbe' and 'Ubba') arrived in the Milford Haven Waterway with twenty-three ships and around 2000 fighting men. They wintered there. Hubba and his two brothers Halfdene and Hinguar had just spent the past fourteen years raiding Britain. It seems likely that upon first entering the waterway, they first sheltered in Angle Bay on the south side near the two mile wide entrance. Shortly afterwards they probably moved to a better site with a hidden safe and sheltered harbour at present unknown but was probably on the north side of the waterway. A popular missconception in Pembrokeshire today is that Hubba built his winter camp or 'tun' in what is now Hubberston. However this is not correct as studies of old maps names show.

The following spring (AD 878) Hubba and his fleet sailed south to Devon to attack a stronghold of King Alfred on Exmoor. Despite having the famous enchanted banner – the Dannebrog – woven by the King's sisters, what happened was a catastrophe for the Vikings. They found the Saxons inside their fort at Cynwit in Somerset. The Vikings besieged the fort, expected the defenders to die of thirst. Unexpectedly at dawn the Saxons led by Odda of Devon, broke out of the fort and attacked the Vikings. It is remembered as the Battle of Cynwit. The Vikings were taken by surprise. Hubba and about 800 of the Vikings were killed with the rest fleeing in the ships. Even the enchanted banner was captured. And there the story of one of Pembrokeshire's most infamous visitors ended.

Hubba is well remembered in Milford Haven and Hubberston and Plate 12 shows the 2011 Milford Haven carnival with a large contingent of 'warriors' with a fake Viking ship. Surprisingly in 2010 the small village of Appledore in Devon, where Hubba is believed to be buried, erected a large memorial stone to him.

In 1021 Olaf Haroldston ravaged Dyfed and Menevia. He returned to Norway were he unified the country and completed the country's conversion to Christianity. He became king for twelve years but went into exile in 1080. He was killed on his return from exile.

Slavery was important to the Vikings. Some slaves were necessary to work the land, and others to work in the house holds. To the Vikings a slave was valuable and needed protection. If a female slave who worked in the household became pregnant, then the man responsible had to provide another woman who was as good a worker as the pregnant one, to take her place until the child was born. If the pregnant slave died then the man responsible had to pay her worth to her lord.

Despite the abundance of Viking place names in Pembrokeshire the metal detectorists of the Pembrokeshire Prospectors (who publish their best findings) have found very little Viking metalwork. Their best Viking find to date is a broken coin of either King Eadred or Eadmund of the Viking Kingdom of York of the mid-tenth century. Eadred lost his kingdom to Eric Bloodaxe. The coin was found on the coast near St. Davids cathedral. A bronze Viking pennanular brooch of the eighth century (used for fastening a cloak) was found at Goodwick. The petals of flower designs at the two ends of the brooch still retained red enamel. Two sword pommels were found of Viking type. A bronze strap end with an intricate Viking interlaced pattern of the tenth or eleventh century was found at Monkton in the western outskirts of modern Pembroke.

Suggested Further Reading

Charles, B.G., 1992, *The Place names of Pembrokeshire*: National Museum of Wales, Aberystwyth, vol.1, 394 p., vol. 2, 867 p.867 p.

Laws, E., 1888, *The History of Little England beyond Wales*: Reprinted 1995, Cyngor Sir Dyfed County Council, Haverfordwest, 458 p.

Rees, S., 1992, *A Guide to Ancient and Historic Wales – Dyfed*: MNSO, London, 241 p.

16. WHERE WAS THE WINTER CAMP OF UBBE RAGNARSSON?

A particularly nasty Viking called Hubba Ragnarsson (also Ubbe and Ubba) arrived in 877 in the Milford Haven Waterway with twenty-three ships after fourteen years of butchery, looting and rapine mainly in what is now England. Hubba wintered here with 2000 warriors as well as slaves and concubines. The site has not yet been identified archaeologically. A common missconception in Pembrokeshire today is that Hubba built his winter camp or 'tun' at the site of what is now Hubberston village on the outskirts of Milford Haven. This is not correct. Charles (1992) has shown the name to lack Scandinavian roots. The village is referred to as 'Villa Herbrandi' in the thirteenth century and also in a 1291 tax return. This suggests the origins lie in 'Hubert's farm or manor'.

The Vikings were fearsome heathen raiders of long ago with brightly painted shields and banners. They dressed in captured finery and stolen gold, and would advance fearlessly into battle rhythmically clashing their swords and axes against their shields and calling out to their Gods. Afterwards there were the spoils to be shared along with the best of the captured young women. The war chiefs practiced polygamy and concubines were common. When Limerick in Ireland was recaptured from the Vikings in AD 936, the victorious Irish were astonished at the beauty of the young captured women and at their fine silks and embroidered clothes. To go 'a'Viking' was a far more attractive alternative to young Norse men than just being farm boys. They gained fame as warriors, enjoyed adventures and gathered treasure and also had the pick of young women captured. In fact to be decked in fine silks and embroidery would have been a not unattractive alternative to being a farm girl for some. There are few written records and much information comes from the sagas. However there are great variations in the details of these tales and what follows is only one version and is probably not entirely accurate.

March 28th is celebrated by some people in Scandinavia as Ragnar Lodbrok day after this great Viking chieftain captured and ransomed Paris in AD 845. He had led a fleet of 5,000 Vikings in 120 ships and ravaged a wide area of France. He was known as 'Hairy Breeches' and was a fighting man, who claimed descent from Odin (a Viking God who ruled Asgard and was the father of Thor). From around AD 835 to 865 he was a fierce Viking chieftain who led pirate raids on several countries. His favoured style was to raid Christian settlements on holy feast days because many of the Christian soldiers would then be in church. He accepted huge ransom payments to leave an area reasonably intact. After the capture of Paris it is said that the king of West Francia Charles II ('the Bald') paid 7,000 pounds of silver to save the city from destruction. From the point of view of his victims, he and his men were a band of murderous heathen given to rapine, looting and slavery. His life, adventures, death and the revenge that was exacted by his sons is one of the great sagas, still sung today.

Ragnar Lodbrok was born in Norway but had family links with the ruling family of Denmark. In 865 he landed in Northumbria. Here it is claimed that he suffered his only defeat in battle, for he was captured by King Aelle II (or Ella) of Deira in Northumbria. Unfortunately King Aelle was not a magnanimous, forgiving man like King Alfred, who eventually defeated the Vikings and then offered them land and lived peacefully. An act that in the view of another fighting man - Sir Winston Churchill in his book 'The History of the English Speaking Peoples' (published immediately after World War II and the defeat of facism) showed that King Alfred's far seeing statesmanship had added another ingredient to the rich amalgum that was smelted to forge the English speaking peoples. A people who eventually spread forth and built the biggest empire ever.

King Aelle decided on a horrible death for the Viking warrior King, who was cast into a pit filled with snakes. There the defiant Viking's last words were a warning that his tormentors ignored but which had astonishing consequences. One of which is that the words have been handed down from generation to generation to the present day. 'The little pigs would grunt now if they knew how it fares with the old boar'. Then amidst the writhing vipers he sang his death song and departed through the gates to join the immortal warriors in Valhalla.

When his four sons heard of his end and his words, as they were all chips off the old block and also fighting men, their wrath was immense and they vowed to avenge their father's death and swore that King Aelle would die even more horribly. They pledged he would die by the method of the 'blood red eagle'. This involved cutting out the flesh and ribs through the back and then pulling out the still-working lungs of the victim. Viking warriors flooded to the call of the sons to avenge the death of their father. In AD

866 three of the sons led an army of 10,000 against the hapless King Aelle. The consequences for what became England were immense.

This Viking army became known as 'The Great Heathen Army'. The mastermind behind the invasion which eventually led to the capture of vast tracts of England (East Anglia, Deira in Northumberland and Mercia) and the formation of Daneland, was Ragnar's son Ivar 'the Boneless'. He obtained the name because of his lanky gangling appearance. He had been happily raiding and fighting in Ireland but turned in 865 to East Anglia. By the spring of AD 866 he had stolen enough horses to mount his vast army of fighting men. He then advanced rapidly north along the old Roman road and was ferried across the River Humber to invade Yorkshire. He was accompanied by his two half brothers Halfdene and Hubba. They carried with them an enchanted banner – the Dannebrog – with the great black two headed raven upon it. This had been stitched together in a single day by their three sisters - the daughters of Hairy Breeches. It was flown before battle and if the Gods directed the banner towards the enemy, then victory was assured. If it hung limp or blew the opposite way, then the Gods were not in favour and battle would not be enjoined.

In November AD 866 York was sacked by the fast moving Viking army. However this event united the people of Northumbria and their two leaders King Aelle of Deira and King Osbert of Bernicia against the Danes. On 23rd March 866 King Aelle was captured in battle trying to recover York and King Osbert killed. So the unfortunate Aelle met his horrible fate at the hands of the sons of Hairy Breeches as foresworn. The other side of the story recording one part of 'the grunts of the little pigs' was told by Simeon of Durham who a century and a half after the fall of York wrote:

'The army raided here and there and filled every place with sorrow. Far and wide it destroyed the churches and monasteries with fire and sword. When it departed from a place it left nothing standing but roofless walls. So great was the destruction that at the present day one can scarcely see anything left in those places, nor any sign of former greatness.'

The great Viking army led by the three sons moved on and ravaged Britain for fourteen years. Nottingham, York, Reading, Cambridge, Exeter, Cirencester, Rochester and London fell to these Viking invaders. In AD 873 Ivar the Boneless died in Ireland. He was succeeded by his brother Halfdene who became King of York in AD 875. This left Hubba Ragnarsson at a loose end and in AD 877 he arrived in the Milford Haven waterway with twenty-three ships and around 2000 fighting men. They wintered there. It seems likely that upon first entering the waterway they first sheltered in Angle Bay on the south side near the two mile wide entrance. Shortly afterwards they discovering a better site with a hidden safe and sheltered harbour. The site has not been located and remains unknown today.

So where was the winter camp of Hubba Ragnarsson and his men? The problem they faced is similar to that experienced by the yachtsmen today. There are about 2,000 yachts in the Milford Haven Waterway. Each winter these boats are taken from their summer moorings and placed in sheltered spots where they will be safe from the savage seas of the winter storms. As an invading force at war with the native populations, Hubba and his men would have favoured somewhere where the boats could not be seen from other boats in the waterway. So open bays such as Angle Bay and Dale Bay can be eliminated. This leaves the tidal pills mainly on the north side of the waterway. These are:

a) Sandy Haven Pill.

b) Hubberston Pill. This one is a particularly good as boats could reach what is now Havens Head and Lower Priory. Both have been in the news recently. The construction of Milford Haven Docks across the pill as well as the infilling of part of the pill to create land for Tesco, the Public Library and other shops, has blocked the drainage. The underground piped drainage has proved inadequate and has resulted in the two sites now being prone to flooding at times of heavy rainfall.

c) Castle Pill on the east side of Milford Haven.

d) Neyland Pill now used as a marina.

d) Pennar Gut on the south side of the Waterway.

Surprisingly in 2010 at the small village of Appledore in Devon, where Hubba is believed to be buried, a large memorial stone was erected to him.

How to identify a Viking wintercamp was recenty described by Hadley and Richards (2013). The AD 872-873 winter camp of the Viking great army was recently identified in fields at Torksey in Lincolnshire. How it was found is most interesting. The discovery resulted from a study of twenty years of finds by metal detectorists by Mark Blackburn, then Keeper of Numismatics at the Fitzwilliam Museum in Cambridge. Over 1,500 items were logged and can now be seen on the Portable Antiquities Scheme website (www.finds.org.uk). Items that identified the winter camp were about 100 silver Arabic dirhams all cut into halves and quarters, English coins dated AD 860 to 870, fifty pieces of cut up silver, ten pieces of cut up gold, and a hundred weights for weighing out gold and silver. There was an abundance of Anglo-Saxon, Frankinsh and Irish copper alloy jewellery, a smiths set of tools, as well as spindle whorls, needles and awls. Leisure activity was recorded in 300 lead gaming pieces.

It is interesting to speculate on what Hubba and his men might have left when he and his 2,000 fighting men sailed away in their twenty-three ships. They may have had plans to return to their well hidden winter camp. It is likely that he left the camp with slaves, some women and perhaps a few old or injured warriors. The data necessary to pinpoint the exact site of the winter camp is probably already available through the efforts of local metal detectorists, but has not yet been analysed

The story of Hubba and his men finished when during the following spring (AD 878) they sailed south to Devon to attack a stronghold of King Alfred on Exmoor. They landed at a bay called Boothyde and marched to Kenwith Hill Fort. Despite having the enchanted banner with them, what happened was a catastrophe for the Vikings They found the Saxons inside their fort at Cynwit. The Vikings besieged the fort, expected the defenders to die of thirst. Unexpectedly at dawn, the Saxons led by Odda (or Odun) Earl of of Devon, broke out of the fort and attacked the Vikings. It is remembered as the Battle of Cynwit. The Vikings were taken by surprise. Hubba and about 800 of the Vikings were killed with the rest fleeing in the ships. Even the enchanted banner was captured. Hubba and his men were buried at Bone hill. A plaque was erected by Charles Chappell that reads:

Stop. Stranger. Stop.
Near this spot is buried
King Hubba the Dane
Who was slayd in a bloody retreat
By King Alfred the Great.

Suggested Further Reading

Charles, B.G., 1992, *The Place names of Pembrokeshire*: National Museum of Wales, Aberystwyth, vol.1, 394 p., vol. 2, 867 p. 867 p.

Hadley, D., and Richards, J.D., 2013, *Viking Torksey: Inside the Great Army's winter camp*: Current Archaeology, No. 281, August 2013, p. 12-19.

17. THE FIRST KING OF ALL WALES – GRUFFYDD AP LLYWELYN (DIED 1063).

After three and a half centuries the Roman legions withdrew from their province Britannia. The power vacuum they left resulted for the common people in centuries of dark years with fighting, fear, brutality, famine, poverty and misery in the aptly named Dark Ages. Rome had ruled the Celtic tribes who had arrived in Britain five centuries before the Roman invasion. In Wales the main Celtic tribes were the Deceangli in the north, the Ordovices in the north-west , the Demetae in the south-west and the Silures in the south-east. With their new found freedom rivalries soon broke out between them. Without a unified defence, Britain was ripe for exploitation.

Anglesea was invaded by a Celtic tribe, the Votadini who travelled from Strathclyde in Scotland. Their leader was Cunedda. His grandson Cadwallon drove the Irish settlers out of Anglesea. His son Maelgwyn Gwynedd considerably expanded the captured area into north-west Wales and gave the province its name Gwynedd. Meanwhile the Saxons already established in England tried to expand westwards. But they were stopped by a Celtic warrior now traditionally known as King Arthur.

Present-day Pembrokeshire was influenced in the fifth and sixth centuries by Irish dynasties who exploited the power vacuum left by the Romans. There are records in both Ireland and Wales of an Irish tribe known as the Deisi who migrated into Pembrokeshire and became the rulers. They brought with them the Ogham script and the custom of erecting memorial stones with both Ogham and Latin inscriptions of prominent people. They became the rulers of the Demetae and their Kingdom of Dyfed. It was not until AD 905 that the male royal line died out. The land was then incorporated into a larger kingdom of Deheubarth that survived until the Norman conquest.

In the fifth and sixth centuries in the east of Britain, a series of invasions and migrations of Saxon people was taking place with the arrival of Angles, Jutes and Saxons from north-west Europe. Eventually the western Saxons from Wessex, with the middle Saxons from Mercia and the northern Saxons from Northumbria succeeded in driving back the Celts. Towards the end of the eighth century King Offa of Mercia had Offa's Dike built before he died in AD 796. The dike became the first political boundary between the Saxons and Celts.

The next invaders were the Vikings who not only attacked Britain but also travelled to Spain, Italy, Iceland, Russia, and France. In Britain they raided and settled in the Faroes, Shetland, the Orkneys, the Hebrides and on the mainland in Scotland, Northumbria, Cumbia, Lancashire, the Isle of Man, Wales and Ireland. They were fierce sea raiders and they terrified the native populations by suddenly appearing, killing and looting, and then disappearing back to the seas in their long ships.

Egbert, the king of Wessex ruled from AD 802 to 839. He defeated Mercia in AD 839 and after that time he received homage from every ruler in England. This made him the first king of a Unified England since the Romans departed. The unification of Wales began in the ninth century when Rhodi the Great (Rhodi Mawr) eventually ruled Gwynedd, Powys and Seisyllwg being north, central, east and much of south Wales. The next to rule much of Wales was Rhodi's grandson Hywel the Good (Hywel Dda). He married Elen, the daughter of the last king of Dyfed (South-west Wales) who brought Dyfed as her dowry. This was then joined to Seisyllwg to form the kingdom of Deheubarth. Hywel died in AD 949 or 950.

In the century before the Norman invasion of 1066, Britain continued in turbulent times. Hardicanute the last of the Danish kings of England died in AD 1402. Viking raids continued from Ireland into Wales. Anglesea was attacked by Vikings in 987. Between 951 and 1091, St Davids was attacked eleven times and two bishops were killed. Out of the turmoil two strong contemporaries emerged. They were the Welsh leader Gruffydd ap Llywelyn and Harold Godwinson, the Saxon Earl of Wessex. They were destined to be arch enemies.

Gruffydd's father was Llywelyn ap Seisyll, king of Seisyllwg, Gwynedd and Powys, who was murdered by his own men in AD 1023. Gruffydd's date of birth is unknown. He led a normal quiet life until suddenly with his father's death responsibility came to him. He responded strongly and attacked and routed the Mercians. He then turned to Duheubarth that was ruled by Hywel ap Edwin whom he defeated in 1041 and carried off his wife. But in 1047 Gruffydd ap Llywelyn was expelled from Duheubarth by Gruffydd ap Rhydderch. This was reversed in 1055 when Gruffydd ap Llywelyn killed his rival. He then went on to subdue Morgannweg and Gwent. This made Gruffydd ap Llywelyn the first king of all Wales. In AD 1056 he joined forces with Earl Harold's enemy Aelfgar the king of Mercia and married his daughter Ealdgyth. The two forces then attacked Hereford and drove out the defenders and burned the cathedral.

Harold was determined to remove Gruffydd and made detailed and careful plans to attack in AD 1062. He first trained his men on how to fight in the Welsh manner using mountain and river terrain. Harold based himself in Gloucester and appeared to be making ready to attack from the south. He sent his fleet to attack the Welsh coast from Bristol. He planned a spring offensive to march his Wessex forces along the south coast from Bristol. At the same time he organised another army from Northumbia led by his brother Earl Tostig to attack Gwynedd from the north. Gruffydd found enemy troops had penetrated Gwynedd and that his home at Rhuddlan was at risk. Gruffydd was driven back into Snowdonia. The offensive continued through the summer.

The Welsh people thought their king was in hiding in the mountains saving himself while their lands were being devastated. Harold offered a reward of 300 cattle for Gruffydd's head. Up until AD 1063 there were many clashes between the two sides. But the great battle between the Saxons led by Harold and the Celts led by Gruffud never occurred because Gruffydd's own Welshmen turned on him and killed him in AD 1063. They sent his head as a peace offering to Earl Harold. Surprisingly Harold then married Gruffydd's wife Eadgyth and awarded the overlordship of Wales to Gruffydd's two brothers Bleddyn and Rhiawallon.

In 1066 when King Edward the Confessor died, Harold seized the throne, only to be killed later that year at the Battle of Hastings opposing the Norman invasion.

Gruffydd left a legacy in Wales which he had united politically, instilled a national spirit and a determination to resist the Saxons. But history never again provided opportunities for another king of Wales as the Norman invasions spread across the country. Wales was invaded by the Normans in AD 1081 and had mostly fallen by AD 1094. However Wales did later spawn one British King who was Henry Tudor or Tewdwr, born at Pembroke Castle and who won his kingship at the Battle of Bosworth Field in 1485.

Suggested Further Reading
Gater, D., 1991, *The Battles of Wales*: Gwasy Carreg Gwaleh, Conway, 127 p. ISBN 0-86381-178-1

18. THE NORMAN WAR MACHINE

Throughout the Dark Ages, the British Isles were an agglomeration of small kingdoms and princeships that warred with each other as well as against the many waves of invaders who came for the easy pickings of a land lacking central government and a protective army. The battle strategy was fairly straightforward with armies preferring to fight on foot and face to face. In 1066 Earl Harold Godwinson led his men with swords, axes and shields and the shield wall was the main battle tactic. The Viking invaders preferred shields and axes. The Irish fought in linen tunics using light axes, swords and spears. Into this came the Normans led by Duke William, who arrived with 2,000 knights and 3,000 archers and squires. He had however carefully brought horses for his mounted knights, who proved invincible over the next centuries. So how did these battle-ready Norman's with their well-trained armies and advanced battle tactics evolve?

They can be traced back to a great Viking warrior called Rollo who invaded the Seine valley. He defeated the French in battle and captured the cities of Rouen and Bayeaux. He was so powerful that he negotiated a land grant with King Charles III (Charles the Simple) of West Francia in return for not attacking any more and for providing protection to the French against other Viking raids along the River Seine. The Duchy of Normandy was formed in AD 911, Rollo taking the title of Count of Rouen. Part of the agreement was that Rollo would become a Christian, which he did and changed his name to Roland. When he captured Bayeau he carried off Poppa, the daughter of Berengar, Count of Bayoux and Rennes. They were married and had a son William Longsword who became Rollo's heir. Rollo became the ruler of Normandy from AD 911 to 927. Rollo died around AD 930 and his grave and effigy is in the Cathedral of Rouen.

The Norman's were hungry for land and under Rollo they developed their war skills into a business both to hold their lands and to expand them. The objective was to capture land and then build a castle upon it. This provided a defendable base. The assets were then divided between knights and manors built. Taxes would be levied and a lifestyle set up for a baron and his knights each of whom would supply a number of fighting men on demand. William of Normandy, a descendant of Rollo, was born in one of these Norman stone castles. Immediately after landing in England at Pevensey, Duke William ordered a castle to be built there. The Normans expanded their territory over the next 150 years and extended themselves into southern Italy, Sicily, Malta and North Africa. Some worked as mercenary soldiers even further afield.

Following the Battle of Hastings, the Normans systematically took over the land from the Saxons, so that by the end of William's reign there was no land left in Saxon ownership. There were revolts in Yorkshire, Northumbria, the West Midlands, the West Country and the Fenlands of the East coast. The risings in the north and east were aided by the Danish Armies of King Svein Estrithsson. William reacted savagely, particularly in the north where large areas were depopulated for generations in an action known as 'the harrying of the north'. In 1070 William ordered the plundering of the monasteries where much of the Saxon wealth had been entrusted. With the land subdued and many Saxons having gone into exile, William in 1085-86 ordered a great survey of England to produce a catalogue of property known as the 'Domesday Book'. It provided the values of properties and a basis for taxation. It also demonstrated the ruthlessness of the Norman occupation.

Meanwhile in Pembrokeshire things were very different. Wales remained a country of warring princes after the Norman invasion. In 1077 Rhys ap Tewdwr returned from banishment in Brittany and laid claim to his kingdom of Deheubarth. He was joined in Pembrokeshire by Gruffydd ap Cynan of North Wales with a large force of Irish. They were victorious and divided South Wales between them. In 1081 William the Conqueror (William Ist) made the pilgrimage to St. Davids in Deheubarth. He brought with him a huge military force to demonstrate his power to the warring Welsh Princes. At the time there were considerable numbers of Norse settlers in Pembrokeshire and they welcomed their Viking relations who had crushed the Celts. Rhys ap Tewdwr responded by meeting William and paying homage to him. Rhys agreed to pay William a tax of £40 per year for his kingdom that resulted in good relations between them until William died.

When William the Conqueror died in AD 1087, the princes of North Wales with a large army invaded Deheubarth. Rhys ap Tewdwr again went into exile this time in Ireland. But he returned and in AD 1088 Rhys defeated his enemies in a great battle at St. Dogmaels. Then in AD 1093 Rhys was defeated, captured and executed by a group of Norman knights on a private expedition against him. His eldest son also died with him. But he left a daughter Nest and two young sons Gruffydd ap Rhys and Hywel ap Rhys. Each would play major roles in the future struggle for Wales.

At first the Norman invasion did not extend into Wales. But Wales was weak from all of the infighting between the princes, but it was a land of rich pickings. It did not take long for a war-loving Norman adventurer to take advantage of it. Martin de Turribus had already been awarded lands in Devonshire and Somersetshire by William the Conqueror. But his thirst for adventure was such that he gathered his supporters and sailed for Wales. They landed at Fishguard Bay, at a poor fishing village called Abergwaun. On learning that the Welsh were massing at Morvill, he marched his men there and defeated them in a sharp skirmish, and then pursued them across the Preseli Mountains. On the south side of the mountains the men of Meline, Nantgwyn and Eglwyswrw came out to meet the Normans. But they were poor villagers and on seeing the well-armed disciplined and battle-hardened Normans they threw down their arms without fighting.

So the hundred of Camaes was taken without further bloodshed. It became a Norman lordship marcher, that is such land that might be won from the Welsh by a Norman or English adventurer with his own force and at his own expense. The Lord could then exercise sovereign jurisdiction. This put Martin de Turribus in a much stronger position than with land granted by the king, for such favours could be withdrawn. He favoured his own won land of Cemaes to the extensive lands granted to him in Devonshire and Somerset by the king.

Martin de Turribus divided the land he won at Cemaes into twenty knights fees each with its own manor, thirty-four plough lands and four boroughs. He built his castle at Newport. The borough of Newport contained 280 burgages (tenements), while that of Nevern contained eighteen. The other two boroughs were Fishguard and St. Dogmaels. The Lord founded towns and abbeys. His followers established the town of Fishguard. He exercised the law with a prison nearby for felons and a gallows for executions. The Lords of Cemaes continued to exercise their powers without control by the King's courts until the system was abolished by a statute of King Henry VIII. An earlier attempt to curb the powers of the marcher lordships of Wales by King Edward I (1277-83) was thwarted by Earl Warren who drew his sword crying out 'By this warrant my ancestors won their lands and privileges, and by this I do and will maintain mine!'

The castle at Newport was the Lords palace and court. Around it the town built up with the Lord's followers. As late as the seventeenth century the citizens names in Newport, as listed by Fenton (1811), were still lacking Welsh identity being Mendus, Devenalt, Revell, Dier, Runway, Genthill,

Cotton, Picton, Lopin, Chapelin, Allman, Tucker, Belward, Jordan and Herring. These non-Welsh names were also recorded in place names such as Larman's kiln, Gile's Lake, Hitchman's Cross, Kadman's Park, Brown's Cliff, Magget's Ditch, Hangingstone and Clerkenwell.

The marcher lords had the unique rights to tax their Welsh country tenants who held their land directly from them and not the king. Some of these taxes persisted until the reign of Queen Elizabeth I and later. All tenants had to labour for three days a week for the Lord. Plough money (Arian aredig) was an annual rent of four pence per acre for permission to plough. Way money (Arian y Vidir) was payment for houses having a way through the Lord's land. Prise ale was five pence paid for either brewing or selling ale. Free fare (Ymando) was a payment of five shillings by any tenant wishing to leave. Turf heriot was a payment of one shilling and four pence for any tenant who died, servants and children excepted. At the death of every burgess, the Lord was paid twelve pence. The Lord appointed a mayor for each new community who was responsible for collecting the taxes. A court was held every fifteen days before the mayor. The Lord collected tolls for each market held of seven shillings from anyone for the right to either buy or sell.

An unexpected consequence of the Norman conquest of Pembrokeshire was the displacement of the Welsh population of south Pembrokeshire by Flemish people. William the Conqueror's queen was Matilda of Flanders and Flemish mercenaries fought alongside the Normans during the invasion of 1066. The Normans found them useful and loyal. In 1108 the sea inundated Flanders and many Flemish refugees came to England seeking land. By then William's son was King Henry I and he tired of the Flemish flood. He put them as far away as possible by giving them the hundred of Roos in Pembrokeshire. This corresponds today to the Dale peninsula. But it soon expanded into the Castle Martin Peninsula including the sites of the future towns of Tenby, Pembroke and Haverfordwest.

The colonists arrived by sea and landed at Sandy Haven on the Milford Haven Waterway. The Flemish colonists provided the barons with a source of loyal men for battles against the Welsh. The Flemings displaced the native Welsh people from south Pembrokeshire and Haverfordwest became their main stronghold from which they settled on the Dale Peninsula and along the Milford Haven Waterway. Records show that the hundreds of both Roos and Manorbier soon lacked any Welsh names.

One Norman knight named Stephen Perrot settled at Narberth and built his castle there and it was later replaced by stone. He garrisoned it with Flemish colonists and gathered them about him to form the town.

This was repeated in many places in Wales and the record of the founding lords, barons and knights is preserved today in the names of their towns and villages: Prendergast after the de Prendergast founder; Roch after the de La Roche family; Steynton founded by Adam de Stainton. The Marcher Lordship of Camaes in North Pembrokeshire alone created and supported twenty knights. The Norman system resulted in Pembrokeshire abounding in knights who held their manors and were able to muster troops in support of the barons.

Another development affecting Norman Pembrokeshire was the success of the Knights Hospitallers. Fenton (1811) describes the rise of the Knights Hospitallers or the Knights of St. John who later established a Commandary at Slebech in Pembrokeshire. In 1104 the order of Hospitallers or Brothers of the Hospital of St. John of Jerusalem became military. In 1113 Raymond de Puy became first Grand Master and drew up the code of written laws. This included dividing the hospitallers into three classes. First were gentlemen who would defend the faith and protect the pilgrims. Second were the chaplains and priests to supply the church. Third were the serving brothers who formed the militia of the order. The reputation of this military order diffused all over the world and they had seminaries in most of the countries of Europe. Geraldus Cambrensis toured Wales with Archbishop Baldwin in 1188 to preach the crusades and gather volunteers.

The Knights Hospitallers acquired immense possessions. In Pembrokeshire the Flemish Lord Wizo (Wiz) and his son Walter donated to them land at Slebech as part of the Lordship of Daugleddau being the land lying between the two Cleddau Rivers. There a Commandery was built. The Norman and Flemish settlers generously gave donations of their newly aquired property. The Earls of Pembroke greatly favoured the establishment and greatly enriched it with gifts. Finally before the dissolution of religious houses under King Henry VIII, the order is believed to have had over 20,000 manors in Christendom. At the time of the dissolution, the immense lands at Slebech and the Commandery were sold to Roger Barlow for the sum of two hundred and five pounds and six shillings.

Suggested Further Reading
Rees. S., 1992, *A Guide to Ancient and Historic Wales – Dyfed*: HMSO, London, 241 p.

19. EARLY NORMAN CASTLES IN PEMBROKESHIRE

As the Norman invaders arrived in Pembrokeshire, one of their earliest acts was to set up earthwork castles with timber fortifications. These were mainly motte and bailey castles. These were the very first defences thrown up by the Norman invaders and it was not until many decades later that the more important castles and strongholds were rebuilt in stone. Sometimes older earthworks of the Iron Age were incorporated into the structures. A motte is a man-made earth mound surrounded by a ditch and a wooden stake wall or palisade. The top of the mound was also fortified with a wooden stake wall and a wooden tower. Its higher vantage was useful as an observation post as well as being the garrison's stronghold. The bailey is a larger enclosed courtyard also with a wooden stake wall and a ditch where people resided. They were not difficult to build often using forced labour and easily defended.

The Normans introduced the design following the invasion of 1066. The structures spread widely through Scotland, Ireland and on the continent during the twelfth and thirteenth centuries. After this time they were replaced by other forms of fortification. Fifty-five mainly-Norman earth and timber castles in Pembrokeshire are listed here and they record the scope of the Norman struggle to take over and manage the lands of Pembrokeshire. Most of the mottes are in north Pembrokeshire. In south Pembrokeshire many were later replaced with stone castles. The Norman stone castles are described separately.

Immediately after the conquest the Norman hold on many areas was not great and in Pembrokeshire was restricted to a number of scattered motte and bailey castles that were contested by Welsh princes. In order to strengthen their hold on the new lands, King Henry I (William the Conqueror's son) from 1105 encouraged foreign colonists with grants of land formerly in Welsh hands. The most prominent group of these to settle in Pembrokeshire were Flemings. It was one of these - Wizo 'the chieftain of the Flemings' - who established the castle, church and borough of Wiston by 1112. Wizo was a Flemish adventurer who put together groups of Flemish families to come and settle the lands he had been granted in Wales. Later he established a second colony in Lanarkshire in Scotland. Today the histories of many of these early castles is lost. But in the north of the county many have Welsh names. It is likely that a lot of these were built by the Welsh people to defend their lands rather than all being Norman.

The following information given here was largely collected from the Pembrokeshire Coast National Park Authority book 'Castles of Pembrokeshire' by Dillwyn Miles, and the website www.castleswales.com

WOLFSCASTLE is named after a prominent motte immediately along-side and east of the main Haverfordwest – Fishguard Road (A40) on the south side of Wolfcastle village and to the north of Ford village in a position commanding the north end of Treffgarne Gorge. The motte stands on top of a prominent bluff between the confluence of the western Cleddau and Anghof Rivers. A ditched motte stands five meters above a level area with a summit diameter of fourteen meters. It is contained within the north part of a scarp-defined oval enclosure measuring seventy by eighty-eight meters and was probably the bailey. Some indications of building shapes can be seen in the ground. The modern Fishguard-Haverfordwest road has cut through a part of the bailey as well as the motte ring ditch. The Latin name 'Castrum Lupi' appears here on a thirteenth century map. The motte has been cleared and steps lead up to it and there is an information board. Very limited parking exists in a wide gateway on a small side road.

WISTON CASTLE is regarded as one of the best preserved motte and bailey castles in Wales. A nine meter high motte has a deep encircling ditch. The motte is eighteen meters wide at its summit. Wiston Castle is unusual as it survives in an intermediate state between an early motte and bailey castle and a later stone castle. On top of the motte there is a stone shell keep instead of the earlier ring wall of stakes. No traces of wooden buildings inside the stone shell are visible. Internally the shell keep is circular but externally it is polygonal with eighteen sides. Sections of the north wall have fallen outwards towards the ditch. On the south side facing the bailey, is the arched entrance. On either side of this are bar holes for securing the wooden gate. There is a large oval bailey surrounded by a well-preserved earth bank which crosses the motte ditch to reach the motte itself. The bailey would have enclosed the main residence and other buildings of the lord.

NEVERN CASTLE also known as Nanhyfer is a motte and bailey castle on a hill overlooking Nevern village and is defended on the south-eastern side by the River Gamman. It was originally the site of a Welsh ringwork but was seized in the early twelfth century by the Norman Robert FitzMartin,

Lord of Cemaes. The ringwork is triangular shaped and defended by a double ring of earth banks that might be part of an earlier Iron Age hillfort. In the twelfth century Welsh Lord Rhys offered peace to the FitzMartins upon the marriage of his daughter Angharad to William FitzMartin (Lord Robert's grandson). The peace was short lived and in 1191 Lord Rhys attacked and captured the castle and turned it over to his son, Maelgwyn. It is believed that the motte was built at this stage by the Welsh. The FitzMartins moved about two and a half miles to build themselves the fine stone castle at Newport. Some years later the aging Lord Rhys suffered the indignity of being imprisoned in the motte and bailey castle by his sons. But the sons soon disagreed and Lord Rhys was freed.

WALWYN'S CASTLE was built inside an Iron Age hillfort in the administrative district of Rhos. It is situated at the head of Sandy Haven valley three miles from the Milford Haven Waterway at the present village of Walwyn's Castle. The castle was the seat of the Barony of Walwyn's Castle with dependent castles at Benton and Dale. It was never rebuilt in stone unlike the other two. It is a complex motte and bailey castle sited on a promontory bounded by a 'U' bend in the valley. There is an unusual quarter circle 20-foot high motte with a small upper bailey separated from a large outer bailey by a wooden gate. The outer bailey was divided in two with the halves also having a wooden gate between them. The main wooden gate was in the bank of the outer bailey. Earth banks outline the parts of the structure that were once topped with wooden palisades. Despite not being developed as a stone castle, Walwyn's Castle had long use. The Norman-English Baron Guy de Bryan was born there in 1254. His son, also Guy, was born there in 1289 and his grandson of the same name in 1311. The latter became Admiral of the King's fleet in 1361.

OTHER MOTTES IN NORTH PEMBROKESHIRE

Camrose castle was built on the Landsker around 1080 as a motte and bailey. It is overgrown but may have a shell keep like Wiston castle. King William I (William the Conqueror) overnighted there on his pilgrimage to St. David's cathedral in 1081.

Castlebythe castle is near an Iron Age hilltop stronghold. It is near the church in the center of Castlebythe village, situated midway between the motte and bailey castles of Henry's Moat and Puncheston. The motte is about 7 meters high and 12 meters wide at the top. The adjacent bailey is 220 by 170 feet with banks 12 feet high. It has a spring and the site possibly reutilises an earlier earth ring structure.

Castle Manorowen or Fartin is situated close to the village of Manorowen. It is a small motte developed within an Iron Age earth ringed fort 65 feet long, 50 feet wide and 12 feet high. The ditch is well preserved on the north side. The site is partly ploughed out.

Castell Haidd at Hayscastle village is a motte and bailey lying within the Lordship of Pebidiog, about three miles from the stone keep of Roch. It lies about three and a half miles inland at the head of a valley running inland from Newgale Sands. It was probably the base of one of the knights of the Bishop of St. David's like Poyntz Castle and Castle Morris nearby. The large motte still stands 20 feet high but much was removed to make a site for a church. There is a bailey. The castle is defended by marshland on the south-west and a wet moat at the opposite end.

Castell Hendre is situated in Henry's Moat village immediately behind the church near an Iron Age fort in a small river valley in the foothills of the Preseli Mountains. The motte is 15 feet high and 30 feet across the top. The remains of a ring ditch lie on the west side but quarrying has destroyed most of it.

Castell Mael in the village of Puncheston may have been a motte and bailey castle as traces of a motte were reported in 1914 by the Royal Commission for Ancient Monuments. Today all that remains is the bailey occupying about four acres with an 8 foot high earth bank. One side is a steep natural scarped river bank. Outside was a 12 foot wide ditch that today is largely infilled. The fort was built by the Norman war lord Robert FitzMartin who seized the Camaes district at the end of the eleventh century.

Pointz Castle is a motte surrounded by a ditch. A depression on the summit suggests that a stone keep may have stood there. No trace of the bailey remains as there is a modern farm on the site. The castle is named after Pons who in the 1180s was a tenant of the bishop of St. David's and who probably built the castle. It was later occupied by the bishops.

Castle Morris is a motte and bailey castle built in the Lordship of Pebidiog in support of St. Davids. The bailey can clearly be seen with a farm inside it, but the motte was removed to site a barn.

Maenclochog castle was identified only by excavation in 2007. There is no motte but a stone wall was built attached to a rock outcrop, sometime after the 1093 Norman conquest of Pembrokeshire. The Norman castle was twice attacked and destroyed by relatives of Lord Rhys of Deheubarth. The first attack was in 1215 by his grandson Rhys Ieuanc. The second attack was in 1257 by Maredudd ap Rhys Gryg of Dinefwr, grandson of Lord Rhys. The Norman fort had been built over a defensive occupied site protected by a ditch and an earth ring with a wooden palisade. Inside was a settlement dating to the ninth and tenth centuries with a large wooden hut. A central fireplace revealed the crops grown by the people living there were oats, rye and wheat. The site demonstrates that people were still living 'Iron Age style' in the area right up until the time of the Norman conquest. Immediately adjacent to the site is the now derelict public House 'The Castle'. The site is now a car park with toilets and has an information board.

OTHER MOTTE AND BAILEY CASTLES OF NORTH PEMBROKESHIRE.

1) Castell Cynon, Lampeter Velfry; 2) Castell Dyffryn Mawr; 3) Castell Eglwywrw; 4) Castell Llainfawr; 5) Castell Pen yr Allt; 6) Castell Pengawasi; 7) Castell Poeth; 8) Castle Villa, Brawdy; 9) Clyn Pattel Mound; 10) Dinas Island castell; 11) Crundale (At Crundale just north of Haverfordwest, the Normans used the Crundale or Rudbaxron Iron Age fort as a defensive ringwork); 12 Dingstopple, Llawhaden; 13) Drim Castle. Llawhaden; 14) Dyffryn; Little Newcastle; 15) Llan-fawr; 16) Llanfyrnach Motte; 17) Llangwathen Motte; 18) New Moat Motte; 19) Newport Old Castle; 20) Parc Castell, Scleddau; 21) Parc Castell, St. Nicholas; 22) Parc Moat, Letterston; 23) Parc y Castell, St Davids; 24) Pengawsai; 25) Pen-yr-allt; 26) Poyntz Castle; and 27) Y Castell, Llys y Fran.

MOTTES IN SOUTH PEMBROKESHIRE.

1) Amroth Castle Park; 2) Camrose; 3) Castlemartin Castle; 4) Castle Pill, Milford Haven; 5) Castle Ring, Begelly; 6) Dingstopple Motte, near Llawhaden; 7) Great Rudbaxton Mount; 8) Little Newcastle; 9) The Tump, St. Ishmaels; 10) Moat Meadow, East Williamston; 11) Picton Motte, The Belvedere; 12) Rosemarket Rath; and 13) Sentence Castle, Templeton.

Suggested Further Reading.

Miles, D., 1986, *Castles of Pembrokeshire*: Pembrokeshire Coast National Park Authority, 32 p.

Rees. S., 1992, *A Guide to Ancient and Historic Wales – Dyfed*: HMSO, London, 241 p.

20. THE NORMAN STONE CASTLES OF PEMBROKESHIRE

Pembrokeshire has been called 'the County of Castles'. Following the Norman invasion of 1066 by an all-male Norman-Flemish mercenary army of opportunists whose reward was the land, buildings, animals, crops, treasures, and women must have been a most unpleasant time for the local population. William the Conqueror kept a firm control of England and ensured that all castles built to subdue the conquered population were held by himself or his trusted deputies. The land was administered from a network of royal castles. Barons had to obtain permission to build a castle. At first only earthwork castles were built, these were mainly motte and bailey castles. A mound of turf, soil and stones was thrown up often with a ditch around the base. On top a wooden defensive wall was built with a defended gate and a lookout tower. Below was the bailey, a defended area for the residential and workshop buildings. These included the new lord's house and feasting hall. All the buildings were of wood and a wooden defensive wall surrounded the whole.

In Wales the situation was different. William did not conquer Wales. Instead he formed a buffer zone with three earls awarded border lands. They were William FirtzOsborn of Hereford, Roger de Montgomery of Shrewsbury and Hugh d'Avranches of Chester. The three were ordered to defend the realm against the Welsh. They all regarded this as an opportunity to privately colonise Wales. What lands they conquered became known as the Welsh Marches and they became 'Marcher Barons' who could build their castles and rule without interference from the king. In England stone castles began to replace the earth motte and bailey castles in the twelfth century. But in Wales stone castle building was delayed because of the resistance of the Welsh princes to the more insecure marcher barons.

It was King Henry I who encouraged Norman and Flemish settlement in south Pembrokeshire where Norman rule stabilised, so that stone castle building took place starting in the late twelfth but mainly through the thirteenth century. The stone castles are concentrated in the south of the county in the Norman-Flemish settled 'Little England beyond Wales'.

Around fifteen major early castles were rebuilt in stone to provide the main fortresses and long term administrative centres in Pembrokeshire. Figure 1 shows the locations of twenty-two stone castles in Pembrokeshire. These were the ones that could be accessed by the sea, either directly on the coast, as at Tenby, or accessed from the tidal creeks of the Cleddau River and its estuaries. Sea access meant that the stone castles could be easily supplied by sea in times of unrest, but also that the abundant limestone in south Pembrokeshire used in their construction, could be transported to the castle site by boat. There remain around fifty-five earthwork castles surviving in Pembrokeshire today.

The magnificent Norman castles are now crumbling ruins in part because they were deliberately wrecked at the orders of Oliver Cromwell after they had been used by Royalist forces against his parliamentary forces. The greatest of the Pembrokeshire castles is the magnificently restored Pembroke Castle, where one can spend a whole day exploring the towers, battlements, rooms and dungeons. This castle alone initiated the Tudor Dynasty and was the base for the Anglo-Norman invasion of Ireland. It was captured only once and that was during the Civil War.

The castle is one of Pembrokeshire's top tourist destinations with over 80,000 visitors annually. Interestingly the Norman stone castles were painted white and stood out prominently in the landscape. Most of the stone castles are situated in south Pembrokeshire, but notable exceptions are Newport and Cilgerran Castles on the north coast. There are many photographs of the castles and descriptions on the internet (e.g. www.castlewales.com/listings.html and www.visitpembrokeshire.com) Most are open to the public with information boards and some have bookshops. The castles are not described here, only a brief outline of the history of each with dramatic events noted is given as a record of the subjugation of the Welsh peoples of Pembrokeshire, and the rapid integration of the Normans into what is today modern Britain and Ireland.

The castles are grouped here as 'Landsker Castles', 'Milford Haven Waterway Castles' and 'Others'. Included in the latter are two bishop's palaces both built by the very powerful bishops of St. Davids Cathedral. This is because William the Conqueror not only brought feudalism to his new kingdom but he also invited various religious communities to establish themselves here. Cistercians, Benedictines, Premonstratensians, Carthusians and other monastic groups came to Britain and built large abbeys and priories. The leaders of these orders had much the same powers and gained the same wealth as the new lords of the realm. The Bishops palaces were fortified and contained garrisons, servants and the bishop's luxurious apartments.

They had battlements, curtain walls, moats, and gatehouses but (with the exception of Llawhaden Castle) were not as strongly fortified as the castles.

The landsker chain of stone castles separating 'Little England beyond Wales from the Welsh north, are from west to east: Roch; Haverfordwest; Picton; Wiston; Llawhaden; and Narberth. The Milford Haven Waterway stone castles are: Angle Tower; Dale; Pembroke; Carew; Benton; and Upton. Others include the north coast castles of Newport and Cilgerran, and the south coast castles of Tenby and Manorbier. Also included are the Bishops Palace at Lamphey and the Bishops Palace of St. Davids. Most of the castles are in ruins but a few of the smaller ones are still occupied, but only two are whitewashed today - Benton and Roch castles. Today these pictureaque ruins are relics of the subjugation of the Welsh people. Their individual histories record the intimidation and resistance of some of the local leaders to the Norman invaders.

1. THE LANDSKER CASTLES.

ROCH CASTLE is a small keep castle in a spectacular setting on top of a tooth of volcanic rock – hence the name. It commands a wide view of west Pembrokeshire and has a famous story about a snake. The castle was built during the second half of the thirteenth century by Adam de Roche. The Roche or de Rupe family were followers of Earl Strongbow and participated in the invasion of Ireland with him in 1167. They became lords of Rocheland with their seat in Astramount in County Wexford and also lords of Fermoy. The family died out in 1420 and the castle changed ownership several times. Its small mullioned windows are a later Tudor addition. It was owned by the Walter family at the time of the Civil War. The castle was garrisoned by the Royalists but was captured by the Parliamentarians in 1642. It was recaptured by the Royalists but again taken by the Parliamentarians. The castle was neglected after the Civil War. In 1900 there was only the shell standing, Viscount St. David began extensive restoration and later owners have continued this work.

Adam de Rupe had his fortune told and learned that he would die of a snake bite. The only poisonous snake in Wales is the adder. Adam decided to keep himself well away from snakes and so resided in the top room of his castle tower. One cold winter night with a gale blowing in from the sea, Adam ordered his servants to bring up logs to make a large fire to keep his tower room warm. But there as an adder in the wood pile and next morn-ing Adam was found dead with a look of disbelief on his face. The tower with its views across St. Brides Bay proved a valuable lookout during the times of the Viking raids. Later it was owned by the Walters family. Lucy Walters became a consort of King Charles II and the mother of the Duke of Monmouth who led the 1685 rebellion.

HAVERFORDWEST CASTLE dominates the centre of the present day market town of Haverfordwest. It guards the lowest fording point of the Western Cleddau River and marks the highest point at which sailing ships could reach. The castle was very seriously destroyed at the orders of Oliver Cromwell. A castle was first established as an earth and timber fortification by Gilbert de Clare, Earl of Pembroke in the mid twelfth century. It is first mentioned by Geraldus Cambrensis as a place he visited in 1188 when it was an earth and timber structure in possession of Richard FitzTancred. The castle became the central stronghold for 'Little England beyond Wales' – an area settled by the Anglo-Normans who replaced the Welsh people with Flemish immigrants.

The castle was probably built of stone by 1220 when it withstood an attack by Llywelyn the Great after he had burned the town. The castle was acquired by Queen Eleanor (wife of Edward I) in 1289 and she began building on a grand scale so the castle became known as 'the Queens castle at Haverford', but she died in 1290. In the fourteenth century the castle passed through several hands including Edward – the Black Prince - from 1359-1367. Back in the hands of the Crown from 1381-1385, the castle was repaired. It withstood an attack in 1405 led by Owain Glyndwr in his War of Independence. In 1407-08 a new tower was added and a new draw-bridge near the inner gate. Henry VII granted the castle to his uncle Jasper Tudor, Earl of Pembroke. When he died in 1495 it passed to Henry VIII who granted it to Anne Bolyn whom he created Marchioness of Pembroke.

By the sixteenth century the castle was derelict but was hastily re-fortified during the Civil War when it changed hands four times between Royalists and Parliamentarians. At this time several of the windows were walled up for protection against Civil War bombardment. In 1648 Oliver Cromwell ordered the castle destroyed, but this was only partially successful with the town's people complaining that they did not have enough gun power to complete the job. Part of the castle became a prison in the eighteenth century and was used until well into the nineteenth century. Today it houses the County Archives.

PICTON CASTLE overlooks the Cleddau River where it divides into two branches. It probably started as an earth and timber structure in the twelfth century. A Flemish settler Wizo had established himself at his castle at Wiston and began granting estates to his knights. Picton Castle is only three miles from Wiston Castle. The names of the early lords at Picton are not known. By the end of the thirteenth century, Picton was held by the Wogan family – Barons of Wiston. The present castle was built by Sir John Wogan between 1295 and 1308. The Wogan line at Picton ended with an heiress who married Owain Dwnn. The Dwnn line ended in an heiress Jane, who in the late fifteenth century married Sir Thomas Philipps of Cilsant.

The castle has remained in the Philipps family to the present day. During this time it was converted from a castle into a stately home. In 1400 the windows in the hall were replaced by large traceried ones. In 1697 Sir John Philipps made extensive alterations. In 1697 Sir John Philipps (fourth bart.) pulled down part of the curtain wall, built the terrace and created a main entrance at first floor level. He also built an extra storey above the great hall and altered some of the windows. Between 1749 and 1752 Sir John Philipps (sixth bart.) remodelled the interior of the castle. It was completely redecorated above basement level, had new plasterwork, panelling and joinery floors, sash windows and at least four marbled fireplaces.

In 1405 the castle was damaged by French forces fighting with Owain Glyndwr. In the Civil War in 1645 the castle was captured by Royalists but was recaptured by Parliamentarians after a three-week siege. Throughout the seventeenth and eighteenth centuries the Philippses of Picton Castle were the most powerful family in Pembrokeshire.

WISTON CASTLE is remarkable for being one of the best preserved motte and bailey castles in Wales yet it has a stone shell keep, so that it remains at an intermediate stage of development. It was built by an early Flemish settler called Wizo before 1112. The castle was briefly captured by the Welsh in 1147. It was again captured by the Welsh in 1193 when it was taken with the aid of treachery by Hywel Sais, son of the Lord Rhys but was recaptured in 1195. In 1220 it was captured by Llywelyn the Great, prince of Gwynedd who destroyed it.

King Henry III ordered William Marshall the Younger, Earl of Pembroke to restore the castle and the local people were told to help William Marshal of Pembroke with the work. The stone shell keep may date from this time. However the arch in the shell keep suggests an older date, so it is possible that no rebuilding occurred and the fallen part of the wall on the north side was brought down during the attack of Llywelyn the Great. When Sir John Wogan built Picton Castle as the seat of his barony, Wiston Castle was abandoned and fell into ruin. During the Civil war in 1643 the Royalists established a small outpost at Wiston. They withdrew quietly when the Parliamentarians led by Major-General Rowland Laugharne approached in 1644. A famous route of Royalists took place by Laugharne's men at Colby Moor just to the south-east of Wiston.

Plate 1. The entrance to Hoyle's Mouth Cave where Upper Paleolithic hunters sheltered thousands of years ago. The author is sitting where the hunters gathered around their fire.

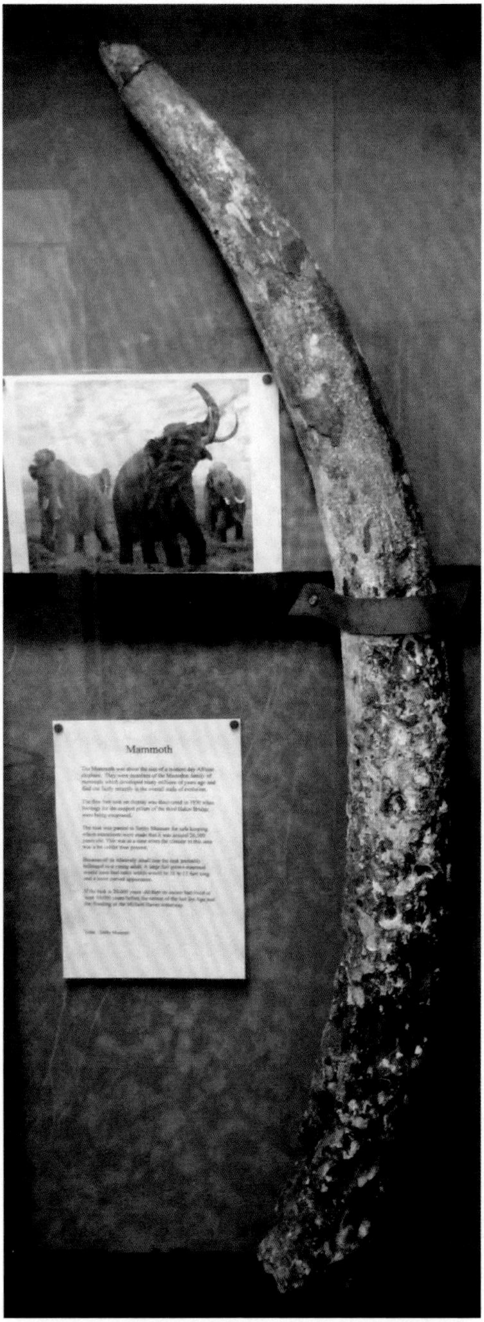
Mammoth

Plate 2. Tusk of woolly mammoth found when digging foundations for Hakin Bridge, now in Milford Haven Museum. The tusk is approximately one meter long.

Plate 3. Pentre Ifan Neolithic burial chamber, the author's wife Anne gives the scale of the structure.

Plate 4. A large fallen oak tree 5,000 years old, sunken forest, Marros.

Plate 5. The lookout on Foel Eryr, looking south over Llys-y-Fran reservoir.

Plate 6. The Bronze Age stone circle of Gors Fawr.

Plate 7. The Bronze Age stone circle of Dyffryn Syfynwy.

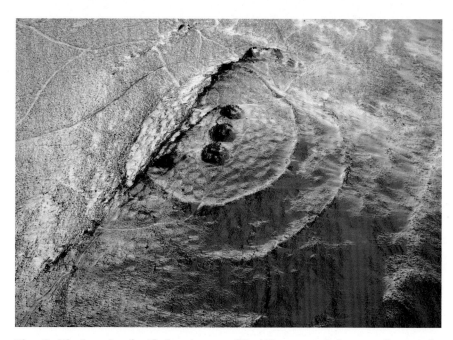

Plate 8. The Iron Age fortified settlement of Foel Drygarn in light snow showing the defensive walls, the three Bronze Age cairns and numerous depressions marking the sites of round huts (Toby Driver, 02/02/2022).

Plate 9. Iron Age round houses at the reconstructed fortified settlement of Castell Henllys.

Plate 10. Carew Celtic Cross.

Plate 11. Nevern Celtic Cross.

Plate 12. Hubba and his Vikings remembered in a Milford Haven carnival.

Plate 13. Pembroke Castle viewed from the north.

Plate 14. Carew Castle viewed from the east.

Plate 15. Pembroke Castle and the adjacent part of the town to the east (right) with a single street and long narrow gardens surrounded by the city wall.

Plate 16. Effigies of Sir John Carew and his wife Dame Elizabeth on their tomb in St. Mary's Church, Carew Cheriton village.

Plate 17. The three sons of Sir John and Dame Elizabeth on their parents' tomb in St. Mary's Church, Carew Cheriton village.

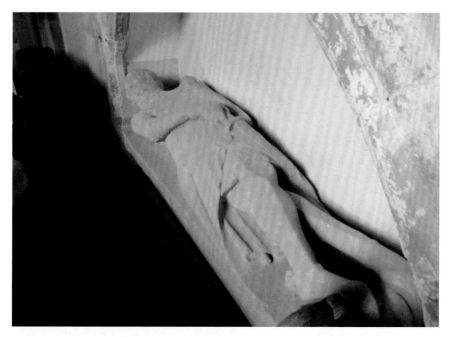

Plate 18. Effigy of unknown knight with crossed legs in a recess at St Mary's Church, Carew Cheriton village.

Plate 19. Effigy of Sir William Malefant on his recessed tomb in Upton Church.

Plate 20. Effigy of a lady on her recessed tomb in Upton Church, possibly Margaret Malefant.

Plate 21. The ruins of Haverfordwest priory with its raised garden beds.

Plate 22. The chancel arch of Pill Priory showing the roofline of the choir and on the right the flight of night steps leading from the monks sleeping quarters into the choir.

Plate 23. Stack Rock Fort – a Palmerston folly.

Plate 24. Five-meter long palm tree trunk with a heavy coating of goose barnacles on Newgale beach in January 2023.

Plate 25. Two sea beans or tropical drift seeds from Pembrokeshire beaches. Lower left is a snuffbox sea bean (*Entada rheedii*) common on Caribbean beaches, found on Freshwater West beach. Upper right is a bull's eye seed (*Dioclea sp.*) from the Amazon River, found on Lindsway Bay.

Plate 26. Five 'floating stones' collected from Sandy Haven beach. Black scoria of basaltic andesite composition and cream-coloured pumice of dacite composition have travelled 5,000 miles from the Caribbean volcanoes. A fifty pence coin is shown for scale.

LLAWHADEN CASTLE was built not as a castle at all but as a fortified Bishops Palace – one of three for the powerful Norman Bishops of St. Davids Cathedral. Construction is likely to have begun as an earth and timber fortification in the twelfth century on land granted to the Norman Bishop Bernard. It was one of three Bishop's Palaces built by the bishops of St. David's, but what resulted was a true fortified castle. It was refortified with stone in response to a siege led by Welshman Lord Rhys in the late twelfth century. In the thirteenth century Bishop Thomas Bek (1280-1293) added the hall block with stone vaulted undercrofts, service rooms and a kitchen. He also had built the elaborately adorned bishop's chambers above. In the late fourteenth century the castle was refortified again by Bishop Adam de Houghton, in response to fear of a French invasion from the nearby Eastern Cleddau River. The bishop added the impressive twin-towered gatehouse, at the same time a range of domestic buildings including apartments and a chapel were added to the south side of the castle. A chapel tower next to the chapel has a fireplace, a latrine, vaulted rooms, a dungeon in the basement and access to the battlements. With the Dissolution of the Monasteries in the sixteenth century, the bishop's palaces of Pembrokeshire, including Llawhaden Castle were abandoned. The latter became a quarry for local building material.

NARBERTH CASTLE has been extensively destroyed. The site was used as a fortification by Welsh Princes before the Norman invasion. The first record of a Norman castle was in 1116. The stone castle was built by Andrew Perrot in the thirteenth century. It was destroyed by Llywelyn the Last's men in 1257. It was probably rebuilt by Roger Mortimer after Narberth was granted to him in 1282. In 1404 Thomas Carrewe was granted the lordship after defending the castle against Owain Glyndwr's French allies in his War of Independence. Previously it had been held by Sir Edward Mortimer, but was forfeited when he took sides with Owain Glyndwr after his capture. The castle later reverted to the Mortimer family when King Edward V granted the lordship to Sir Edmund Mortimer. When the latter died childless in 1425, Narberth Castle reverted to the Crown.

2. CASTLES OF THE MILFORD HAVEN WATERWAY

ANGLE CASTLE overlooks Angle Bay at the entrance to the Milford Haven Waterway. A French army landed here in 1405 in support of Owain Glyndwr. It is a single-tower fortified residence and was built by the powerful Shirburn family in the fourteenth century. These structures are common in Ireland and Scotland, but are not common in Wales. There was a walled and moated enclosure to the north, with the south and west protected by marshy ground.

DALE CASTLE is a private house incorporating parts of a much earlier castle. The original castle was built by the de Vale family. When Robert de Vale died in 1303 his estate passed to his four daughters. Dale passed to the Walter family of Roch and Rosemarket. Later the castle was owned by a succession of families – the Paynters, Allens and Lloyds. The present castle is mainly a Victorian mansion owned by the Lloyd-Philipps family.

PEMBROKE CASTLE is the mightiest of the Norman castles in Pembrokeshire and was never captured by the Welsh (Plate 13). It has a long and remarkable history and is best remembered as the site for the organisation and jumping off point for the Norman invasion fleets that captured much of Ireland only eighty miles away across the Irish Sea. It was first established as an earth and timber structure in 1093 by Arnulf son of Roger Montgomery, Earl of Shrewsbury. Three years later it was successfully defended against the Welsh by Gerald de Windsor.

Work on the stone structure was begun when King Richard I granted the earldom to a then-poor knight William Marshal in 1189. The latter proved very capable and started building in stone – the work continued for thirty years. First he built the inner ward with its splendid round keep over 22 meters high and a domed stone roof. The keep had four floors connected by a spiral staircase that led to the battlements. A ring of sockets in the stonework outside the battlements shows where in times of attack a wooden fighting platform could be erected outside the battlements above the heads of the attackers. The keep was enclosed by an inner ward curtain wall with a large horse-shoe shaped gate of which only the footings remain. The castle was enlarged and strengthened by William's third son Gilbert between 1234 and 1241.

The castle next passed to William de Valence (a half brother of Henry II) through his marriage to William's Marshal's granddaughter Joan. The Valence family held the castle for seventy years and built the walls and towers of the outer ward. They also walled and fortified the town. On the death of Aymer (William de Valence's son), the castle passed through marriage to the Hastings family who held it from 1324 to 1389, when the castle reverted to Richard I. There followed a series of short tenancies and the castle began to fall into disrepair. In 1400 the castle was attacked by Owain Glyndwr, but he was paid to go away. The castle passed to Jasper Tewdwr (Tudor), Earl of Pembroke and his nephew Henry Tewdwr was born in the castle in 1457. Henry later defeated King Richard III at the

Battle of Bosworth Field and established the Tudor Dynasty, becoming King Henry VII.

In the Civil War in 1648 Oliver Cromwell laid siege to the castle and captured it after seven weeks. He ordered the castle destroyed which proved impossible, but the castle was seriously damaged. The castle then remained an overgrown ruin until 1880 when Mr. J. R. Cobb of Brecon spent three years in restoration work. Nothing then happened until 1928 when Major-General Sir Ivor Philips of Cosherton Hall acquired the castle and began an extensive restoration program. When he died a trust was set up to continue the restoration that continues to this day.

CAREW CASTLE is a beautiful ruin standing alone on a low ridge overlooking the Carew River that flows into the Cleddau River (Plate 14). It was first built as an earth and timber castle by Gerald of Windsor around 1100 after he obtained the site as a dowry when he married the beautiful Princess Nest. Owain ap Cadwgan was overwhelmed by Princess Nest's beauty and with a few men broke into the castle and kidnapped the Princess and her children. Six years later Gerald killed Owain in revenge. Apart from one attack by Lord Rhys in 1192, the castle remained free of Welsh wars.

A stone castle probably stood by 1212 when it was seized by King John when passing through Pembrokeshire on his Irish expedition. The castle long remained in the hands of the Carew family who built most of the stone castle visible today. In the late thirteenth and early fourteenth century Sir Nicholas de Carew constructed many of the stone buildings that surround the inner ward. Around 1480 Sir Edmund Carew passed the castle to Sir Rhys ap Thomas. Sir Rhys was knighted in return for services rendered to Henry Tewdwr (who became King Henry VII) during his victory at the Battle of Bosworth Field. Sir Rhys is credited with killing King Richard III on the battlefield. Sir Rhys converted Carew into a home and built the gatehouse.

Sir Rhys held a great tournament at the castle in 1507 for which he set up the arms of his patron King Henry VII together with Arthur, Prince of Wales and his wife Catherine of Aragon for the tournament. The arms are still in place on the castle walls. The castle was granted to Sir John Perrot in 1558 who converted it into an Elizabethan Mansion by knocking down the north-east tower and north curtain wall and building a new northern range with typical Elizabethan great windows. Unfortunately the castle was not occupied for long as Sir John was accused of treason and sent to the Tower of London. During the Civil War the castle was refortified and outside the middle gatehouse a 'V' shaped bank for guns is still visible.

In the seventeenth century Sir Roland Rhys lived at the castle and owned a pet ape. He was killed by the ape and the tale exists that the ghost of the ape can still be seen on the battlements late at night. The castle was then let out to tenants but was abandoned in 1686.

BENTON CASTLE stands on a rock above the Cleddau River. It is believed to date from the thirteenth century and may have been built by the de la Roche family. Little is known of its history. The remains show it to have been a small enclosure castle with a round keep and a round tower on the exposed side. It lacks staircases and the floors must have been accessed by ladders. There is a polygonal ward. The surviving parts were restored from ruins in 1932.

UPTON CASTLE lies on the west bank of the Carew River near where it flows into the Cleddau River. It was built in the thirteenth century but is partly replaced by a later house. The original was built by the Malefants, a Norman family who held it until the sixteenth century. The male line died out in the Tudor period and it went out of the family. The castle was modernised in the eighteenth century and today is privately owned. It is more of a fortified mansion but has three remarkably strong round towers with a gate house between two of them. There is also a building that was once apparently a hall.

3. OTHER CASTLES.

NEWPORT CASTLE was built by William FitzMartin who married the daughter of the Lord Rhys. William was ejected from Nevern Castle by Lord Rhys in 1191 and came to Tresdraeth or Narberth. There he built his castle along with the town and a church. Twice in the thirteenth century Newport castle was destroyed by the Welsh, first by Llywelyn the Great in 1215 and again by Llywelyn the Last in 1257. The present stone castle may have been built after this time. The castle consists of a massive gatehouse flanked by two circular towers – the Dungeon Tower and the Hunters Tower. The castle passed to the Audley family in 1326. It was bought by the Owen family. In 1859 the Lloyds of Bronwydd made a residence of the gatehouse.

CILGERRAN CASTLE stands on a promontory overlooking the junction of the rivers Teifi and Plysgog. It was probably built as an earth castle by Gerald de Windsor who married Princes Nest. It is possible that Princess Nest and her children were kidnapped from Cilgerran Castle. The castle has a stormy history. It was first captured by Lord Rhys in 1165 and two Norman attempts to recover it failed. It was retaken by William Marshal, Earl of Pembroke, in 1204. It was recaptured by the Welsh during Llywelyn the Great's campaigns in 1215. It was retaken by the younger William Marshal (son of the above William Marshal) Earl of Pembroke, in 1223 who built the impressive stone castle.

Five Marshall brothers successively held the castle and earldom of Pembroke. The curtain wall and buildings on the north-east and north-west side of the ward probably date to the second half of the century. The castle next passed by marriage to the de Cantelupe family and then in the fourteenth century also by marriage to the Hastings family. In the 1370s a French invasion was feared and King Edward III ordered the then rather derelict castle to be refortified. The north-west tower may have been built at this stage. In 1389 when the Hastings family died out, the castle passed to the Crown. It was much damaged and may have been captured and held for a short time in 1405 during Owain Glyndwr's War of Independence. In the Tudor period the castle was granted to the Vaughan family by King Henry VII and was occupied by the family until the early seventeenth century, when they built a house nearby. The castle then fell into ruin. The artist Turner painted and sketched the ruined castle several times.

MANORBIER CASTLE stands on a narrow ridge overlooking Manorbier Bay. It is famous as the birthplace and home of Geraldus Cambrensis – Gerald the Welshman. The castle began as an earth and timber fortification built by the Norman knight Odo de Barri. This was gradually replaced by the Barri family as a stone castle. The hall block was built by William de Barri in the 1140s and includes a dove cote. Gilluame de Barri had a son, Gerald de Barri who became known as the great twelfth century scholar Geraldus Cambrensis who was born in the castle in the twelfth century. His maternal nephew was David FitzGerald, Bishop of St. Davids. He was a grandson of Gerald de Windsor, Constable of Pembroke castle and his famous wife Princess Nest, daughter of Rhys ap Tewdwr, last prince of south west Wales. In 1260 a chapel was built in the inner ward and today patches of medieval wall paintings survive inside.

Richard de Barri stormed the castle in 1327 to reclaim what was rightfully his. The de Barries then owned the castle until 1359. After the Barri ownership, the castle changed hands several times. The castle became property of the Crown in the late fifteenth century. In 1630 Queen Elizabeth I sold the castle, then in ruinous condition, to the Bowen family of Trefloyne. In 1645 during the Civil War, the castle was seized by Oliver Cromwell's Roundheads and slighted. A series of earth banks and ditches outside the castle date from this time. The Philippses of Picton Castle bought Manorbier Castle in 1670. The family leased it to Mr. J. R. Cobb in the late nineteenth century, who undertook much restoration work (as he also did for Pembroke Castle). During the First World War soldiers were stationed at the castle and small fireplaces built for them can still be seen.

TENBY CASTLE stands on a high rocky headland and the old town occupies an adjacent promontory and retains most of its defensive wall. The castle was built by the Normans in the twelfth century as an earth and timber structure. It was captured by Rhys ap Gruffydd (the Lord Rhys) and his brother Maredudd in 1153. Lord Rhy's son Maelgwn sacked the town in 1187. Llewellym the Last sacked and burned the town in 1260. In response the stone castle, a defensive wall across the headland and most of the town walls were built during the thirteenth century. Work commenced by William de Valence who became Lord of Pembroke around 1264. In 1328 the D-shaped barbican was added to defend the gate as well as two D-shaped towers to the north and south of the gate. Tenby resisted a siege by Owain Glyndwr's French allies in 1405. In 1437 the moat was widened to thirty feet, the walls heightened and a second, higher series of arrow slits was built, reached by a parapet walk. At the same time a square tower was added to the cliff top on the south of the town and a large rectangular bastion with two towers built further north with gun ports, a fireplace and latrine.

In 1457 Jasper Tewdwr and his young nephew Henry Tewdwr escaped by boat from Tenby and reached Britanny. Henry remained there for fourteen years before returning and winning the throne at Bosworth Field.

During the Civil War the castle was in Parliamentarian hands. In 1648 Royalist rebels held the castle for ten weeks but were starved into surrender. In 1588 with the Spanish Armada threatening, parts of the town wall were rebuilt and strengthened. Parts of the medieval town defences remain well preserved although of the original three gates and twelve towers, only one gate and seven towers remain.

AMROTH CASTLE has largely disappeared with only a much restored fourteenth century gateway remaining incorporated into a later residence. It is only recently that the name Amroth was used and the original name of the castle was Earwere. The castle was built by Pigot de Say who was a follower of Arnulf de Montgomery. Pigot's daughter married the Welsh Prince Cadwgan ap Bleddyn of Ceredigion. It was his son Owain who abducted Princes Nest in 1108. As a result, King Henry I sent Cadwgan into exile and his son fled to Ireland. The Elliot family were long term residents of the castle. Today the castle is part of Amroth Holiday Centre.

4. BISHOPS PALACES

LAMPHEY BISHOP'S PALACE is not a castle but a lavish fortified country seat used by the bishops of St. David's Cathedral. It began as the seat of the last Welsh bishops before the Norman invasion. After the invasion Norman bishops considerably extended and embellished the palace. In particular they added the Old Hall, the West Hall and the Great Hall. Building extended from the thirteenth to the sixteenth centuries. After the reformation the palace was acquired by the Earl of Essex and his descendants, but quickly became a ruin.

BISHOPS PALACE, ST. DAVIDS. When the Normans arrived in Pembrokeshire in the eleventh century, they took over St. Davids cathedral and appointed a Norman Bishop. They protected the cathedral with a motte and bailey castle. They then built a stone protective wall around the cathedral buildings including the palace. Thomas Bek carried out a program of building between 1280 and 1293 to produce the chapel in the south-west corner, the hall, private apartments and the gate. Bishop Henry de Gower between 1328 and 1347 carried out major works on the cathedral and at the palace built the Great Hall with its wheel window in the east gable, the distinctive arcaded parapet and the majestic porch. Later bishops made further additions and alterations to the palace. With the reformation the palace fell into disrepair and ruin.

Suggested Further Reading

Miles. D., 1986, *Castles of Pembrokeshire*: Pembrokeshire Coast National Park Authority, 32 p.

Rees. S., 1992, *A Guide to Ancient and Historic Wales – Dyfed*: HMSO, London, 241 p.

Stickings, T.G., 1972, *Stories of the Castles and Strongholds of Pembrokeshire*: H .G. Walters (Publishers) Ltd., Tenby, 132 p.

21. PRINCESS NEST

The Welsh princess Nest (or Nesta) was born around 1085 (died c. 1136). This was a time of great conflict immediately following the Norman invasion of 1066. Nest is described in ancient accounts as being very beautiful and 'the Helen of Wales'. She is reputed to have created a fatal attraction in all men that she encountered. She had a remarkable life in these turbulent times. Born the daughter of a Welsh prince, she became a king's mistress, married two Norman barons, was abducted by a Welsh prince and had at least nine children by five different men. She was the progenitor of three great Cambro-Norman and Anglo-Norman families - the FitzHenrys, FitzGeralds and FitzStephens. Many of the details of her life are unknown including her birth and death dates. It is not clear how many children she bore and whether she married the last two Normans in her life.

Wales in the eleventh century comprised several Celtic minor kingdoms each ruled by their prince and warring with each other. In 1075, Nest's father, Prince Rhys ap Tewdwr (c.1040 -1093), was the last ruler of Deheubarth (south-west Wales corresponding to modern Pembrokeshire, Ceredigion (Cardiganshire) and Carmarthenshire). Her welsh name was Nesta ferch Rhys and her mother was Gwladys ferch Rhiwallon. She had two younger brothers - Gruffydd ap Rhys and Hywel ap Rhys - as well as several older illegitimate half brothers and half sisters. Her life as a young girl in the court of her father would have been colourful and interesting.

The family would travel around Deheubarth from royal seat to royal seat as her father, the lord, administered his land and visited the households of other senior men. Taxes were not paid in money but in goods and animals collected. Rhys ap Tewdwr ruled by supplying his supporters with the wealth he gathered. They were a large party including the prince, his queen, the captain of the guard, his men at ams or warband of young aristocratic warriors, bards from another country, the royal horses, dogs, and hawkes with their custodians, his household and his warband. All these were supported by Rhys ap Tewdwr and whom he was obliged to feast and give gifts from the taxes collected.

In 1081 Rhys ap Tewdwr was driven out of his castle at Dinefawr by an invading army led by other Welsh leaders from Powys and Morgannwg. He fled to St. Davids. There he met Gruffydd ap Cynan the rightful heir to the throne of Gwynned who had landed at Portclais nearby from Ireland. He brought with him an army of his followers including Irish and Danes. Together the two armies marched east for a day to the vicinity of the Preseli Mountains, where the battle of Mynydd Carn took place. Rhys and Gruffydd were victorious

Later that year Rhys ap Twedwr met with King William 1st (William the Conqueror) during the latter's pilgrimage to St. David's. He negotiated peace at a price of forty pounds per year, so that for the last six years of William's life Deheubarth was at peace with the Normans. However when King William died in 1088 Deheubarth was attacked by the ruler of Powys. For a short time Rhys ap Tewdwr fled to Ireland but returned shortly and with the help of Vikings defeated the army of Powys. Three years later Powys attacked again and Rhys ap Tewdwr was victorious at the Battle of St. Dogmaels in north Pembrokeshire. But he and one of his sons (Nest's half brother Goronwy) were killed in 1093 near Brecon in battle against the Normans under Robert FitzHamon's leadership

Critcal to the future of Nest was the success of Roger of Montgomery, Earl of Shrewsbury. He had commanded the right wing of the Noman army at the Battle of Hastings, was a staunch supporter of Wlliam the Conqueror and had been richly rewarded with land in Sussex. When Welsh resistance sprang up William also awarded Roger Montgomery Shropshire, where Montgomery constructed a line of castles. Roger had an arranged married with Mabel de Belleme in 1051 and she brought much dowery land. They had nine children, five sons and four daughters. The children were well provided for. Their eldest son Robert de Belleme would inherit the holdings in Normandy. The second son Hugh was awarded lands in England. Roger arranged an advantageous marriage for his third son Roger. This left his two younger sons Philip and Arnulf and the daughters to be provided for.

A great family opportunity arose when Rhys ap Tewdwr was killed by Normans in 1093. Roger de Montgomery and his three land-hungry sons Robert, Hugh and Arnulf, invaded Deheubarth sweeping along the Severn Valley into modern Pembrokeshire. Hugh was already Earl of Shrewsbury and strove to establish a Lordship for his brother Arnulf. By the end of 1093 Arnulf regarded himslf as Lord of Pembroke and the rich farm land of much of the former Deuhebarth. He brought many of his friends and followers with him.

Sometime after the death of Rhys ap Tewdwr, Princess Nest and her younger brother Hywel ap Rhys were captured by the Normans and came into the hands of Arnulf Montgomery. The latter was a great fighter but a very cruel man who enjoyed torturing his prisoners. Hywel was castrated and kept as a prisoner in one of Arnulf's castles. Nest's older brother Gruffydd ap Rhys escaped to Ireland. Nest was taken as a hostage for the good behaviour of the Welsh people and in particular her two brothers. The conquest of Wales was completed shortly afterwards.

It is unknown how Nest felt but she was very young, perhaps only fifteen years old (old enough to be married in those times). She had lost her parents (nothing is known of the fate of her mother) and her brothers and found herself alone in an alien Norman world where people spoke Norman French, dressed and behaved very differently and the men wore a strange hair style. She was probably afraid of the Montgomery brothers. To the Normans she was a great prize as in the absence of her brothers, her marriage might be used as a claim for the land of Deheubarth. She would have made an ideal wife for Arnulf and a great help to him in consolidating his new gained lands.

But such things were not to be. William the Conqueror died in 1087 and his son William Rufus became the king. He did nor want Arnulf to marry Nest because he might become too powerful in distant west Wales. So Nest became a royal ward probably in Windsor, where she came to the attention of Prince Henry, son of William the Conqueror, shortly before he became King Henry I (1100-1135). Roger de Montgomery and his sons Roger de Belleme and Arnulf de Belleme did not support William Rufus and joined a revolt against him in 1068. It became known the Belleme Rebellion. King Henry Rufus died in 1100 in a mysterious hunting accident at which his younger bother Henry was present. Henry rushed to Winchester and seized the treasury and was crowned King Henry I three days later. Roger and Arnulf were eventually defeated in battle by King Henry I and his army and the two brothers accepted exile as their punishment.

King Henry was a great womaniser who had at least twenty illegitimate children before and after his marriage. Princess Nest became a concubine and bore Henry a son. The child was named Henry FitzHenry. Nest was now safe from the Montgomery brothers and under the Kings protection. King Henry was closely attached to Nest and he sought her advice throughout his reign. However as king he found it necessary to make a political marriage to the daughter of the King of Scotland. So King Henry arranged the marriage of Princess Nest to Gerald de Windsor - Constable of Pembroke Castle in the Norman stronghold of South Pembrokeshire.

Gerald was born Gerald de FitzWalter of Windsor and his father Walter was a Saxon and Custodian of Windsor. King Henry I decided to keep his only son Henry FitzHenry with him in London as he feared for his safety in Wales. He later gave him lands in Narberth in Pembrokeshire. Henry FitzHenry died in battle in 1157 but left children who formed the FitzHenry dynasty.

King Henry made a political marriage to Edith-Matilda of Scotland to strengthen his claim to the throne. When King Henry I offered Gerald of Windsor, castellan of Pembroke Castle, the hand of Nest in marriage, he probably saw the offer as a measure of trust from the King. He accepted. Land at Carew was included as a dowry. So after an absence of seven years Princess Nest returned by sea to Pembroke castle to meet her future husband Gerald, in what had been a part of her father's kingdom.

Now her people had been conquered and reduced to serfs in a new feudal system. The rich lands of south Pembrokeshire had become a Norman stronghold with a ring of Norman castles built to defend the area from the Welsh people who remained in the colder and somewhat barren mountainous north of the county. How did she feel leaving an infant son behind fathered by the current King of England, to be sent back into her former lands for which her father and a half brother had died, to go into an arranged marriage with a Norman Lord opposed to her brothers. Her future husband already had a Welsh concubine Myfanwy with whom he had fathered two sons - John and Llinos. Gerald was much older than Nest..

The Norman - Welsh integration did in fact proceed surprisingly rapidly as the Normans strengthened their hold on the conquered lands by marrying the daughters of the Welsh rulers. Princess Nest and Gerald were married in 1100. With the marriage came land at Carew (Nest's dowry). The power of the king was enormous as he granted lands and castles to favourites and removed them at will. Gerald seems to have been very aware of this as he made the best he could by building himself a castle on the dowry land brought with Princess Nest. This castle was at Carew and was Gerald's own private stronghold as distinct from his official post at Pembroke. The move meant that he was no longer dependent on the king's favour as at Pembroke.

Life proceeded well for Nest and her husband. They had three children. In 1108 Gerald built himslf another earth and timber castle at what is now Cilgerran Castle near Cardigan castle that was another stronghold of his Lord at Pembroke - Arnulf de Montgomery. This may have been in anticipation of trouble in Ceredigeon to the north. He put Nest, the children and his treasures there. It was probaly a shrewd move by Gerald, as the presence of Nest there might deter the wesh princes of Ceredigeon, some of whom were related to Nest in their drive against the earldom of Pembroke. But events turned out very differently.

A major event in Nest's life began when Cadwagn ap Bleddyn, prince of Powys, held a great feast at which his son Owain ap Cadwagn (second cousin to Nest) heard of the great beauty of Princess Nest. During Christmas 1109 Gerald and Nest were visited by Owain ap Cadwagn. Owain was enchanted by Nest's beauty. He returned with fifteen warriors and attacked their castle (most likely Cilgerran Castle) by tunnelling under the gate and setting fire to it. Nest persuaded her husband Gerald to escape through the garderobe (lavatory chute). Owain robbed the fort and carried off Nest with four children (three were hers with Gerald and a fourth was from a concubine by Gerald). There are rumours that Nest may have born Owain two sons, Llywelyn and Einion, although this is very speculative and unlikely. She did persuade Owain to release the children.

King Henry I was not at all pleased with Nest's abduction. He decided that Cadwagn was incapable of keeping his son under control. He took his petty kingdom from him and gave it to Gilbert de Tonbridge, father of Gilbert de Claire. It is unknown when Nest returned to her family. But she did and life settled down again with Gerald. Another child – Maurice - was born. Meanwhile Owain returned from Ireland and set about raiding and plundering Norman lands. In 1114 King Henry was provoked into coming to Wales with an army to put an end to the troubles there. Peace was established and Owain received his fathers land and gave hostages for his good behaviour.

But in 1113, after twenty years in exile, Gruffydd ap Rhys, prince of South Wales, returned from Ireland. He spent two years with his former kinsmen and much of it with his sister Nest and Gerald. He stayed with them at Pembroke Castle. To the Normans he was seen as a social and political threat. But for the Welsh people of the former Deheubarth he was seen as hope for a Welsh future. It also gave Nest time to get to know her brother who would prove himelf not a diplomat but more of a trouble maker. He did not approach King Henry and he made no claims on the former lands of Deheubarth. But Nest had a role to play in helping her brother make contacts with the key people of former Deheubarth and his presence was seen by the Normans. It placed Gerald in a difficult position as his loyalties could be questioned. For Nest it also must have been a trying time with her brother and husband on opposite sides of the conflict.

In 1115 Nest's youmger brother Hywel escaped and joined Gruffydd. Possibly Nest had something to do with this. As Gerald's role was to keep the peace in the earldom of Pembroke, his hosting Gruffedd was clearly the work of Nest. King Henry became suspicious of his loyalty and eventually removed him as castellian of Pembroke castle. In 1115 Gerald was near Carmarthen with an army of Flemish supporters when they encountered Owain with his army who had been fighting in the area. At the time both armies were fighting on the same side. But Gerald seeking revenge for the abduction of his wife and the attack of his fort at Cilgerran, attacked. Owain was killed by arrows. This is the last historic record of Gerald, and it seems he died soon afterwards.

Gruffydd ap Rhys eventually made his peace with King Henry I and accepted a small area of land where he lived and raised a family. Gruffydd ap Rhys never achieved success in restoring the Welsh soverignity of Deheubarth. But his son Rhys ap Gruffydd became known as Lord Rhys and rebuilt southern Wesh power in the second half of the twelfth century.

After Gerald's death around 1116, in order to survive in the male-dominated world of the twelfth century Wales, and as a potential heiress, it was necessary for Nest to remarry. She is next recorded as living with and probably married to William Hait, the Flemish Sheriff of Pembroke, who replaced Gerald. This was another cultural change for Nest for she was now amongst the Flemish people. For Hait, the aquisition of a fomer princes of Duheubarth was a major step forward and may have assisted him in obtaining the position of castellan to Pembroke Castle. He would have met Nest when she was Gerald's wife at Pembroke and Carew castles. They had a son William FitzHait or FitzHay. But neither the son nor father played any prominent role in the future of the area. The marriage did not last long but what happened is unrecorded.

The next known event is that Nest's sons later married her off to Stephen de Marisco, Constable of Cardigan in about 1120. She would have met Stephen when she and Gerald were at Cilgerran Castle. As castellan, Stephen's role was much the same as that of Gerald. At this stage of her life Nest's sons with Gerald were now adults and knights and they rode with Stephen in his battles with the welsh. Unfortunately at this time her Welsh brother Gruffydd was also at war with the Normans. Nest found herself in a similar position to what she had been in with Gerald. But this time her sons and husband were fighting with the Normans and Flemish settlers agains her brother and his Welsh supporters. Nest and Stephen had two sons. The eldest was Robert FitzStephen, born around 1121-24. The name of the younger son is unrecorded but might be Hywel.

Princess Nest died around 1136. But the details are not recorded. Her mixed Norman and Welsh interests are recorded in the Wesh names of three of her children – Hywel, Angharad and Gwladus. It was quite an achievemnt for Nest to have some of her children given Welsh names. No Norman would like to have a son named after an enemy he had fought. For example in 1105 Gerald had fought Hywel ap Goronwy, who was eventually killed in a Norman ambush. Hywel was also Nest's younger brother who fought against the Normans. The fact that Angharad was given a welsh name during the life time of Gerald suggests that he was sympathetic to the welsh side of his wife Nest.

Gerald of Wales was a grandson of Nest. In his autobiography he names ten children of Nest. They are William FitzGerald, Robert, Henry, Maurice, William Hay, Hywel, Walter, David, Angharad and Gwladus. Henry was Nest's son by King Henry I. Stephen was fathered by Stephen, Constable of Cardigan after 1009. William FitzGerald, Maurice, David, Angharad and Gwladus were fathered by Gerald. William inherited Gerald's welsh property after his fathers death. Nest's children and grandchildren - the FitzHenrys, FitzGeralds, FitzStephens and the Barrys - became Pembrokeshire knights who undertook the first Norman invasion of Ireland.

The invasion was led by Robert FitzStephen and his nephew Meilyr FitzHenry – the Kings grandson and Robert de Barri (the son of Nest's daughter Angharad). They were followed later by Nest's son and grandson, Maurice and Raymond FitzGerald. From these descendants of Nest arose the noble Cambro-Norman families of Ireland whose names became famous in the following centuries of Irish history – the FitzStephens, Barrys, FitzHenrys and most famous – the FitzGeralds. President Kennedy in America was also a descendant of Nest's FitzGerald dynasty as his mother's maiden name was Rose FitzGerald. Gerald's eldest son William adopted the local surname de Carew. David became Bishop of St. Davids in 1148. Angharad married William, Lord of Barri and became the mother of Gerald of Wales. Hywel might have been another son of Stephen of Cardigan, as he laid claim to one of Stephen's former holdings – Lampeter. Nothing is known of the fathers of Walter or Gwladus.

The Norman hunger for land persisted. Princess Nest's son David FitzGerald became the third Norman Bishop of St. David's in 1148. He used the bishopric to enrich his family in land and offices. He gave his brother Maurice the manors of Llanrhian, Priskilly and Castle Morris (Maurice). Bishop David had at least one son (Miles) and several daughters. Miles joined the Norman invasion of Ireland. For many years the Cathedral demanded the return of the property. By 1300 the properties were returned by Sir John Wogan of Picton Castle who was the Chief Justice of Ireland for King Edward I. Only Castle Morris and Priskilly are shown in the Black Book of St. Davids (1324). It seems that Sir John Wogan kept Llanrhian for himself.

The welsh Princess Nest by her actions and her large number of Cambro-Norman children considerably bridged the two warring sides of the conflict in Wales and her children created some of the leading Welsh-Norman and Irish-Norman families who went on to play major roles in the formation of modern Britain and Ireland. Her actions ensured the survival of much of ancient Britain and helped lay the foundations of modern Britain where the different peoples are now reasonably integrated and very many of the present day population have some Norman ancestry.

Suggested Further Reading
Maund, K., 2007, *Princess Nest of Wales – Seductress of the English*: Tempos Publishing Ltd., Stroud, 192 p. ISBN 978-0-7524-3771-2.

22. THE DEATH OF PRINCESS GWENLLIAN AND A GREAT WELSH VICTORY AT CARDIGAN

The Welsh people have survived many invasions and are historically proud with a long record of defensive fighting to preserve their lands and traditions. An early Welsh hero was Prince Caractacus or Caradog in Welsh. His father was King Cunobelinus, whose lands were seized by the Roman General Aulus Plautinus. Caractacus then led the Silures and Ordovices in a guerrilla war against the invading Romans. He was finally defeated but escaped to the Brigantes in Yorkshire, where their queen Cartimandus betrayed him to the Romans. Taken to Rome in chains as a prisoner, he was pardoned by the Emperor because of his noble bearing.

The Norman invasion along with the Norman program of bringing in Flemish settlers to act as their foot soldiers provided a huge challenge. Many rose to defend Wales and there follows one example but it illustrates the complexity as the Normans married into the Welsh royal families producing conflicting loyalties. This story begins when Princess Nest's father, Rhys ap Tewdwr, the last Welsh ruler of the south-west Wales Kingdom of Deheubarth (including modern Pembrokeshire) was killed in battle with the Normans in 1093. Princes Nest was taken as a hostage, probably to Windsor, for the good behaviour of her two younger brothers - Gruffydd ap Rhys and Hywel ap Rhys. Gruffydd ap Rhys went into exile in Ireland

Gruffydd ap Rhys returned to Pembrokeshire determined to regain his rightful but lost kingdom. Princess Nest persuaded her husband Gerald to support her brother. Having gained his support Gruffydd ap Rhys then proceeded to North Wales to the court of his father-in-law Gruffydd ap Cynan, Prince of North Wales. This Gruffydd was a famous warrior who earlier had returned from exile in Ireland bringing with him an Irish army with which he captured the kingdom of Gwynedd and went on to oppose the Normans.

King Henry learned of the meeting of the two Welsh princes and feared the revival of Deheubarth and the uniting of the two forces. He invited

Gruffydd ap Cynan to London, where he feasted him and showered him with gifts of plate and jewels and extracted a promise to send his son-in law to him either dead or alive in chains. While drunk on the king's wines Gruffydd ap Cynan was overheard boasting of what the king was doing for him by a relative of Gerald of Windsor. A messenger was immediately sent to Pembroke with the news. Gerald immediately sent a rider to his brother-in-law Gruffydd ap Rhys telling him to seek sanctuary. This he did with the monks of Aberdaron Church. There he was found with his brother Hywel, by Gruffydd ap Cynan who demanded the monks give them up. The monks refused and while the argument raged, a ship arrived from Pembroke that took him and his brother Hywel to Cardigan.

There Prince Gruffydd ap Rhys raised his standard and made his stand. He gathered supporters and then attacked the Normans and their Fleming supporters in the Cardigan area. He then moved to attack Swansea Castle but failed. So he burned the suburbs and retreated through Gowerland. He next attacked and completely destroyed Carmarthen. His war brought him much plunder and many recruits. In England, King Henry was unable to raise forces to counter attack because of pestilances in the country. So he paid some other Welsh leaders to attack instead. However this attempt achieved little. So King Henry tried again by importing another wave of Flemings. This was some eight years after the first Fleming refugees arrived after the flooding of their land due the washing away of protective sand dunes. He sent the Flemings to Pembrokeshire along with men to teach them the English language. In return they would fight with the Normans against the Welsh.

The immigration of the Flemings further roused the Welsh of south Wales. The Cardigan area rose in support of Gruffydd and he marched against Kidwelly Castle and captured it from William de Londres. King Henry, still unable to raise an army, offered forgiveness and reward to any Welshman who would attack Gruffydd. One who responded was Owain ap Cadwagn, the abductor of Nest. In 1112 he travelled to Wales with King Henry and took the field against Gruffydd. When Gerald de Windsor learned this, he gathered his men and set out to find his wife's abductor. They met and Owain was killed in the fighting by an arrow. Gerald died soon afterwards and Princess Nest then married Stephen, the castellan of Cardigan.

Meanwhile Prince Gruffydd ap Rhys continued to harrass the Normans. He lost his battle at Aberystwith. Then Robert, King Henry's illegitimate son led a strong force against Gruffydd from Glamorgan. But the Welsh portion of his army deserted him and joined Gruffydd. The war continued until 1121 when a peace was agreed. On the death of King Henry in 1134, Stephen became King. He summoned Gruffydd to answer complaints made by Norman and Flemish settlers. Gruffuyd ignored the summons and went to North Wales taking his eldest son, to seek assistance from his father-in-law Gruffydd ap Cynan.

In South Wales Gruffydd's wife Princess Gwenllian learned that reinforcements had landed in support of the Norman occupied Kidwelly Castle, seat of the Norman Lord Maurice de Londres. Princess Gwenllian was Nest's sister in law and the daughter of a Welsh king – Gruffydd ap Cynan of Gwynedd. Unlike Nest her father and brother both sided against the Normans and her father had retained some of his lands. She lived in a Welsh world. Princess Gwenllian decided to intercept the advancing Normans before they reached the castle. She assemble a small mounted force including her two sons Maelgwn and Morgan and set out. When they reached Mynydd y Garreg by the River Gwendraethn, her scouts reported that the force had not yet reached the castle but were on the march.

Princess Gwenllian then sent a large detachment of her troops to intercept. This did not happen. Instead the Norman reinforcements led by a Welsh traitor named Gruffydd ap Llewellyn attacked over the summit of Mynydd y Garreg. At the same time Baron Maurice de Londres left the castle and attacked with his men. Princess Gwenllian and her small force were outnumbered and soon cut to pieces. The princess saw her son Maelgwn killed at her side as he tried to protect her. The small number of prisoners were gathered together. The Princess was wounded. Baron de Londres was not a chivalrous man and ordered the immediate execution of the princess and her son Morgan. Both were beheaded before the jeering crowd of the Baron, the Welsh traitor and the Normans. The 516 dead from both sides were left on the field to be devoured by wolves. The field is known today as 'Maes Gwenllian'. She is remembered in song:

> Sleep, Gwenllian, my heart's delight
> Sleep on thro' shiv'ring spear and brand,
> They bretheren battle with the foe,
> Thy Sire's red strokes around him sweep,
> Whilst thou, his bonny babe, art smiling through thy sleep
> All Gwalia shudders at the Norman blow!

The execution of Gwenllian aroused and incensed both her father's kingdom in North Wales and her grandfather's former kingdom in South Wales. The fighting men of both areas joined together for revenge. From

North Wales the two sons of Gruffydd ap Cynan – Owain Gwynedd and Cadwaladr marched with an army of 2,000 horse and 6,000 infantry, all fully armed and with considerable supplies. They subdued the country as they passed and the joint forces invaded the Cardigan area and north Pembrokeshire. They went into battle shouting 'Maes Gwenllian'! Nothing could stop them and the Normans and their Flemish settlers fled before them.

The Norman forces were under the command of Stephen the castellan of Cardigan whose wife was Princess Nest – the sister of Gruffydd. The Normans were augmented by another force led by the Earl of Chester comprising Normans, Flemish and English with several powerful barons. The two sides met in battle at Cardigan in October 1136. All the foreign people had congregated there for safety. It was an exceedingly bloody battle with many casualties. The Welsh were victorious and claimed 3,000 of the Norman side were killed. Norman power in South-West Wales was completely destroyed. Cardigan was burned. Besides the male prisoners, it was claimed that 10,000 widows were captured. Their menfolk had been either killed in battle, had burned in the town or drowned in the River Teifi. The fleeing defeated army crowded across a narrow bridge over the River Teifi, many falling into the river until the bridge collapsed under their weight throwing many of the armed Norman soldiers into the river. It was said that even though the bridge was down, there were so many bodies of men and horses in the river that it was possible to walk across with dry feet.

The remnants of the defeated army tried to escape to nearby Norman castles but large numbers of prisoners were taken. There were so many prisoners that some had to be guarded by Welsh women. A prominent Norman who was killed was Richard, the eldest son of Gilbert de Clare who had conquered Cardigan. His wife and her ladies were besieged in their small castle at Caerwedros. But the ladies were rescued in the nick of time by a party of determined Norman horsemen led by Milo FitzWalter who had ridden day and night to rescue them. It was a close thing as the Normans had to cut their way through much larger numbers both on the way into the castle and again on the way out.

The victory was so complete that the Kings of England were unable to do anything for some years afterwards. Gruffydd then led his men to capture the Rhos area of central Pembrokeshire – the Flemish stronghold - and took the town of Haverfordwest. However he spared his sisters former castle at Pembroke. This was the end of the war. Gruffydd celebrated with a great entertainment held at Ystrad Towy to which he invited all the dignitaries of Wales. His ally Prince Gruffydd ap Cynan attended with his two sons and very many people flocked to Carmarthen. There the festivities went on for forty days. There was feasting and drinking and music with bards singing and even play acting.

After the celebrations the two princes - Gruffydd ap Rhys and Gruffydd ap Cynan - got together and established a new system of jurisdiction throughout Wales, with a court in every hundred and a sub-court in every commot. The remaining Normans in Wales appealed to King Stephen for help, but the king was too busy with his affairs in England to even reply to them. But only a year later Gruffydd ap Rhys was dead. He was slain in his greatest hour while at the peak of his powers. His end was ignominious for he died through the treachery of a new wife. But he had had six sons with his first wife Gwenllian. Two had died with her, but four remained – Andarawd, Cadell, Maredydd and Rhys. These four brothers then jointly ruled their father's land without animosity, following their father's example set as a great patriot, a warrior and a politician.

Suggested Further Reading
Gater, D., 1991, *The Battles of Wales*: Gwasg Carreg Gwalch, Conway, 127 p. ISBN: 0-86381-178-7

23. PEMBROKE CASTLE AND ITS TOWN WALLS

Pembroke castle (Plate 13) is the biggest and most impressive of the Norman castles of Pembrokeshire and it has a remarkably well-preserved Norman town with surviving town walls with defensive towers (Plate 15). This was the great Norman stronghold where the invasion of Ireland started off by sea along the Milford Haven Waterway. The coming of the conquering Normans to south west Wales was the start of a long and turbulent history for this area.

It all began with Rhys ap Tewdwr (1065 -1093) who was the prince of the Kingdom of Deheubarth or south-west Wales. In 1081 when William the Conqueror visited Deheubarth on a pilgrimage to St.Davids (he brought his army with him), he is believed to have met with Rhys who paid homage and agreed at pay £40 a year for his kingdom. This ensured good relations with the Conqueror which lasted until his death in 1087. Afterwards Rhys was unable to withstand the pressure of the Norman advance into South Wales and was killed in battle with the Normans at the Battle of Brecon in 1093. His daughter Princess Nest played a remarkable historic role and became the progenitor of four major Cambro-Norman families.

Rhys's death led to the Normans taking over much of his kingdom. Robert de Montgomery, Earl of Shrewsbury advanced from his stronghold to occupy Ceredigion and then Dyfed. He gave Dyfed to his son Arnulf who in 1093 built 'a slender fortress of stakes and turf' (now believed to have strengthened a much older Iron-Age earth works) at Pembroke. However Arnulf was accused of treason by King Henry I and was replaced as castellian by Gerald, son of Walter FitzOther, custodian of Windsor. Gerald married Pricess Nest who was a hostage for the good behaviour of her brothers and who had been a concubine to King Henry I and bore him a son. It was an arranged marriage by the King who made a political marriage for himself with the daughter of the King of Scotland. Nest brought land as dowry and on it at Carew Gerald built them a castle home.

In 1189 when William Marshall became Earl of Pembroke, the earth and timber structure at Pembroke was transformed over the next thirty years into a powerful stone fortification in the form of the great tower and much of the inner ward. William was succeeded by each of his five sons in turn. It was his third son Gilbert who enlarged and strengthened the castle between 1234 and 1241. There is a legend that an Irish bishop put a curse on William Marshall saying that all his sons would die childless. When this occurred the castle passed into the ownership of William de Valence, who became Lord of Pembrokeshire through his marriage to Joan the granddaughter of William Marshall. The Valence family held the castle for seventy years. They strengthened the castle by building the walls and towers around the outer ward. They also fortified the town with a surrounding wall with three gates and added a postern gate.

Pembroke castle has been the site of many major historic events. The Norman conquest of Ireland was organised from the castle and came about in an unusual manner. Irish King Dermot MacMurrough was driven out of his kingdom by other Irish kings. In 1167 he appealed to King Henry II for aid to recover his throne. Henry authorised any of his barons to give assistance. First to respond was Richard de Clare, second Earl of Pembroke and like his father was known as Strongbow. He drove a very hard bargain when they agreed that Earl Strongbow would lead an army into Ireland in return for the hand of Dermot's daughter Aoife and the succession of his kingdom. Dermot made another deal with Robert FitzStephen and Maurice FitzGerald who were promised the town of Wexford and its surrounding areas.

In May 1169 Robert FitzStephen, with thirty knights, sixty squires and 300 archers and foot soldiers embarked in three ships in the Milford Haven waterway as the first invading wave of the Norman invasion of Ireland. He was soon followed by Maurice de Prendergast with 200 men and joined by Irish king Dermot with 500 men. The combined forces advanced on Wexford and took the town that was handed over as promised by Dermot. Maurice FitzGerald landed at Wexford with reinforcements in late 1169. Earl Strongbow finally landed in August 1170. He arrived in the Waterford estuary and had to decide on which side to land. On one side was the tower of Hook and on the other the church of Crook – hence the saying 'by Hook or by Crook'.

He captured Waterford where he met Dermot who gave his daughter in marriage. Dermot died the following spring and Earl Strongbow succeeded to his kingdom. Shortly afterwards Earl Strongbow returned to England, where he met King Henry II at Newnham and surrendered his conquests to him. King Henry II sailed for Ireland with a large fleet in October 1171. He landed at Waterford and then moved on to Dublin where he received the submissions of the Irish kings. He left Wexford in April 1172 having laid the foundations of English rule in Ireland without a battle.

Another major event occurred when Henry Tewdwr (1457-1509) was born in Pembroke Castle. Henry defeated King Richard III at the Battle of Bosworth Field to become the first monarch of the Tudor Dynasty as King Henry VII. He was the last king of England to win his throne on the field of battle. Although he had spent his childhood in Pembroke he never returned to Wales but made his son Henry, Prince of Wales and Earl of Pembroke.

There followed a very long period of peace at Pembroke during which the Earls of Pembroke held their own courts in the Chancery of Pembroke Castle. They dispensed their own justice and the King's Writ was unknown in the area. This period of self-governance that had started in 1189 was ended in 1535 when King Henry VIII abolished the status of Earldom, so that the Earldom of Pembroke became the shire of Pembroke. This was achieved through the parliamentary 'Laws in Wales Acts of 1535 and 1542' by which the legal system for Wales was annexed to those of England. The laws are sometimes referred to as the 'Acts of Union'. The purpose was the creation of a single state and a single jurisdiction referred to as 'England and Wales'.

Pembroke Castle played a major role in the Civil War (1642-1651). Most of South Wales was Royalist but fortified Pembroke declared for parliament. The castle was besieged by Lord Carberry but was saved when Parliamentary reinforcements arrived by sea along the Milford Haven water-way. The roundheads then attacked and captured Tenby, Haverfordwest and Carew. However in 1648 when the Civil War was almost ended, Pembroke's leaders changed sides. In particular Major General Laugharne and Colonel Poyer felt themselves ill-treated by parliament and seized Pembroke and Tenby and declared for the king. As their strength grew parliament became concerned and Lieutenant General Oliver Cromwell was ordered on 1st May 1648 with additional forces to South Wales. Cromwell, despite suffering gout, succeeded in capturing Pembroke Castle after seven weeks, mainly by destroying with cannon fire the staircase leading down to the water source in a cellar of the castle. Three of Pembroke's leaders were found guilty of treason but the lives of two were spared by drawing lots. Colonel Poyer alone was shot in Covent Garden on 25th April 1649.

Cromwell ordered the castle to be destroyed. It proved difficult to destroy such a massive castle, although it was seriously damaged. It remained a ruin plundered for stone by the local population until 1880 when Mr. J. R. Cobb of Brecon spent three years restoring what he could. Then nothing happened until 1928 when Major General Sir Ivor Philips of Cosherton Hall acquired the ruins. He restored the walls and towers to be as close to the original appearance as possible. When the general died, a trust was set up managed jointly by the family and the town council to maintain the castle and to continue the work of restoration.

Pembroke Castle is today one of the major tourist attractions of Pembrokeshire and has its own website which includes photographs, history, descriptions and a virtual tour at www.pembroke-castle.co.uk Less well known is the remarkable state of preservation of the Norman town that developed to the east of the castle running along a ridge with a single street of buildings each with long strip gardens and surrounded by a wall with fortifications along it. This layout remains unchanged today and large portions of the town wall survive. The town has its own website describing its long history at www.pembrokestory.org.uk. Not to be missed is the town walking guide that can be downloaded with a map from www. pembroketownguide.co.uk.

The ancient layout of the town is most unsuitable for modern cars and lorries. So the best way to see the town is on foot. The guide describes a walking town trail. This begins at Pembroke quay - a once busy but tidal port which was the main site for bringing in goods by sea as the road system overland was not good. The walk circles the castle passing the Wogan Cave beneath the castle. Next are buildings dating from the fourteenth and fifteenth centuries. The walk then enters the main street with its quaint shops and historic buildings.

A completely new display (not yet described in the walking guide) are the murals in the town hall which describe the long history of Pembroke and its castle. These are available in book form. The walk then follows the city walls on the south side with its medieval towers with arrow slits and then returns to the High Street. A small circular tower on the north-east was originally attached by a now broken stretch of wall to Bernard's Tower. This impressive three-story tower is isolated at the north-eastern end of the town, almost half a mile from the castle. The tower has a forebuilding over the entrance, a bridge pit, portcullis and gate. The roof dome of the tower is intact and it had a fire place and lavatory, being originally self contained. The walk then returns to the trail. Start by following the Mill Pond Walk alongside the former tidal creek that was dammed to provide power for the corn mill that stood at Pembroke quay. The Mill Pond Walk follows the site of the northern defensive town wall.

Suggested Further Reading
Gater, D., 1991, *The Battles of Wales*: Gwasg Csarreg Gwalch, Conway, 127 p. ISBN: 0-86381-178-7

24. THE NORMAN INVASION OF IRELAND

Figure 9. Robert FitzStephen sets out with three ships, 390 men and horses to invade Ireland, leaving the Milford Haven Waterway in May 1169

William the Conqueror gained England in the single battle at Hastings in 1066. The colonisation of Wales later followed and was mainly completed by 1100. William thought about a Norman conquest of Ireland, but was kept too busy controlling his recently gained lands to follow through. One of his sons - King Henry II - took up the idea and obtained the permission of the English pope Nicholas Brakespear to carry out the invasion. But he also was busy with other matters, being king of Britain and much of France. It took trouble in Leinster in SE Ireland (an area corresponding to the modern county of Wexford with parts of Kildare, Carlow and Wicklow) to precipitate the events that led to the actual invasion. Dermot MacMurrough was king of Ui Ceinnsealaigh – the largest kingdom in Leinster. He was described by Geraldus Cambrensis as:

'A man of warlike spirit and a brave one in his nation, with a voice hoarse from frequent shouting in the din of battle. One who preferred to be feared rather than loved, who was obnoxious to his own people and an object of hatred to strangers. His hand was against every man, and every man's hand against his.'

Dermot's downfall began at the age of forty-two years, when he abducted the forty four year old wife of a rival king – Dervorgilla wife of Tiernan

O'Rourke – the one eyed king of Breifne. It was probably with her approved, for she had all her possessions packed and her cattle ready to move. She was recaptured within a year and returned (with her possessions and cattle) but O'Rourke and Dermot hated one another. Fifteen years later when Dermot was defeated in battle, O'Rourke arranged for his exile from Ireland.

Dermot with a small group of followers went in search of King Henry II to request assistance in regaining his Kingdom. He landed in Bristol and finally tracked the king down in Aquitaine, France in 1167. He was favourably received and obtained a letter of support that has survived through the writing of Geraldus Cambrensis:

'Henry, King of England, Duke of Normandy and Aquitaine, and Count of Anjou, to all his liegemen, English, Normans, Welsh and Scots, and to all nations subject to his sway, greetings. Whensoever these letters shall come unto you, know that we have received Dermot, Prince of Leinster, into our grace and favour; wherefore whosoever within the bounds of our territories shall be willing to give him aid, as our vassal and liegeman, in recovering his dominion, let him be assured of his favour and license in that behalf.'

Armed with the letter, Dermot returned to Bristol but failed to raise any support. He then crossed into south Wales and travelled to what is now Pembrokeshire. There in the Noman strongholds he found what he sought. First to be recruited was Earl Richard FitzGilbert de Clare, Earl of Pembroke and known as 'Strongbow' as he was a famous archer and a veteran of many battles. His meeting with Dermot was most timely as he had lost his lands and possessions that had been confiscated by King Henry II because he had opposed him. Earl Richard's father was Gilbert de Clare, a former Earl of Pembroke, whose grandfather Richard de Clare had fought at the Battle of Hastings. At the time Earl Strongbow was between fifty and sixty years old and a widower. Geraldus Cambrensis describes him as:

'His complexion was somewhat ruddy, and his skin freckled. He had grey eyes, feminine features, a weak voice, and short neck. For the rest he was tall in stature, and a man of great generosity, and of courteous manner.'

Earl Strongbow however drove a hard bargain. Dermot eventually agreed to the terms. In exchange for military support he would provide Strongbow with his daughter Aoife in marriage, plus make him King of Leinster after he, Dermot, died. Recruiting Earl Strongbow was a masterful stroke for it opened the doors to recruiting many other Norman warriors. The progeny of Princess Nest and her multiple families, were to play a major role in the invasion and most would settle in Ireland to give rise to the great Norman-Irish families there. Key leaders were Earl Strongbow, Robert FitzStephen, Maurice FitzGerald. Princess Nest's son by King Henry II had two sons Meiler and Robert FitzHenry who also joined the invasion. Princess Nest's daughter Angharat married William de Barri and they had three sons. One was Geraldus Cambrensis the chronicler, and Robert and Phillip who both joined the invasion. So Nest's progeny gave rise to the FitzHenrys, FitzGeralds, FitzStephens and Barrys (latter through her daughter Angharad) for the invasion and they went on to become prominent families in the future history of Ireland.

Dermot then set out on the road to St. Davids, stopping along the way to recruit. His objective was a tipoff from Strongbow that Rhys ap Gruffydd, the Welsh Prince of South Wales, was holding an important prisoner. This was Robert FitzStephen, a son of Princess Nest by Stephen, Constable of Cardigan. After three years in prison, Stephen had been offered his freedom to take up arms against King Henry. But he had refused. Now he was offered freedom if he would join Dermot in Ireland. He agreed.

With two key Normans recruited, others began to flock to his standard. Dermot's offered rewards were most impressive. He promised Maurice FitzGerald and Robert FitzStephen the town of Wexford plus the adjoining cantreds of land if they would join him in battle the following spring. A cantrad was land containing one hundred manors or townlands of 1,000 acres each. For the new generation of land-hungry Normans after the conquest of 1066, this was opportunity indeed.

The distance from Pembrokeshire across to SE Ireland is only 80 miles. The mountains of Wicklow are visible on a clear day from the Preseli Mountains of Pembrokeshire. Geraldus Cambrensis paints a picture of Dermot at this time:

'...sniffing from the Welsh coast the air of Ireland. Wafted on western breezes and, as it was, inhaling the scent of his beloved country. He had no small consolation feasting his eyes on the sight of his land, though the distance was such that it was difficult to distinguish between the mountains and cloud.'

En route to St Davids, Dermot also stopped at the small Roch castle perched on a rock. There he recruited Richard FitzGodebert who because of the rock under the castle took the name 'de la Roche'. His brother Robert also joined.

Dermot then returned to Ireland in 1167 bringing with him a small reconnaissance party of Normans, Flemings and Welsh, led by Richard FitzGodebert, to plan the Norman invasion. They landed in a small creek on the open coast of Wexford about twelve miles south of Arklow Head and moved to Ferns. News of Dermot's return reached the ears of High King Ruairi O'Connor who called up Dermot's old enemy Tiernan O'Rourke and they marched against him. Dermot was defeated with twenty-five men killed including a Welshman. The High King took two of Dermot's sons as hostages but granted Dermot ten cantreds of land on condition he recognised the High King and abandoned his plans for kingship of Leinster. Dermot also had to pay one hundred ounces of gold to O'Rourke as reparations for abducting his wife.

Back in Pembrokeshire preparations were in full swing for the invasion. The Norman army was well organised with three military ranks. Those knights on whom the order of chivalry had been conferred fought in armour on horseback with shields and long lances. The men at arms were landed gentry, usually relations of the knights, and fought in armour with swords and shields. Many were on horseback. The archers fought on foot, were lightly armoured and carried their deadly long bows. The armour of the mounted men was a mail shirt covering the body, arms and thighs. A conical iron helmet had a guard over the nose and chain guarding the neck and throat. In contrast the Irish fought in linen tunics with light axes, swords and spears. For the Normans war was a business and as soon as land was won a castle was constructed and the area socially reconstructed with a manor or barony set up.

The first landing of the invasion took place in late April/early May 1169. It comprised three ships each carrying 120 men, some horses and provisions. They were led by Robert FitzStephen (Figure 9). Their long ships were typically Norse with long hulls that were open, a single mast and a square sail. They were steered by an oar on the starboard side near the stern. The shields of the men hung along the sides to protect the crew. The ships, when not sailing, were propelled by long sweeps with two men to each sweep. This small expedition of three ships would prove to be of immense importance in both Irish and Norman histories. That such a small force would even set out, let alone succeed, is surprising.

The small fleet rowed down the Milford Haven Waterway from Pembroke to the entrance at St. Ann's Head, where they met the swell of the Irish Sea and turned for the Wexford coast. After a few hours, the mountains of Ireland began to rise from the horizon. FitzStephen kept his fleet to the south to avoid shipping from the Norse port of Wexford. They entered Bannow Bay and landed near what is now Bannow in Durmot's territory of Ui Ceinnsealaigh on May 1ˢᵗ 1169. A messenger was sent to Dermot and a camp set up. They were about 390 men but only a half days sailing from Wexford or Waterford. They were not discovered and Dermot sent his son ahead to meet them while he gathered his fighting men. The next day two more ships arrived from Milford Haven bringing Maurice de Prendergast from Rhos district in Pembrokeshire with ten men at arms and a large number of archers. There were now around 600 men camped at Bannow and Dermot arrived with 500 more men.

Dermot and the Normans confirmed their contract and battle banners were unfurled and the army set out to capture Wexford about twenty miles away. On route at a place now called Duncormick, they had their first clash with the Irish and had to fight their way across a river but defeated the enemy. Wexford was a Norse port and the inhabitants were familiar with the rather ragged attacks from the native Irish. The townspeople were confident of defeating the invaders and about 2,000 men went outside the town walls to meet them. When they saw for the first time the well-armed disciplined and ordered Norman army with accompanying horsemen they turned back into the town to man the walls. The suburbs outside were set afire. FitzStephen attacked, but his men were repulsed by the citizens throwing rocks and timbers down onto them. FitzStephen called off the attack. Geraldus reports that his elder brother Robert de Barri was injured in the attack.

Next morning the Normans again approached the town walls but the citizens had had a change of heart. Two bishops who were visiting the town negotiated a peace. Dermot, true to his word awarded the town and all the country east and west of it to Robert FitzStephen and Maurice FitzGerald. Two cantrads of land were awarded to Hervey de Monte Marisco, Strongbow's uncle. This 200,000 acres was astonishing to Hervey as he had fallen on hard times with no armour nor money and had been sent as an observer by Strongbow. Other Norman and Flemish knights also received land grants. These grants initiated intense Norman and Flemish colonisation into southern Wexford. Dermot then retired to Ferns where for three weeks he and his supporters feasted and celebrated.

Dermot next decided to invade the kingdom of Ossory (most of present day County Kilkenny and part of Laoighis). This had formerly been a part of Dermot's Leinster and the king there – Donal MacGiolla Phadrig - had blinded Dermot's eldest son when he was a hostage there. Dermot's army was now around 2,000 men and a long and fierce battle followed in thick woodland. Towards evening the enemy were driven into the open where they were cut down by the Norman cavalry. Around 200 Irishmen were killed and their heads cut off and thrown at Dermot's feet. The Normans camped for the night and over the next three days persued their enemies. At this point Maurice de Prendergast had a change of heart about Dermot and left his army and joined King Donal against Dermot. But he eventually returned with his men to Wales. This caused King Donal to sue for peace with FitzStephen. This was granted and King Donal had to acknowledge Dermot as king of Leinster. Dermot and his army returned to Ferns,

Rauri O'Connor, High King of Ireland at the time, assembled his forces and marched on Ferns. Dermot and his men retreated into woodland and dug in. Battle was avoided by the intervention of the clergy. The terms were that Dermot was to send his troops back to Wales and bring no more. One of his sons was taken as hostage to his compliance. Dermot had no intention of sending his troops back to Wales and was now intent on becoming King of all Leinster again.

Towards the end of 1169 a third landing of Normans occurred. Maurice FitzGerald, then about sixty years old, arrived with two ships carrying ten men-at-arms, thirty mounted retainers and a hundred archers. Heartened by the fresh troops, Dermot marched his army against Dublin, where the Norsemen had killed his father. The king of the Norsemen there – Asculf MacTorkil - submitted to Dermot and gave him treasures and hostages.

Around this time Dermot considered his army strong enough to send a small party of Normans under the leadership of Robert FitzStephen across Ireland to Limerick. There he was to assist his son-in-law – Donal O'Brian – in a conflict with High King Ruairi O'Connor. The mission was a success and Dermot realised that his Norman warriors were invincible against the large army of High King Ruairi O'Connor. He began to consider himself as a possible High King of Ireland, if he could get a bigger Norman army. He discussed this with FitzStephen and FitzGerald. They agreed and suggested sending to Wales immediately for more men. Dermot was so pleased that he offered either of them his daughter Aoife in marriage. They both declined as Aoife was already promised to Strongbow. Dermot sent letters to Earl Strongbow asking him to keep to his promises of 1167 and again offered the kingship of Leinster and his daughter in marriage.

Earl Strongbow began to make his preparations to join the invasion. Immediately he sent an advance party out under the leadership of Raymond 'Le Gros' FitzGerald de Carew who was a nephew of both Maurice FitzGerald and Robert FitzStephen. Raymond brought with him ten men-at-arms and seventy archers. Their landing in Ireland was the fourth of the invasion and occurred around 1st May 1670. They landed at a place today known as Baginbum near Waterford and near Bannow. It was in Dermot's territory and they constructed a fort there of turf and the boughs of trees. He sent men out to round up as many cattle as possible and they were brought into the stockade. He was joined there by Hervey de Monte Marisco with three knights. The party then totalled around one hundred men.

Around three thousand Irishmen and Waterford Norsemen gathered to oppose the small Norman group. As they advanced Raymond gathered his men in the small fort, and addressed them. Next he drove the cattle out into the advancing enemy causing confusion. He then led his men in attack into the advancing enemy and slew one man letting out a great battle cry. This inspired his men to attack. Another Norman who showed outstanding courage was man-at-arms William Ferrand. He had leprosy and hoped to die gloriously in battle. But he survived to eventually found the Leper Church of St. Magdalen outside Wexford town. The enemy was routed and about 1,000 killed by the Normans. Seventy important prisoners were taken that Raymond wanted to ransom. But Hervey thought they were too many to safely hold. So he and his supporters broke their limbs and threw them into the sea where they drowned. Another version suggests that a woman called Alice who had followed her man from Wales, beheaded the captives because her man had been killed. Raymond proved to be wise man for he spent the summer holed up with his men inside the small fort awaiting the arrival of Earl Strongbow with his main force.

King Henry II did not like Earl Strongbow, who had opposed him. So Earl Strongbow had sought King Henry' approval to invade Ireland. The king approved but in a joking manner urging Strongbow to go away as far as his feet would carry him. Before departing Earl Strongbow made a pilgrimage to St. Davids collecting young men along the way. He embarked his men, taking about two hundred men-at-arms and other troops to a total of around 1,000 men. The wind was fair and they sailed across to Waterford. This was the fifth and largest part of the Norman Invasion so far. The fleet sailed along the south coast of Wexford, around Hook Head and entered the Waterford Estuary landing on 23rd August 1170. Their passing was seen by Raymond and his men who immediately marched for Waterford. They arrived there before Earl Strongbow and his men. Then the two forces combined to attack the town.

Waterford was then a Norse town but also contained a group of Irishmen with their chief Maelseachlann O Faolain. The latter group had taken part in the earlier attack on Raymond. The town was defended by stone and clay ramparts with round towers at intervals. The Normans twice attacked the walls and were repulsed. Then Raymond spotted a weakness in the wall. At one point a small wooden house protruded outside the wall and was standing on a wooden post. Raymond sent men in armour to cut down the post. They did this and the house with a large part of the wall came tumbling down. The Normans entered the town. The towers were harder to take and one put up a great resistance. It was called Reginald's Tower.

Inside were two Norse Earls both called Sitric and another called Reginald as well as chief O Faolain. When at last it was captured the two Sitrics were executed. Robert and O Faolain were saved by the arrival of Dermot who pleaded for the men. The date was 25th August.

Dermot had brought with him Robert FitzStephen, Maurice FitzGerald and his daughter Aoife. There amidst the smoking town with the dead and wounded strewn about, Earl Strongbow and Aoife were married in agreement with Dermot's promise. It was a great historic occasion. The ceremony took place in Waterford Church which was filled with the mail-clad Normans, and their Flemish, Welsh and Irish allies. It was the first Norman-Irish marriage of the invasion and by it Earl Strongbow became heir-in-succession to the Kingdom of Leinster and the Norse towns of Dublin, Waterford and Wexford. Dermot had achieved much of his early ambition.

The next step was to take Dublin – a small but important well-fortified Norse trading centre. High King Ruairi O'Connor gathered a large army said to be composed of 30,000 troops and marched there to protect the town. With him he brought Dermot's enemy Tieren O'Rourke. Meanwhile Dermot and Strongbow with a mixed force of 5,500 men had marched through Wexford into Wicklow and reached Dublin without being discovered. Two Norman forces led by Milo de Cogan and Raymond 'Le Gros' attacked from two directions without consulting Dermot or Strongbow. They broke into the town. Asculf MacTorkil, the king of Dublin and the senior citizens barely had time to reach their ships and escape. Many citizens including women and children were slaughtered and much gold and silver plunder was taken. Dublin had fallen on 21st September 1170. The town was left in the hands of Dairmaid MacMurchadha to avenge the killing of his father by the people of Dublin who had buried his body with that of a dog. The great opposing army never appeared, for when it was learned that the Dublin leaders were negotiating with the invaders, the army turned away.

Dermot set out in persuit of his enemy O'Rourke and large areas were devastated. But Dermot overstepped the mark by leaving the kingdom of Leinster and entering the territory of the High King O'Connor in his rampage. The High King sent warning messages. To these Dermot replied that he intended to defeat the High King's army and claim the high king-ship for himself. The high king was furious and executed his hostages, Conor the son of Dairmaid and heir to Leinster and also his grandson. After this Demot retired to Ferns and was no longer active. He died in early May 1172 at the age of sixty-one years.

The death of Dermot was a major turning point in the invasion of Ireland. Milo de Cogan had been appointed governor of Dublin and Earl Strongbow returned south to strengthen his garrisons at Waterford and Wexford. Previously the Irish kings and chieftains had regarded the situation as a fight between Dermot MacMurrough and High King Ruairi O'Connor with a few Normans assisting one side. But when Earl Strongbow took the throne of Leinster so easily the picture changed. The Irish law of succession had been bypassed and worse was that Earl Strongbow was appointing his own officials to set up a different and new form of government. There was a strong reaction.

As early as late 1170, the church convened a synod in Armagh. They ruled that the invasion was a judgement for the sins of the Irish people who had purchased English men from traders and pirates to use as slaves. The synod decreed that all English slaves should be set free. There was a great uprising of the tribes of Leinster against the invaders. Robert FitzStephen found himself besieged in his fort at Ferrycarrig by a revolt by the Wexford Norse. It was led by Dermot's nephew Murchadh. Dermot's son Donal Cavanagh remained a supporter of Earl Strongbow. High King Ruairi O'Connor rallied the provincial kings and their supporters to gather together to drive the invaders out of Ireland. Lastly the defeated Norse King Asculf MacTorkil of Dublin returned with a fleet of sixty ships and 1,000 fighting Norsemen to recapture Dublin.

Earl Strongbow, the new King of Leinster, now found himself in an unenviable position as the forces opposing him were far greater than his own. Worse was that King Henry II had ruled that no more of his subjects were to go to Ireland. He also ordered all those there to return before Easter. In addition King Henry II banned the export of supplies to Ireland. The English King had blocked Earl Strongbow from his Welsh base. Yet he and his father William the Conqueror had both desired to conquer Ireland. Evidently he was not pleased that Earl Strongbow had taken the initiative and succeeded.

But Earl Strongbow was in modern terminology 'a cool customer'. He did not relinquish his hard won Irish Kingdom and return home. Instead a wrote a letter to the king and sent it to him in Aquitaine with his trusted baron Raymond 'Le Gros'. In it he offered the king all his Irish possessions. He pointed out that he had with Henry II's permission, gone to assist Dermot the king's liegeman. He ended by stating that he would hold the possessions to the will and disposal of the king. It was an offer not to set up a rival Norman state in Ireland.

King Henry did not reply. He may have regarded Earl Strongbow's position as hopeless or he just preferred to await the outcome and see how events turned out. It was a difficult decision as the delay might have cost him his chance of gaining Ireland. Earl Strongbow, his barons and knights now stood alone facing the overwhelming forces of High King Ruairi O'Connor, the tribes of Leinster, the aroused Norsemen of Waterford, Wexford and the Norse fleet at Dublin.

Waterford was recaptured by Dermot MacCarthy of Desmond. King Asculf MacTorkil disembarked his thousand Norse warriors outside Dublin where Earl Strongbow awaited attack. The Norse were led by the beserker John the Wode (Mad John) who immediately attacked Dublin without waiting for the arrival of the great army of High King O'Connor. Milo de Cogan led an attack on the advancing Norsemen but had to retreat because of overwhelming numbers. But his brother Richard de Cogan led a cavalry attack on the rear of the Norsemen. This broke and scattered the Norsemen who fleeing back to their ships were cut down by the Norman cavalry. The beserker John the Wode was killed and Asculf MacTorkil was captured and later beheaded.

Meanwhile the great army of High King Ruairi O'Connor of 60,000 men was approaching Dublin. The great force was spread out with most in the Castleknock area. The Munster and Leinster men were at Kilmainham and Dalkey. The Ulster men were at Clontarf. In addition further support for the High King arrived in the form a fleet of thirty ships carrying Norse warriors from the Isle of Man and the Hebrides. The fleet entered Dublin Bay and was commanded by King Gottard of Man.

Dublin was under siege from July into August and food became scarce. Earl Strongbow decided to negotiate. He sent Archbishop O'Toole offering to submit to the high king if he could still hold Leinster. The high king replied that he would leave Strongbow the three Norse centres of Dublin, Waterford and Wexford only and that should the earl reject this offer he would storm Dublin immediately.

At a war council Earl Strongbow's key men Milo de Cogan, Maurice FitzGerald and Raymond 'Le Gros' argued to attack the high king immediately while they still had food. So a sortie was planned. Three all-Norman detachments each of 200 fighting men would advance, Milo in the lead, Raymond in the centre and Strongbow bringing up the rear. The Normans crossed the Liffey River and attacked the high king's encampment. It was around September 1st and the attack came as a complete surprise. The high king and many of his men were bathing in the Liffey. About 150 Irish men were killed and the high king barely escaped with his life. His army was dispersed. The Norman superiority in arms had been demonstrated again. The Irish camp contained enough supplies for the Normans for a year. The high king would remain in Connaught and not challenge the Normans again.

When King Henry II learned of Earl Strongbow's success, he greatly feared the establishment of a rival Norman state in Ireland. He called a meeting of his barons in Argentan and obtained their approval for his own invasion of Ireland. The timing of his invasion would remove him from the criticisms he was receiving for the murder of Thomas Beckett in late 1170. King Henry crossed from Normandy to Portsmouth and marched to Gloustershire where his main army was being assembled. At Winchester he found Dermot's brother Murchadh MacMurrough and several of the Norsemen of Wexford awaiting him. They reported that they held a prisoner – Robert FitzStephen. On reaching the army near Gloucester, the king found Earl Strongbow waiting for him in response to a summons. Earl Strongbow repeated his earlier offer to the king and the two were reconciled after some argument. The king granted Earl Strongbow all of Leinster except Dublin and a coastal strip that he kept for himself.

King Henry then embarked his army on 16th October 1171 into 400 ships and sailed for Ireland. The well-equipped army comprised 500 knights and 4,000 men at arms with much equipment and food. On 17th October they landed at Crook on the west side of Waterford harbour. Next day all entered Waterford where Earl Strongbow formerly surrendered the town and did homage for Leinster. Shortly afterwards the Norse of Wexford brought Robert FitzStephen there in chains. The king condemned him for invading Ireland and setting up an independent state and imprisoned him, but soon quietly released him.

The English army was never engaged in any fighting for most of the Irish kings submitted to Henry's rule, took oaths of fealty, gave hostages and agreed to pay yearly tributes. In return they received back their kingdoms. Henry had of course papal approval and he had his large army with him. Most of the Norman invaders were confirmed in their earlier grants of land. The submission of the Irish kings might have been because Henry presented himself as the protector of Ireland to save it from his invading Normans. King Henry spent Christmas in Dublin entertaining Irish kings and chieftains with feasts and gifts. He placated the Irish church.

Most critically the king appointed his own Norman followers to key administrative positions, thereby weakening Earl Strongbow's supporters. The knights Robert FitzStephen, Maurice FitzStephen, Meiler FitzHenry and Miles FitzDavid were placed in the Dublin garrison under the command of Henry's supporter Hugh de Lacy. King Henry added Milo de Cogan and Raymond 'Le Gros' to his own personal retinue and took them back to England with him. The king's visit to Ireland lasted only six months but he had gained Ireland in a bloodless victory and destroyed for ever the dream of Earl Strongbow of a Norman state in Ireland.

After Henry departed from Ireland, the invasion proper was finished. What remained were dark days that became nothing more than a rather dirty and often dishonorable land grab. King Henry was far too busy with his affairs in England and France and quite unable to act as the protector of Ireland. A number of Irish chieftains mysteriously died. In particular in 1172 Dermot's brother Murchadh MacMurrough, a claimant to the throne of Leinster, died at the hands of 'the English', so Earl Strongbow's claim to the kingship of Leinster remained unchallenged. The two groups of Normans (Earl Strongbow's men and King Henry's men) vied with each other to gain land and the Norman sphere of influence with Norman castles expanded. The land grab was halted briefly in spring of 1173 when Earl Strongbow and de Lacy were called by King Henry for military service in Normandy. Earl Strongbow returned to Ireland in the autumn with Raymon 'Le Gros' to find the Irish leaders in revolt against the Normans. A process of 'pacification' began. Under Norman rule the Irish people were reduced to tilling the land and herding the cattle. But within the Norman lands peace reigned. Earl Strongbow died in Dublin in 1176. Within eighty years of the invasion three quarters of Ireland was in the hands of foreigners.

Suggested Further Reading.
Roche, R., 1970, *The Norman Invasion of Ireland*: Anvil Books, Republic of Ireland, 134 p.

25. HENRY TEWDWR AND MULLOCK BRIDGE ON THE DALE PENINSULA

There is a lovely old stone causeway with two bridge arches that crosses the tidal stream of the Gann a short way outside Dale on the road to Milford Haven. It has long been called Mullock Bridge. This old bridge is built of Old Red Sandstone – the local rock. It is rather narrow for cars, so the Council replaced it with a road that crossed alongside it with the stream piped under it. The new road has two lanes of course whereas the old bridge, built for horses and carts, has only one lane and rather steep arches. So today the two crossings lie side by side. However today on high spring tides when the sea backs up the Gann, it is only the new road that floods. The old causeway remains high and dry but cannot now be used by cars as concrete posts have been placed across the approaches. So today when there are several feet of sea water over the new road, the old Mullock Bridge proudly stands high and dry alongside it. It seems there was something that the Victorian and Edwardian bridge builders knew that we in the computer and space age have forgotten.

In 1485 an earlier version of Mullock Bridge was the scene of a drama that marked a great adventure that culminated in the death in battle of King Richard III (at the age of only thirty-two years) after only a two year reign. This ended the Plantagenet royal dynasty and replaced it with the new Tudor dynasty that lasted for the next 118 years. The story is told by Sir Winston Churchill (1956) in his 'The History of the English Speaking Peoples' Volume 1, The Birth of Britain, p. 392. The second half of the fifteenth century (1455 to 1484) was a turbulent and miserable time in England when a series of dynastic civil wars were fought for the throne of England and Wales. The battles were between two rival branches of the royal house of Plantagenet. At war were the houses of Lancaster and York, with heraldic symbols of a red or white rose. It was known as the War of the Roses.

In April 1843 King Edward IV died and his twelve year old son Prince Edward would be the next King Edward V. Edward IV's brother Richard was proclaimed Lord Protector of the realm for the twelve year old king.

Richard accompanied the twelve year old boy to London for his coronation planned for 22nd June and placed him in the Tower of London – then a royal residence. He was joined there by his younger brother Prince Richard. Sadly dirty dealing began immediately.

Before the planned coronation, King Edward IV's marriage to the two prince's mother was declared invalid making the princes illegitimate and ineligible for the throne. Richard was hastily crowned King Richard III on 6th July. Next the two princes disappeared for ever. They were last seen in August and accusations were made that they had been murdered by King Richard who could not produce them. Sir Thomas More, chancellor to King Henry VIII wrote his 'history of King Richard III' in 1583. In it he identified Sir James Tyrell as the murderer, acting on King Richard III's orders. Tyrell made a confession stating that he rode sorrowfully to London and committed the deed on the King's orders. The murder of the princes and rightful king by their uncle Richard was regarded as an atrocious crime.

In 1674 workmen altering a staircase leading to the white chapel in the Tower of London, uncovered the skeletons of two young boys. They were examined by the royal surgeon who found they were of the correct ages to be the two missing princes and he confirmed this. On the order of King Charles II, the remains were reburied in Henry VII's Chapel at Westminster with a Latin inscription blaming their uncle described as 'the usurper of the realm'. In 1933 the grave was opened to see what light modern forensic study might reveal. The skeletons were identified as belonging to two children, one aged around seven to eleven years and the other around eleven to thirteen years.

The disappearance of the princes reduced any threat to King Richard III of a rebellion led by his enemies. Richard was the eighth and youngest child of Richard Plantagenet, Third Duke of York. He was to be the last Yorkist king. There followed two rebellions against King Richard. The first in October 1843 was led by Henry Stafford, Second Duke of Buckingham which collapsed and the duke was executed. The second rebellion was led by Henry Tewdwr, second earl of Richmond, and was successful. Henry was of the house of Lancaster but married Edward IVs daughter Elizabeth of York and united the two houses. In 1499 King Henry VII executed Edward, Earl of Warwick (son of Richard III's brother Clarence). So ended the War of Roses.

Henry Tewdwr was born in Pembroke Castle in 1457 and became the Earl of Richmond. He became a claimant to the throne of England when in 1484 the only son of King Richard III died. Henry had had a very turbulent upbringing, for seven years of his childhood he was besieged in

Harlech Castle. At the age of fourteen he and his uncle Jasper both fled from Tenby to Britanny in France. There Henry lived in impoverished exile. King Richard was not popular after the matter of the two young princes.

Many of the Earls did not want Richard as king and with the death of his only son, they contacted Henry Tewdwr to return to England and claim the throne. During the first rebellion led by the Duke of Buckingham, Henry had sailed to join him but fortunately for him contrary winds prevented him from landing in England. For the second attempt Henry obtained from the Duke of Britanny between 1000 and 2000 seasoned fighting men and started to assemble an invasion force at the mouth of the River Seine, where he was joined by supporters crossing from England. King Richard feared this invasion and prepared his troops.

On August 1st 1485 Henry Tewdwr embarked with his English supporters both Yorkist and Lancastrian, sailed around Lands End and landed at Mill Bay near Dale on the Milford Haven Waterway on 7th August. There he knelt, recited a psalm, kissed the ground, crossed himself and gave the order to advance in the name of God and St. George. He had only two thousand men with him but he proclaimed King Richard as the usurper of the throne against him. Henry was very conscious of his need to swell his army and had come all the way around to Pembrokeshire because his uncle Jasper Tewdwr was Earl of Pembroke and could provide Henry with more fighting men. Also the Welsh people were delighted to have Henry as a Welshman to claim the throne. They saw in him a way for the ancient Britons to attain a national dream.

Henry's arrival presented a major problem for Rhys ap Thomas of Carew Castle – King Richard's leading supporter in south Wales, who had made an oath to the king 'Whoever ill-affected to the state, shall have to land in these parts of Wales, where I have anie employment under your majestie, must resolve himself to make his entrance and irruption over my bellie'. His moral dilemma was resolved by none other than the Bishop of St. Davids who offered to absolve him of his oath and suggested that he lay himself on the ground and allow Henry to step over his belly. Instead a more dignified version was employed where Rhys ap Thomas lay under Mullock Bridge while Henry walked over the top. In this way Rhys ap Thomas was absolved of his oath and with his troops joined Henry. Henry Tewdwr stopped at St. Ishmaels village for a drink and the well used was long after called 'The King's Well'.

The joined forces of Henry and Rhys proved to be a major factor in deciding the Battle of Bosworth Field. Rhys brought with him a large contingent of Welsh men and 500 trained cavalry. It was at the Battle of Bosworth Field that one of his troops, a commoner named Wyllyam Gardynyr was reputed to have killed King Richard with a poleaxe, when his horse became trapped in a marsh. The credit went to Rhys ap Thomas who was then known as the man who killed a king. Henry Tewdwr was delighted with his support and knighted Rhys three days after the battle.

The battle of Bosworth Field was a match of King Richard with about 8,000 troops and Henry Tewdwr with around 5,000. However several of Richard's leading supporters switched sides or refused to fight, that considerably depleted Richard's army. When John Howard, the Duke of Norfolk and a close companion of King Richard was killed, Richard probably realised that things were not going in his favour. He led an impromptu cavalry charge deep into Henry Tewdwrs's ranks in an attempt to end the battle suddenly by killing Henry Tewdwr. It has been suggested that it was the seasoned core of French troops that broke this charge and the battle was soon ended.

So history shows that at Mullock Bridge a dramatic scene was acted out and Rhys ap Thomas defected from King Richard III. So began a chain of historic events that led to Rhys ap Thomas becoming known as the man who killed a king, who was knighted and who returned to Pembrokeshire as Sir Rhys. Many years later after long service to King Henry, he was rewarded by being made a Knight of the Garter. He threw the greatest tournament ever held in Wales at Carew Castle to celebrate this and his ascent to becoming the most powerful man in Wales and a favourite of King Henry VII. The story of the evil King Richard III and the little Princes in the tower was dramatised as a play by William Shakespeare who came up with the famous line well known today of the death of King Richard who is reputed to have cried out when bogged on the battlefield 'A Horse! A Horse! My Kingdom for a horse!'

Suggested Further Reading
Churchill, W. S., Sir, 1956-58, *Volume I: The History of the English Speaking Peoples - The Birth of Britain*, p. 392, Casswell, London,

26. THE GREAT TOURNAMENT AT CAREW CASTLE

Figure 10. The champions jousting at the Carew Tournament of August 1507

When King Henry VII raised Sir Rhys ap Thomas to a Knight of the Garter in 1505, the fifty-six year old Sir Thomas decided on a very big celebration. He arranged for the first and last tournament ever held in Wales. The event took place over five days from 21st to 25th May 1507 at his stronghold of Carew Castle. Happily accounts exist of the tournament that was attended by 1,000 people so we can today follow the events.

Invitations were sent out to all parts of Wales to all of the leading men of the time. The first day of the tournament was taken up with the arrival and greeting of the guests. From Pembrokeshire Sir Thomas Perrot and Sir John Wogan attended along with Arnold Butler and Griffith Dunn. Breconshire provided Vaughan of Tretower. Glamorganshire provided Jenkin Mansell known as 'Jenkin the Valiant' who had welcomed Henry Tewdwr when he landed at Dale. He had also married a grand-daughter of King Edward IV. Monmouthshire provided Sir William Herbert of Colebrook. From North Wales Griffith of Llansadwrn, Wynn of Gwydir and Robert Salisbury attended. The most senior men were quartered in the castle and the others in tents in the park outside the castle green.

On the second day – St. George's Day – Sir Rhys led the party to Lamphey Palace where they were received by Robert Sherborne (the Bishop of St. Davids), the Abbot of Talley Cathedral and the Prior of Carmarthen. All attended mass in the chapel of Lamphey Palace. Then Sir Rhys led the party back to Carew for feasting in the great banqueting hall.

Great preparations had been made. As the party approached the castle they saw a picture of St. George and St David embracing one another hanging over the castle entrance. Inside two hundred of Sir Rhys' men dressed in blue livery formed an avenue through which the guests passed into a lesser court. Inside this were men in armour bearing the escutchons and coats of armour of Sir Rhys' ancestors. They next entered the Great Hall that was richly hung with tapestries. At the top end was the King's table covered in red velvet (although the King was absent). On either side of the King's table a long table ran down either side of the hall. Sir Rhys had his own table and the guests were grouped according to seniority. All men stood bareheaded before the tables, as though in the presence of royalty until a great fanfare of trumpets sounded. The master of ceremony was Griffith – Sir Rhys' only legitimate son, as he had been brought up at court and understood the ceremonial customs.

The feasting began and the health of the King, Queen and the Prince was drunk repeatedly. The bards sang eulogies praising the guests and their ancestors to the accompaniment of harp music. The party became extremely merry and the feast was so prolonged that there was no time left that day for jousting.

On the third day, after the assembly was sounded, Sir Rhys appeared as a splendid knight astride a richly caparisoned fine charger. He was wearing a suit of gilded armour. Two pages followed him on horseback and there were two footmen on either side of him. One hundred of his men wearing blue liveries preceded him and another one hundred followed. He formed his own procession and proceeded to the park where a tilting yard had been set up. At opposite ends of the yard were two tents. One was for the appellants (challengers) and the other for the defenders. Sir Rhys then sat in the judge's chair near the centre of the yard near where the clashes would occur. His servants stood around him each armed with a halberd (a combined spear and axe on a five to seven foot long pole) and a basket hilted sword strapped on.

The trumpets sounded and the four defending champions rode up. They were Sir William Herbert and Roger Salisbury of North Wales and Jenkin Mansell and Vaughan of Tretower. Next the four challenging champions rode up. Griffith ap Rhys led the way, followed by Sir Thomas Perrot, then

Sir William Wogan and Griffith Dunn bring up the rear. They all paraded around the tilt yard and presented arms to Sir Rhys. Around them 1000 people watched the splendid scene of armed knights ready for combat. Their flags and pennants flying and their shield insignias identifying them. The sight would never be seen again in Wales until modern Hollywood movies arrived.

The knights picked up their long lances and each made six charges (Figure 10). They then discarded the lances and took out their swords and fell to hacking at each other. The crowd roared with excitement as they watched and heard the champions exchanging stout blows, some landing and some being parried. Perhaps they wanted to see blood flow. But in this they were to be disappointed for Sir Rhys had some of his men standing by with stout staves to block the swords if the fighting became too real. This completed the mornings entertainment. The knights then attended mass and went on to a lunch (dinner).

In the afternoon the crowds reassembled and the tournament continued with a wide variety of knightly sports. There was wrestling, throwing the bar, and tossing the pike. A most popular activity was quintain. This was a medieval training where a knight would tilt at a figure set up on a post which was also fitted with a sandbag or a sword, so that if the knight was too slow the item would swing around and strike him.

At supper that night, Griffith ap Rhys challenged Sir William Herbert to tilt on the next day and offered a supper on his success to be eaten at Carmarthen after the tournament. Sir William accepted but insisted that the young heirs Penrhyn and Gwydir join in. Sir Rhys disagreed as he feared the two lads might be injured – the oldest was only sixteen. Finally after much argument from the young men he agreed.

On the fourth day, the morning was again occupied with tilting. Sir Rhys judged and gave the award against his son's party. In the afternoon they hunted in the park and killed several bucks. These were sent to Carmarthen for the supper that Griffith ap Rhys had to give for Sir William Herbert. In the evening there were theatricals and a comedy was played. This brought the tournament activities to an end. The fifth and last day was spent assisting the guests to pack and saying goodbys.

The tournament was been a great success and 1000 people had spent five days together amicably enjoying the great spectacle. There had been no disagreements nor injuries to mar the event. The tournament was long afterwards humorously referred to as 'St. George's pilgrimage to St. Davids'.

Sir Rhys had evidently used the tournament for self glorification and that of his ancestors. His daily use of his 200 blue liveried men was but a small part of it. He was at his most powerful after his long allegiance and many rewards from Henry Tudor. Did he still entertain doubts about his abrupt about face and breaking his oath to Richard III? Perhaps, like the large portion of Richard's army who stood by and did not fight at the critical Battle of Bosworth Field, perhaps he had secretly detested a king who had murdered the two legitimate heirs to the throne - the two young princes in the Tower of London.

Suggested Further Reading
Spurrell, W.G., 1921, *The history of Carew, Pembrokeshire*, W. Spurrell and Son.

27. VIEW THE NORMAN EARLS AND KNIGHTS OF PEMBROKESHIRE

The Normans were proud warriors and conscious of their historic roles, so when they died they marked their graves with fine effigies, so that later generations might still observe and admire them. Effigies are life-sized sculptures of deceased persons wearing the costume of their station. The first UK effigies appeared in the twelfth century. By the fourteenth century they had their hands together in prayer. They were often painted. Many show knights in armour with sword and shield, often with their legs crossed possibly indicating that the knight served in the crusades. These fine recumbent life-sized statues show not only the earl/knight but often with him is his lady dressed in her finest robes. Others show tonsured monks in their habits.

Some idea of the age of an unidentified knight's effigy can be obtained from the armour worn. The Normans of eleventh century, as shown in the Bayeux tapestry, wore the Norman conical metal helmet with a long metal plate covering the nose. Their bodies were protected by hauberks – a quilted garment with attached metal plates with the tunic and breeches in one piece. This was replaced by a head covering of chain mail sewn onto a leather hood that fitted over the head and shoulders. The hauberks were replaced with mail clad surcoats and jupons with brightly emblazed heraldic ensignia. In the fourteenth century articulated plate armour made a coat of mail unnecessary. A visored helmet was worn with the plate armour. Much of the finest armour was made in the fifteenth century. But the increased use of firearms in the sixteenth century rendered metal plate armour unnecessary.

Today, almost a thousand years later, despite the ravages of time, a surprising number of effigies have survived. There is a publication listing 248 known effigies in South Wales. Many effigies have been lost in wars and accidents, others deliberately cut up by the impoverished landless tenants for repurposing the stone. Those that remain permit us to gaze upon the likenesses of these dominant people who shaped our history.

One of the most renowned of the Pembrokeshire Normans was Richard de Clare known as Earl Strongbow because of his prowess with the long bow in many battles. At the age of between fifty and sixty years he took 1000 fighting men in ships and joined the invasion of Ireland. There he led the well disciplined Normans against far larger armies of both Irish and Norse settlers and defeated them. He married Aoife the daughter of the King of Leinster and on the death of the latter he became the King. This did not please King Henry II who had tried to stop him by blocking the shipping of troops and equipment from Earl Strongbow's base in 'Little England Beyond Wales'. With such a rival in Ireland, King Henry had to raise his own army of 6000 fighting men and also invade Ireland. King Henry was a master politician and the Irish Kings all submitted to him having tasted Norman battle tactics with Earl Strongbow. In fact King Henry presented himself to them as their protector from his Norman barons. Because of Earl Strongbow's efforts, King Henry won Ireland without shedding blood.

Earl Strongbow's grave and effigy can be found in Christ Church Cathedral in Dublin, as he died there. An inscribed stone with the half-sized effigy reads:

'THIS AUNCYENT MONVMENT OF RICHARD STRANGBOWE CALLED COMES STRANGULENSIS LORD OF CHEPSTO AND OGNY THE FIRST AND PRINCIPALL INVADER OF IRELAND 1169 QVI OBIIT 1177 THE MONYMENT WAS BROKEN BY THE FALLOF THE ROFF AND BODYE OF CRYSTES CHVRCHE IN AN 1562 AND SET UP AT THE CHARGE OF THE RIGHT HONORABLE SR HENIRI SIDNEY KNIGHT OF THE NOBLE ORDER L PRESIDEN WAILES L DEPVTY OF IRELAND 1570'

As recorded, when the cathedral collapsed, the stone effigy was broken. But the effigy there today is not broken nor scratched. The heraldry on the shield is not correct for it is not that of the Earl of Pembroke. The chain mail armour shown by the effigy suggests a date of around 1330. Clearly Sir Henry Sidney replaced Earl Strongbow's broken effigy with another one that he removed from another site. It has been suggested that the present effigy might be that of Earl Strongbow's son the Third Earl, but that is not certain.

A magnificent effigy of the first Earl of Pembroke William Marshall (c.1140 -1219) who built the great round keep of Pembroke Castle, can be seen on his tomb in Temple Church in London.

St. Mary's Church in Carew Cheriton village lies only a half mile from

Carew Castle. It was the family chapel for the Carew family. The name was taken by Gerald de Windsor and a new family coat of arms designed. It has four fine effigies all carved out of what appears to be Portland stone. They were described by Fenton (1811).

Two fine effigies show Sir John Carew and his wife Dame Elizabeth (Preface and Plate 16). Sir John is wearing full armour but without a helmet. He has a neck ruff. His lady is also wearing a neck ruff with a most elaborate dress, bodice and splendid head covering. Sir John and his lady are shown as mature persons and Sir John has a beard (Frontispiece). At the time of Fenton's visit, Sir John's right arm and the hands of both effigies were missing. The inscription provides the following information: 'Sir John Carew (died 21st February 1637) and his wife Dame Elizabeth, also their three sons Thomas, John and George and five daughters Elizabeth, Bridget, Margaret, Mary and Dorothy.' Their three sons are carved kneeling in mourning on the side of the Portland stone base of the tomb (Plate 17). The daughters are shown on the opposite side but cannot be seen against the church wall.

Carew Cheriton Church also contains, two other effigies. One is of a cross-legged knight. He lies in chain-mail and plate armour on his back with legs crossed, his sword is in his right hand and his shield on his left side (Plate 18). The effigy lies in a canopied recess with much carved decoration including six panels with figures along the base. But at the time of Fenton's visit in 1810 the tomb and effigy had so many coatings of white wash that details were obscured. The effigy was identified and described by Fenton (1811) as that of Sir Elidore de Stackpole - first holder of the Stackpole estate and founder of Cheriton Church. This identification was challenged by Laws (1888) who pointed out that this cannot be correct as the mixture of mail and plate armour did not come into vogue until the latter half of the thirteenth century. This suggests that the effigy may not represent a Stackpole, but rather Sir Nicholas de Carew who built the present castle at Carew.

There is also a life-sized effigy of a priest lying in his habit on his back with his feet on a small dog. Also in the church is a small effigy of a lady in a hard yellow stone that has no canopy. She wears a striking costume and an elaborate headdress. She was identified by Fenton as Lady Elspeth, Sir Elidore's wife. The small effigy has crossed hands and is believed to be a heart burial.

Upton Church, adjacent to Upton Castle, preserves the effigies of two possible Malefants. Opposite the entrance, under a rich stone canopy ornamented with carved figures of the apostles up the sides, is the tomb and recumbent effigy of a slim crusader in complete armour believed to be Sir

William Malefant who died in 1362. His head is protected by a conical metal helmet and chainmail (Plate 19). His armoured feet with spurs lie on his hunting dog. The effigy is of alabaster but the right arm is missing. Within the communion rails there is, under a wrought canopy of stone, the effigy of a lady in a robe and headdress (Plate 20). It has been suggested that she is Lady Margaret, Sir William's wife, but the details of her dress suggest a later age.

Lying on the floor of Upton Church is a vast effigy in stone of a knight, being six feet long with the feet broken off. It is partly mutilated with the face broken off, but the detail of the chain mail carving is excellent. It is composed of a purplish stone. Fenton found this damaged effigy at nearby Nash Church. At the time of his visit in 1811 it as lying outside the church under the drippings of the eves. Fenton learned that it had been on a bench at the north end of an isle that became dilapidated. There was no identification but a tradition that he had been an admiral and a giant of a man. He had died abroad and his body was landed at Cosherton Pill near the church. Laws (1888) also described this effigy that was then lying outside in nettles. He illustrated it. It shows the knight in chain mail armour lying on his right side, shield to the left with his head on a pillow. The lack of plate armour suggested to Laws that it belonged to the oldest type of effigy found in Wales. This effigy was later moved to Upton Church.

Another fine example of the effigies of a knight and his lady, both in alabaster, lay in Slebech Church and were described and illustrated by Fenton (1811). The two recumbent effigies lay together. One is of a lady and lies under a carved canopy with white marble. The other is that of a knight over six feet tall, in armour, lying outside the canopy and added at a later date. Both appear youthful. The knight is in full armour of the period 1450 – 1500 with head resting on his helmet on which was placed the crest. The latter is now much mutilated but appears not to be of the Barlow family who lived for many years at Slebech. The badge of the Order of the Golden Fleece is suspended around his neck. The lady is in a long dress with elegant folds below the waist, bodice tightly laced and a cloak thrown back. Her hair is loose and flowing with a wreath around her head. Her dress appears to be of the period of Richard II (1367 – 1400) or of Henry VI (1421-1471).

Fenton believed that the knight was probably Roger Barlow, as the Order around his neck was probably awarded him for his services to Spain by King Charles V of Spain. Lately the badge has been suggested to be the Order of the Sun and Roses instituted by Edward VI (1461-1483) and an alternative identification suggested as that of Sir William Wogan and his wife the Lady Margaret. The Barlow coat of arms on the shield may have been added since Fenton's visit. The church fell into ruins and in 1904 the effigies were removed to the modern parish church without the canopy. Slebech is also the church where Sir William Hamilton is buried along with his first wife Catherine Barlow. Today Slebech Church is abandoned and becoming derelict.

Roger Barlow (1485 – 1553) had a remarkably adventurous life. He and his brothers were made destitute when their father was taken to the Tower of London on suspicion of treason and the family property confiscated. Like his brothers he set out to seek his fortune. Roger travelled to Seville and lived there for fifteen years. From 1526 to 1528 he was employed by King Charles V of Spain to participate in Sebastian Cabot's expedition to the River Plate in South America. Upon returning to Spain he was introduced to Sir Thomas Bullen then on a mission to Spain. Sir Thomas informed his King of Rogers successes and abilities and he was ordered to return to England. This he did in 1531 and was made Vice Admiral under Lord Seymour. It was planned that he would lead an expedition of three ships from Milford Haven to explore for a northern passage to the East Indies. The untimely death of King Henry however quashed this project.

At the time of the dissolution, the immense lands at Slebech and the Commandery were sold to Roger Barlow for the sum of two hundred and five pounds and six shillings. He is believed to have settled there and it became the seat of many generations of the Barlow family who became major landowners in Pembrokeshire. The old Commandery was demolished and replaced by Slebech Mansion.

Another knight's effigy can be seen in Llangwm Church believed to be that of one of the de la Roche family, who built Roch castle (amongst other things). The knight is a recumbent crusader beneath an elaborate canopy. In his right hand is his sword and in his left his shield, with head facing right with strongly marked features resting on his helmet, which has as a crest the head of an eagle. He wears a short coat with chain mail protecting his neck and plate armour on his arms and legs.

The largest collection of effigies in Pembrokeshire is contained in St. Davids Cathedral. Most of these are of religious persons. But there are four effigies of knights. Fenton (1811) describes two knights in armour opposite each other in the chancel. One is of Rhys ap Gruffydd or Lord Rhys, Prince of South Wales and the other is his son Rhys Gryg. Lord Rhys's head rests on his helmet that is surmounted by a lion and his son's head is on a pillow. Lord Rhys spent his life battling the Normans and Flemings who had invaded his lands. There are other but unidentified knights effigies in the cathedral.

In St. Mary's Church, Tenby lying under a plain canopy is the effigy of a knight in chain mail and plate armour as was worn soon after the conquest. His shield bears the Barri coat of arms, but there is no inscription.

During the reformation of Henry VIII many of the effigies were destroyed when the religious houses were closed and sold with their lands. For example fragments of the effigy of a knight were found during the recent excavation of the ruins of Haverfordwest priory. Others were destroyed by the landless peasants of later generations. Fenton (1811) on a visit to Newport church found two stone canopies that were lacking their effigies. An old mason he met there told him that about thirty years previously there had been an effigy of a man (details unknown) and he remembered it being taken away, adding with great exultation, that it served to cut up into fine arches for windows'. Fenton thought that the two missing effigies were probably of Sir William Martin and his lady, the Lord Rhys's daughter, who are believed to have founded the church.

In Herbrandston Church is the worn effigy of a fourteenth century knight holding a sword.

Suggested Further Reading

Fenton, R., 1911, *A historical tour through Pembrokeshire*: Reprinted 2018, Herd Press, 818 p.

Laws, E., 1888, *The history of Little England beyond Wales*: Reprinted 1995, Cyngor Sir Dyfed County Council, Haverfordwest, 458 p.

28. TWO PEMBROKESHIRE PRIORIES

All over England, Wales and Ireland are to be found the splendid and noble ruins of monasteries, priories, convents and friaries. A total of 825 communities were dissolved or suppressed between 1536 and 1540 in what became known as the 'Dissolution of the Monastries'. The ruins record the greatest transfer of property in English history since the Norman conquest of 1066. It happened as a whole series of adverse events came together. The Roman Church of Britain had become extremely wealthy and powerful and also somewhat greedy and corrupt and certain practices were opposed by the newly formed Protestant movement. At this time the printing press was invented and scholars were able to circulate new ideas about religion which fuelled the division of the western church. This invention also rendered one of the main uses of the monasteries obsolete and that was their role in painstakingly copying manuscripts. The final event was the coming of an aggressive King Henry VIII, who not only wanted to remarry (not permitted under the Roman Church) but required considerable funding for his wars against France and Scotland. Against him stood not only the Roman Church but also Sir Thomas Moore – a councillor to King Henry VIII and Lord High Chancellor of Great Britain .

The trouble began during the reign of King Henry VIII (1509-1547). In 1517 the German cleric Martin Luther, along with French theologian John Calvin and other early Protestants precipitated the Protestant Reformation or division of western Christianity. They objected to several practices of the Roman Catholic Church, in particular the selling of pardons for sins. The reformation led to the birth of the Protestant faith. In 1534 the Act of Supremacy was passed by parliament granting King Henry VIII Royal Supremacy meaning he would be head of the Church of England (this is still the legal authority of the sovereign of the United Kingdom). This was followed by the First Suppression Act of 1536 and the Second Suppression act of 1539.

Sir Thomas More, a leading Roman Catholic and Lord High Chancellor was responsible for the functioning and independence of the law courts. He resigned this position in 1532 probably because he opposed King Henry's stand against the Roman Catholic Church. In 1534 the Succession Act was passed that required More to take an oath that rejected the Pope, that declared as invalid the marriage between Henry VIII and Catherine of Aragon and acknowledged that the children of Henry and Anne Bolyn would be legal heirs to the throne. Sir Thomas along with John Fisher, Bishop of Rochester, refused to take this oath in April 1534 and was committed to the Tower of London for treason on April 17th. Sir Thomas was found guilty of treason on perjured evidence. On July 6th 1535 Sir Thomas and Bishop Fisher were both executed by decapitation. His final words spoken on the scaffold where he died were 'the king's good servant but God's first'.

Sir Thomas' body was buried in an unmarked grave in St. Peter's Chapel. His head was placed upon a pike over London Bridge for a month as was the normal custom for traitors. His eldest daughter Margaret rescued the head before it could be thrown into the River Thames. Margaret had married into the Roper family of Canterbury and placed the head in the Roper family vault in St. Dunstan's Church just across the road from Roper House. The head was seen in 1835 during repair work in a niche in the vault in a small casket. Paintings exist of Margaret rescuing Sir Thomas's head.

Sir Thomas was beatified by Pope Leo XIII in 1886 and canonised, along with John Fisher, on 19th May 1935 and his feast day established as 9th July. His feast day was changed and his name added to the Roman Catholic calendar of saints in 1970 for celebration on 22nd June jointly with St. John Fisher. In 1980 Sir Thomas was added to the Church of England's calendar of Saints and Heroes of the Christian Church and jointly with John Fisher is commemorated on 6th July. His life is popularly known from such films as 'A man for all seasons' and his writings are today cited widely as an example of a courageous stand against oppression.

In 1536 (the 27th year of King Henry VIII's reign) there were over 800 monasteries, abbeys, priories, nunneries and friaries (religious houses) with over 10,000 monks, nuns, friars and canons. By 1540 these had gone. The altar plates, goblets and vestments went to King Henry's jewel house. The bells were melted down for cannon. The lead roofing was used for shot, often melted on site over fires of wood from the roof rafters of the religious houses. Roof slates, dressed stones, stained glass windows and wooden furniture and fittings were sold for building materials. A great spree of looting resulted in destruction of tombs and relics of the Saints and past kings. Even the tomb of King Alfred the Great was looted. The wealth considerably helped King Henry in his wars against France and Scotland. At first monks and nuns were given pensions, but later things became harsher. Monks had to declare that the monastic way of life had been a vain and superstitious round of ceremonies that they were ready to abandon, so they could live as 'true Christian men' outside the monasteries.

The land taken amounted to around one third of England and Wales. Much of this land was worked by tenants. Some of the land was kept for the income to benefit the Crown, some was sold for similar reasons and some was given to supporters of the king. By selling and gifting the lands to the gentry and nobility, Henry created supporters beholden to the Crown who could use the land more efficiently. King Henry VIII by his bold and utterly ruthless actions, was able to get divorced, and remarry, to hugely increase his income so that he could fight wars and by redistributing the land, considerably strengthen his position. Many who opposed him were executed. It is estimated that loot from the monasteries raised £150,000 (although £50,000 was used for monastic pensions) and sale of the lands raised 1.4 million pounds (equivalent to £481 million today).

Opposition to the reformation was widespread, as many of the religious houses were centres of hospitality and learning, sources of charity for the old and infirm and provided school teachers to the villages. Mobs attacked men sent to break up the religious houses. In northern England there were a series of uprisings by Roman Catholics. In autumn 1536 there was a great gathering of 40,000 at Horncastle in Lincolnshire. Revolt spread through Yorkshire and the rebels were led by Robert Aske, but the King ordered the rebellions to be put down. Forty-seven of the Lincolnshire rebels were executed and 132 from York. Further rebellions in Cornwall in early 1537 and in Walsingham (in Norfolk) received similar treatment. In Ireland the dissolution proceeded more slowly especially in areas still in the hands of Irish chieftains. By the time of King Henry's death in 1547, only about a half of the four hundred religious houses there had been destroyed.

Although some of the religious buildings dated back to Anglo-Saxon times before the Norman invasion, most had been founded in the 11th and 12th centuries. Today their picturesque remains are well known tourist destinations. In Pembrokeshire King Henry VIII appointed Anne Bolyn as Marchioness of Pembrokeshire and through her influence Protestant Thomas Barlow became prior of the Augustinian Priory of Haverfordwest and soon afterwards Bishop of St. David's Cathedral, so that St. David's then led the way in Pembrokeshire in promoting Protestantism. The splendid Lamphey Palace near Pembroke was the retreat of the Bishops of St. David's. Smaller religious houses existed at the Black Monks of Pembroke, St. Dogmael's, Caldy Island, Pill Augustine Canons, Augustine Priory at Haverfordwest and the Knights Hospitallers at Slebech.

Recently the ruins of two Pembrokeshire priories have been cleared and some stabilisation work carried out. These are Haverfordwest priory and Pill priory at Milford Haven and they make an interesting days visit. Haverfordwest Priory ruins are extensive and open to the public, free of charge, with information boards (Plate 21). The remains of Pill Priory (Plate 22) are partly open where they have been converted to a public house and partly in a private garden, but very visible from the road alongside. Both priory sites have information panels with maps explaining the ruins.

Haverfordwest Priory.

This was a house of Augustinian cannons that was founded in 1200 on land granted by Robert FitzTancard – Norman Lord of Haverfordwest - on the banks of the Western Cleddau River. The ruins lie alongside the new bypass between Haverfordwest and Merlins Bridge and the Western Cleddau River. Car parking is in Quay Street alongside the river.

The major part of the ruins is of a thirteenth century cruciform priory church on the north side of the site. Parts of the walls survive almost to roof height. The nave or long axis was over forty-five meters in length and had a screen in the centre separating the choir from the nave (approach to the high altar). The stone footings of the choir stalls are still visible. In the south-east corner of the church lie the remains of the cloister – a rectangular courtyard surrounded by open galleries. A narrow covered passage alongside the south side of the church was formerly the room for keeping vestments and other furnishings such as sacred vessels and records (sacristy). Beside this was a small building used for meetings (the Chapter House) with a splendid west door. A tomb plinth in the centre may have held the remains of the priory's founder. The toilet block remains unexcavated and also what is probably the infirmary. The canon's refectory was on the southern range and was entered from the west end where a long stone basin lies for washing hands.

Partly excavated buildings to the south are probably work rooms and kitchen. Very striking are the medieval gardens forming a large rectangular area adjacent to the south-eastern side of the church. The gardens comprise eight raised beds with stone borders. This is the only surviving ecclesiastical garden in Britain. It has been replanted as it might have been in the sixteenth century. In the centre of the gardens is a smaller garden believed to be exclusively for the Abbot.

The priory was dissolved in 1536 and acquired by Richard and Thomas Barlow, brothers of William Barlow, Bishop of St. Davids. The two brothers can be regarded as adventurers from an Essex family who in 1546 purchased from the Crown for the price of £705 and six shillings and three pence the Hospitallier Commandery of Slebech as well as Pill Priory and the priory and friary of Haverfordwest including their extensive tracts of land. (Note: after the American Civil War the term 'carpetbagger' was coined for northerners who entered the devastated south and bought cheaply). The Barlow brothers started the demolition work, but it was not entirely completed as the ruins today testify. Archaeological work was carried out on the priory in the 1920's and again between 1983 and 1986 and much decorated rock was found and is on display at Haverfordwest Museum in the ruins of Haverfordwest castle. Sites were found where the lead from the roof had been melted on site.

Pill Priory, Milford Haven.

This was a Tironian house built between 1161 and 1170 as a daughter house of St. Dogmael's Abbey near Cardigan. These were grey-clad monks of a Roman Catholic monastic order. The founder was Adam de Roche of the Barony of Roch. The church was dedicated to St. Budoc in the Celtic tradition and to the Blessed Virgin.

The plan is cruciform and it was built of local Old Red Sandstone probably quarried one kilometre to the northwest and also Carboniferous limestone probably brought by boat along the Milford Haven waterway from quarries in the Carew area. As at Haverfordwest Priory, the church is at the north side of the site with the cloister and monks buildings on the south side. Today the main part of the ruin is the Chancel arch which led into the choir in the east. Three window openings remain high in the wall and the 'V' shaped roofline of the choir is quite distinct. The wall contains a flight of night stairs that allowed the monks to descend from their dormitory to enter the Choir from the sleeping quarters for night-time services. The domestic quarters were arranged around three sides of the cloister but only those on the east have survived. They are now incorporated into two later houses constructed after the dissolution. The base of the central tower remains and the south wall of the south-facing transept.

The site has not been archaeologically excavated but in 1990 repairs to the public road passing through the village revealed numerous graves with skeletons. These were removed but have since been reburied in a small marked area in the garden beside the Chancel arch. The site today is a splendid example of private initiative for the ruins and a stone house within them built of recycled monastery stones was recently bought. These enterprising people have made a great effort of preserve the ruins and obtained a grant from CADW to clear the ruins of ivy and to stabilise the remains. This has been tastefully done and the result is splendid. There is an information board with a map at the site and the owners have a website giving the history of the priory at www.pillpriory.co.uk

The land in the Hubberston and Pill area, including the remains of Pill Priory remained in the Barlow family until the mid eighteenth century when they were owned by Catherine Barlow of Slebech. In 1758 she married William Hamilton (later knighted) and on her death in 1782, he inherited the land in the Hubberston and Pill area. He used this to develop the port and town of Milford Haven which he visited with his second wife Lady Emma Hamilton and Lord Nelson in 1802.

Suggested Further Reading
Woodward, G.W.O., 2018, *The Dissolution of the Monasteries*: Pitkin Publishing Ltd., London, 33 p. ISBN 978-0-85372-617-3.

29. THE CIVIL WAR IN PEMBROKESHIRE

Throughout England and Wales there are many stone castles. Today most are picturesque ruins. But they tell a story of major political changes. From the time of William the Conqueror in 1066, the Kingdom was administered from a network of royal castles and Lordships. After the Civil War and the King had been executed, the new rulers – the people's parliament - further demonstrated their new powers by ordering the destruction or 'slighting' of many of these great and rich castles to symbolise the end of the royal castle rule.

The stone castles of Pembrokeshire (Figure 1) played an important role in the Civil War. Those at Pembroke, Carew, Manorbier, Tenby, Picton, Wiston, Haverfordwest and Roch changed hands, most several times. Haverfordwest and Pembroke castles were ordered destroyed by Oliver Cromwell. Destruction of the castles was never completed as it was found to require vast amounts of gunpowder which was expensive.

At the start of the first Civil War in 1642, only Pembroke and Tenby declared for Parliament. The rest of the county declared their allegiance to the king. Some families played key roles. The Lort family were strong supporters of the King and the three brothers each raised a regiment of Royalists. On the other hand the Laugharne family were staunch Parliamentarians and Roland Laugharne would play a major role in Pembrokeshire. Colonel John Poyer, the mayor and a merchant of Pembroke, was the first Parliamentarian in Pembrokeshire to stand up against the King. For the first year of the war he prepared the defences of Pembroke castle and town.

A man who was to play a sinister, surreptitious, and insidious role in Pembrokeshire with major consequences was John Eliot of Eawar (Amroth), a lawyer and friend of the Lort family. In modern parlance he was a crooked lawyer. His persistent sinister intriguing, accusations and false information, perhaps an early form of propaganda, caused major problems for the three main Parliamentary commanders operating in south-west Wales, far from the government in London. He obtained the ears in London of powerful individuals who would act against the local parliamentary commanders leading eventually to their rebellion and a second civil war. The rebellion was quelled by Oliver Cromwell himself and his Ironsides who took the field in Pembrokeshire to end it. Eliot was a friend of the Lort brothers and they strongly opposed and did their best to bring down Parliamentary commander Colonel John Poyer of Pembroke.

Rowland Laugharne was aged about thirty years at the outbreak of hostilities and would become a major Parliamentary commander during the war. As a youth he had been a page to Robert Deveraux, the third Earl of Essex, who would be the Parlimentary commander in England. Rowland was a devoted follower of the Earl. Rowland's father John of St. Brides was also a supporter of Parliament. Rowland's two nephews Vaughan and James Laugharne also fought with the Parliamentarians.

The Civil War began on August 22nd 1642 when the King raised his standard in Nottingham. In Pembrokeshire, the towns of Tenby, Pembroke and Haverfordwest made preparations for war against the King. Tenby surrendered to a Royalist force led by Roger Lort without a fight. Haverfordwest followed in September, surrendering to Lord Carbery without a fight. Lord Carbery then laid siege to Pembroke Castle. Colonel Poyer held out until a Parliamentary fleet sailed into Milford Haven bringing 200 marines and supporting cannon. The siege was lifted. At this point the Earl of Essex sent Major General Roland Laugharne back to Pembrokeshire to take command of the Parliamentary forces. He joined Poyer in Pembroke castle. This heartened the garrison and Laugharne proposed taking Tenby with the help of Admiral Swanley and six Parliamentarian ships. Admiral Swanley bombarded Tenby unsuccessfully.

At this stage of the Civil War the Royalists in Pembrokeshire were mainly in command. Laugharne and Poyer remained inside Pembroke and John Laugharne brought his family there for safety. Lord Carbery boasted that he would plunder the gentlemen's houses in Tenby and put Poyer in a barrel of nails and roll him downhill into the sea. But Pembroke was impregnable behind its walls so Carbery instead garrisoned Tenby, Haverfordwest, Carew, Manorbier and Roch castles and some smaller houses – near Haverfordwest, also Stackpole House, Trefloyne near Tenby and Dale. Pembroke was surrounded by Royalist positions and the situation looked most favourable for the Royalists.

Major General Laugharne at this time led a small party out to forage. He was attacked by a Royalist party from Carew Castle led by Lieutenant Jones. Laugharne with only seven troopers, charged them and took twenty prisoners including the lieutenant. It was a sign of things to come. He was determined to break the Royalists encircling him. He was assisted by Admiral Richard Swanley who on 23rd January 1644 brought five parliamentary ships into Milford Haven. Three days later they were joined by three more ships. Two Royalist ships, the *Globe* and *Providence* retreated into Prix Pill under the guns of Fort Prix.

Next Laugharne assembled a force of 250 foot soldiers and fifty horse. These included some guns and 200 seamen borrowed from Admiral Swanley's fleet. The Parliamentarians advanced on Roger Lort's garrisoned Stackpole House. It was captured for the loss of two men killed and several wounded. Next Laugharne attacked the house at Trefloyne owned by Thomas Bowen, brother in law of Roger Lort. The house was defended by 150 foot soldiers and forty horse. Lord Carbery came out of Tenby with about 100 foot soldiers and horse to assist, but ran into Parliamentary gun fire and retreated back to Tenby. The Trefloyne garrison surrendered when the defensive walls were breached. Laugharne slighted the defences and took forty saddled and bridled horses and the arms of the foot soldiers. He released his captives and returned to Pembroke. The action incurred for him the wrath of the Lort family that 'was to have major consequences later on'.

Laugharne next decided to attack and capture the Royalist stronghold of Prix Pill to gain control of shipping in the Milford Haven Waterway. This was an earthworks on the west side of what is today Castle Pill, where the town of Milford Haven now stands. (It was removed in the 1970s to enable housing to be built there). On 23rd February Laugharne assembled 250 foot soldiers (a half of them again borrowed seamen from Admiral Swanley), sixty horse and guns. Laugharne took with him his father John, who was well known in the area, to ensure the support of the local people who could assist in moving the guns. They landed on the north side of the haven from boats provided by and protected by Admiral Swanley's fleet. The guns were speedily placed on the eastern side of the entrance to the pill and before nightfall they had opened fire. In addition Admiral Swanley brought his ships in to join the bombardment and engage the two Royalist ships.

Meanwhile Laugharne had marched with most of his force to cut the road from Haverfordwest from which Royalist reinforcements were expected. He placed twenty musketeers in Steynton church tower which overlooked the road. Late in the evening the reinforcements from Haverfordwest (sixty horse and some foot soldiers led by Sir Francis Lloyd) arrived. On seeing the Parliametary forces, Sir Francis immediately retreated back to Haverfordwest without firing a shot. Laughare and his men spent a cold night in a field.

Next morning the bombardment of the fort continued. Laugharne used his horse to charge a Royalist position blocking the road to the south. This succeeded and the attack carried through to reach Pill village and the ruins of an old chapel (St. Thomas a Becket Chapel consecrated in 1180, by far the oldest building in the area, today restored) near it. With the arrival of Laugharne and his men, the Parliamentary bombardment of the fort ceased for fear of hitting them. Before any further action could be taken, Prix Fort raised a flag of truce and the officers surrendered as prisoners. A messenger from Haverfordwest Castle arrived and witnessed the surrender and carried the news back to Haverfordwest. Laugharne captured eighteen big guns, six field carriages and 300 soldiers and the two Royalist ships. The action cost Laugharne one seaman killed accidentally by a shot from *Globe*. The Royalists lost two men during the morning bombardment.

Next morning (25th February) Laugharne and his force arrived at Haverfordwest to find the garrison had fled. The town and castle were taken without a shot being fired. The Parliamentarians received a surprising friendly welcome in the town. Two days later the Royalist garrison at Roch Castle surrendered. The smaller garrisons at Haroldston, Picton and some houses near Haverfordwest quietly dispersed without any fighting. Laugharne's bold actions had reversed the situation in Pembrokeshire and now the Royalists held only Carew and Tenby.

Laugharne left a garrison in Haverfordwest and withdrew to Pembroke. There with Admiral Swanley an attack on Tenby was planned. The Admiral loaned a 27-pounder gun with a crew and as many seamen as he could spare. He sent two of his ships *Prosperous* and *Crescent* to Caldy Roads to bombard Tenby. On 6th March Laughane with 500 men and guns, set out for Tenby. Transporting the guns proved heavy and slow work but they were in place before the walls of Tenby a day and a half later. The officers in charge of Tenby and its fort refused to surrender.

Next morning (7th March) the bombardment began and Laugharne placed his troops in position. But the walls proved strong and the bombardment continued from Thursday 7th March to Saturday. Many houses in the town were damaged, but no breach could be made in the walls. John Gwyn the Governor, Colonel David Gwyn (his brother) and Lieutenant Colonel Butler in Tenby stood firm. Finally a breach was made in the North Gate of the town. Governor John Gwyn led a charge of the defenders through it. But he was shot and carried back inside the walls. They were followed by the Parliamentarians into the town.

Tenby surrendered. The Governor was dying. The officers and 300 men were taken prisoner. The heroes of the action as reported to Parliament were Rowland Laugharne, Walter Cuny, Arthur Owen, John Poyer, Rice Powell,

Thomas Laugharne, Rowland Wogan and John Powell. But Parliament would overlook this.

On 10th March John Poyer reached the now isolated garrison at Carew Castle and called on them to surrender. This was agreed and the officers and men were permitted to go free taking their weapons with them. Poyer and his force installed themselves in the castle for a year. During this time Poyer collected the castle's revenues from its tenants. He needed the money as a stop gap measure to continue funding his operations. The money should have gone to Sir Richard Philipps of Picton Castle. This action by Poyer would lead to considerable trouble for him in the future when he would be accused of embezzlement and expropriation.

Laugharne, now in his finest hour, wrote to the Royalists of Cardiganshire and Carmarthenshire demanding their surrender. He then assemble a force of 400 foot soldiers and 150 horse on Colby Moor only 25 miles from Carmarthen. This caused the garrison at Carmarthen to abandon the town and march out north to Newcastle Emlyn. For the moment this ended the campaigning in Pembrokeshire.

When reports of the successes of the minority Parliamentary forces in Pembrokeshire against the majority of Royalists and also gains in other parts of South Wales reached the House of Common, the response was surprising. Only Admiral Swanley and his Vice Admiral were thanked for their service and each was honored and awarded a gold chain. The actions of Laugharne and Poyer were ignored. Both men had made enemies by their actions and were now out of favour in Parliament. There was a strong reaction by the Royalists who recognised that in South Wales they lacked leaders with military experience. Prince Rupert was appointed as the King's supreme general in Wales and the Marches with powers to raise men as well as money for their equipment and maintenance. In addition a new Royalist Commander, Sir Charles Gerard was appointed. He brought with him similarly experienced officers. They and their troops were battle hardened by experience in Ireland. Towards the end of May, Gerard and his force landed at Black Rock, Chepstow and began their advance across South Wales to reverse the Parliamentary gains.

Meanwhile Admiral Swanley's moment of glory was marred by a report that after the fall of Tenby, he had captured a troop ship off Anglesey and had thrown overboard ('made water rats of') 'Irish rebels' - seventy men and two women - in an anti-Papist action. The Royalists made much propaganda about this matter. The House of Commons appointed a very large committee to raise men, money, horses and ammunition in Pembrokeshire, and also to confiscate or let out the estates of the enemy and 'Papists'. The twenty-eight men on the committee included both supporters and enemies of Laugharne and Poyer. The hostile fraction would render the committee of little use to the two Parliamentary leaders.

Gerard and his force reputedly composed of 'Papists and Irish rebels' had great success. In June they captured Carmarthen and garrisoned it. The force then marched north capturing 200 prisoners at the Cardigan border and then taking Cardigan and Emlyn Castles. On 7th July they captured Roch Castle that was a provisions base for Laugharne. Gerard sent a column of troops to capture Laugharne Castle.

Laugharne with his inexperienced troops fell back on Haverfordwest, Tenby and Pembroke. Haverfordwest was taken by Gerard on 22nd July. In mid-August Laugharne's brother Thomas serving as a sergeant-major took out a troop of horse from Tenby and was captured.

However at this point Gerard's advance was halted. The King was defeated at Marston Moor on July 2nd. Gerard was required in England. He departed taking 500 horse and his Irish soldiers with him. His departure was followed by many complaints about his brutality, his disregard of people and his taking over property. Laugharne was now able to counterattack. In September he attacked garrisons along the borders of Carmarthenshire and Cardiganshire. In August his forces were strengthened by 140 men sent by the Earl of Essex, as well as provisions worth £557 sent by sea. In October Admiral Swanley returned and loaned Laugharne a big gun and a detachment of seamen. Laugharne Castle was captured first with further successes at Clog-y-fran House near St. Clears and Merthyr. On 27th November Laugharne accompanying a force led by Colonel Beale, defeated a Royalist force at Machnynlleth. Laugharne then attacked Cardigan that surrendered immediately, but the castle held out for two weeks until the walls were breached. Laugharne then placed Colonel Rice Powell in charge of Cardigan and advanced on Newcastle Emlyn.

Gerard with a force of 1,200 horse and 1,300 foot soldiers abruptly returned to Cardigan. He seized the town and called on Powell to surrender. Powell refused and sent a messenger to Laugharne. Gerard then broke down a section of the bridge across the River Teifi and assaulted the castle. 150 of his men died for little gain. Laugharne learning that Powell only had eight days supplies left, marched to the Pembrokeshire bank of the river and got supplies across to Powell. 120 of Swanley's men made the crossing in boats while under fire. Next on 22nd January, Laugharne led 250 foot soldiers and 200 seamen in an attack on the town. This was coordinated with a sally from the castle. The Royalists, lacking the stern leadership of Gerard, who was absent, were driven out of the town.

There followed some months of inaction. On 16th March, Laughane was finally appointed commander of all Parliamentary forces in South Wales. In April he began a siege of Newcastle Emlyn. On 27th April Gerard arrived there unexpectedly at 6.00 am on a Sunday morning and completely routed the Parliamentarians. 120 men were killed and 486 taken prisoner including twenty officers. The route extended all the way to Haverfordwest and no serious attempt was made to defend the town and castle. The garrison at Cardigan on learning this, fired the castle and retired by sea. Gerard then advanced with speed and reached Haverfordwest on 28th. That night he speedily captured Picton castle. Powder, arms, plate and £500 were taken. Next Carew Castle was captured. This left the Parliamentarians with only Tenby and Pembroke.

Gerard, now confident of success garrisoned Carew Castle and set up a battery to command the waterway to Pembroke. He offered bribes to Poyer at Pembroke to surrender the castle, but was refused. In London the complaints against Poyer were temporarily forgotten and he was voted fresh supplies of ammunition. But on 14th June 1645 the King's forces were disastrously defeated at Naseby by Fairfax and Cromwell. Gerard, who had been summoned from Pembrokeshire, failed to arrive in time. The King decided that his best chances now lay in Wales and moved to Raglan and Cardiff to raise more troops. There he met strong criticism of Gerard and at a meeting near Cardiff removed Gerard from command and replaced him with Sir Jacob Astley.

Laugharne was now faced by a Royalist force in Haverfordwest led by Major-Generals Stradling and Egerton. He assembled 500 foot soldiers, 200 horse and dragoons and two small guns taken from Tenby and Pembroke at Canaston Wood some three miles west of Narberth. They were joined by 250 seamen who landed from the Eastern Cleddau. On 1st August 1,100 Royalist foot soldiers with 450 horse and four field guns marched out of Haverfordwest Castle towards Narberth. What happened next was a major clash between the Royalists and Parliamentarians in what became known as the Battle of Colby Moor, after the location where the two sides fought. It is near Wiston Castle.

At 6.00 pm on the evening of August 1st, 150 musketeers and two troops of Parlimentarian horse engaged a greatly superior Royalist force. The fight continued very fiercely for one hour. Surprisingly the Parliamentarians won the day. The Royalist cavalry was overcome by the Parliamentarian horse and were persued back towards Haverfordwest. Laugharne with the remainder of his force attacked the Royalist foot soldiers very success-fully. 150 were killed and 700 taken prisoner including thirty-two officers. His own casualties were much smaller. 800 muskets, guns, provisions and gunpowder were captured.

Under cover of darkness the two Royalist major-generals with the remainder of their horse abandoned Haverfordwest Castle and rode to Carmarthen. They left a garrison at the castle. The next day Laugharne arrived in Haverfordwest and after resting for the Sabbath, began to bombard the castle. But the walls proved impregnable. On 5th August he had the castle gates fired and his men scaled the battlements. The castle was taken with twenty officers and 120 men made prisoners. Laugharne reported his total casualties at Colby Moor and Haverfordwest as two killed and sixty wounded, which suggests the Royalists were weakly led.

The King's cause in Wales was now completely lost. On 9th August Laugharne assembled his forces before Carew Castle and by 13th August reported that Carew, Manorbier and Picton castles were all captured. On 12th October Carmarthen declared for Parliament, causing the Royalist garrison to retire to Newcastle Emlyn that was taken before Christmas. Only Aberystwyth held out until April 1846. The House of Commons responded to Laugharne's good news by declaring 28th September to be a Day of Thanksgiving. His services were finally recognised and he was awarded the Barlow Estates at Slebech. It was to be the only occasion that he would be honored by Parliament.

With the ending of battlefield hostilities, local political infighting broke out. In December 1645 Poyer petitioned with justification for financial aid stating that for four years as governor of Pembroke he had spent all of his own money and had borrowed £2,000 from supporters to repair the walls and supply the garrison with arms and ammunition. Some of his supporters had lost heavily to attacks by Gerard's forces and were in urgent need of money. But John Lort set his insidious friend John Eliot to work. In February Eliot claimed that Poyer had in his possession money and goods of great value. Poyer briefly in London was arrested. Laugharne sent a letter on 16th January stating that Lort and Eliot had not taken the side of Parliament until victory was assured and that they were motivated by private malice. But Poyer was not returned to his command and languished in London unexamined and awaiting the decision of Parliament. This brought an end to the First Civil War.

After the war, the main concern in South Wales was taxation. How much longer must county committees raise funds to support parliamentary forces in the area? In August a Parliamentary committee proposed that the three counties of south-west Wales (garrisons of Tenby and Pembroke aside) should have a peace-time force of 100 horse and 100 dragoons. Laugharne was then in command of 1,400 foot and 600 horse. It seems that John Eliot may have intervened here by suggesting that if Tenby and Pembroke were to be garrisoned then each should have a governor from the new Model Army, so the county of Pembroke should no longer suffer the oppression and tyranny of its governor John Poyer. But no action followed.

Next trouble followed for Laugharne. The King had been seized by the army from Parliament's custody and requests for financial assistance for him and Sir Thomas Fairfax (general of all parliamentary forces) were received in the county. Laugharne wrote to Parliament on the matter stating that he had arrested one of the King's supporters and that he remained loyal to the Parliamentary cause.

On 25th March Poyer's nominal arrest in London ended when Parliament confirmed his command of the fifteen strong garrison of Pembroke and he returned to Wales. The insidious Eliot however stated that Poyer left London because he could not explain an absence of £6,000 from his returns to the state. Learning of this, Poyer in great anger arrested the three Lort brothers and locked them up in Pembroke Castle. The Lorts afterwards claimed that Poyer did this to obtain money from them. The dispute was resolved by the judges of the assize who invited Poyer to Haverfordwest and there detained him until the Lorts were released.

But this was not the end of the matter. Poyer busy with the Lort's arrest had ignored a summons of the Committee of Accounts, as well as a direct order from his Commander in Chief Fairfax to release his prisoners. Also claims had to be made for back pay for the army through the Pembrokeshire Commissioners. But these included Poyer's enemies, the three Lort bothers, Sir Richard Philipps and John Eliot. Poyer saw little hope of success and remained behind the walls of Pembroke Castle. The insidious Eliot wrote from Windsor on 12th January stating that Poyer had recruited men to bring the garrison up to 200 men, was pillaging houses, shooting cattle in the fields and was drunk in the afternoons.

On 18th February 1648 a Colonel Fleming arrived outside Pembroke with orders from Fairfax to take over Pembroke Castle from Poyer. Poyer refused to surrender the castle or to meet with Fairfax and was now in rebellion against Parliament. His shortage of money showed when he demanded £1000 of Fairfax to pay his bills before surrendering. Money was also a problem for Laugharne and his men. Laughane claimed to have spent his own fortune of £37,650 on the war effort. He and his men had not been paid for two and a half years and his officers also claimed financial losses and war damage to their estates. Poyer, Laugharne and Powell all felt they had made great personal sacrifices for the cause. They were also exceedingly annoyed with the efforts of John Eliot, who free of the fighting, had the ears of influential men in London. The view was shared by thirty-one of Laugharne's officers, who on 21st of February signed a letter complaining of the malicious aspersions cast by John Eliot upon the honor of their Major-General and his forces and accusing Eliot of delinquency and fraud.

Through January and February 1648 Poyer continued to gather in provisions from the surrounding countryside and to persuade the local market to supply the castle. On 1st March 200 foot soldiers sent by Fairfax arrived from Gloucester. This enabled Fairfax to occupy Pembroke town and stop the supplies to the castle. On 4th March Fairfax again demanded the surrender of Pembroke Castle. Again Poyer replied asking for £1000 to repay his expenses and that his forces be paid before surrendering. This indicated that he had no confidence in the County Committee. He evidently felt strongly about what he and his men were owed in back pay and expenses.

Fleming approached the County Committee who immediately offered to drop all suits and law actions against Poyer. But it was too late. Poyer raised his banner and opened fire on Fleming and his men. On 16th March the rebellion spread when the Tenby garrison decided to join Poyer and it was shortly commanded by Rice Powell, when he returned to Wales. The unrest spread to Laugharne's forces. Two companies led by Captains Addis and Agborow who were in the process of disbanding, marched to Pembroke to join Poyer. Poyer ordered them to attack Fleming and his force and sallied forth with his men. Fleming's men were driven out of the town with casualties and Fleming was wounded. Two guns were captured and taken with thirty prisoners into the castle. Samson Lort on 24th March wrote to the Commons that he feared a new war unless 'this cockatrice in the egg' was not crushed.

On 28th March two companies with 350 men from Bristol landed near Pembroke sent by Fairfax. They were quartered in the church at Pwllcrochan. Next day Poyer attacked and ordered them away from the waters of Milford Haven. Poyer and Powell had written to Prince Charles in St. Germaine asking for the appointment of a royal general, indemnity for their actions, and back payments as they were now in the hands of a few men of avrice and ambition who wanted to disband them. The prince replied on 3rd April appointing Poyer as governor of Pembroke and Powell of Tenby.

On 8th April Colonel Horton under orders from Fairfax, left Brecon with 1,200 men and was joined at Neath by Colonel Okey's dragoons from Cardiff. The objective was to capture the rebellious garrisons of Tenby and Pembroke. Poyer and Powell recruited men until each garrison had about 1000 men. Carmarthen and Llanelli were also in rebel hands. On 27th April Horton sent out Fleming with a party. They were captured and Fleming shot. This caused Horton to retreat back to Brecon. On 29th April Laugharne was in Haverfordwest and next day rode out to join Powell whose forces were advancing into Glamorgan. Like Poyer and Powell, he felt his very best efforts had been discounted and distorted by his enemies.

But history shows that they had seriously misjudged their position. Their defeat began on 3rd May when Oliver Cromwell with his Ironsides, under orders from Fairfax, marched out of Windsor to quell the rebellion in Wales. Horton learning that Cromwell was coming, felt he needed to achieve something first. So on 3rd May he marched his forces out of Brecon hoping to meet Powell and Laugharne before they reached Cardiff. He crossed the River Taf and took up a defensive position between St. Fagans and Capel Llanilltern. Powell and Laughane with around 8,000 men, but few horse, advanced against Horton's position. But they were beaten back on both wings by Horton's cavalry. The infantry fought well but became surrounded and broke and fled. They were persued by Horton's 3,000 seasoned troops and cavalry. They were persued for ten miles with 3,000 prisoners taken with very large amounts of weapons and ammunition captured. Powell and Laugharne both escaped, but Laugharne was wounded and his brother Thomas killed. The flight eastwards continued to Tenby. Horton and his forces arrived at Tenby on 17th May.

Cromwell and his forces arrived on May 23rd. He left Horton to reduce the town and castle and moved on to Pembroke. On May 25th Horton's men killed thirty of Tenby's defenders at an outpost. The garrison then sued for surrender, but Horton refused. On 31st May a breach was made in the wall. At this point Cromwell intervened and offered terms to Tenby's garrison. By 3rd June both the castle and town were in Horton's hands. 300 soldiers, twenty-five pieces of ordnance and thirty officers were captured. On 5th June the Commons ordered the seizing of the estates of Laugharne, Poyer and Powell.

The impasse at the mighty fortress of Pembroke was broken by Oliver Cromwell who arrived there on 24th May 1648. Cromwell set fire to parts of the town and attacked the castle repeatedly including cutting off the water supply. Cromwell hoped to starve out the garrison. At the end of June, Cromwell received heavy guns that he had sent for. The town walls had already been breached in several places, houses demolished, thirty of the garrison killed and 120 of Poyer's men were refusing to fight. Poyer and

Laugharne had persuaded the men to go on fighting for another four days until relief arrived. With the big guns in position and no hope of relief, Poyer sent a message to Cromwell asking for terms. Final terms were agreed on 10th July with Cromwell giving the garrison two hours to decide. The castle surrendered on 11th July 1648. When the articles of surrender were studied it was found that neither Poyer nor Laughane had signed.

When the garrison surrendered, Cromwell ordered the defences of the town and castle destroyed and then left immediately for Scotland taking the key prisoners with him. The key prisoners were left at Nottingham and then sent to army headquarters at Windsor. In Pembroke, the garrison soldiers were freed on condition they agreed to submit to the authority of parliament. Most of the officers were ordered to leave the Kingdom within six weeks and not to return within two years. In April 1649 a military court sat for eight days to hear the charges against Poyer, Laugharne and Powell. On 4th April a military court sentenced the three to death. Poyer petitioned the president of the military court about his personal financial sacrifices, his essential loyalty to Parliament and his despair in obtaining his rights against his enemies. He was ignored. The Council of State reduce the death sentence of the three to the death of one man only. A child was appointed to draw the lots and the death paper selected was for Poyer. On 25th April 1646, Colonel John Poyer was driven to Covent Garden market, placed against the wall of Bedford House and executed by firing squad. He is reported to have died bravely.

Major General Laugharne and Colonel Powell received pardons and were set free twelve days later. Both were heavily in debit from costs incurred in the service of Parliament. Laugharne became a member of Parliament for Pembroke boroughs in 1661 and deputy-lieutenant for Pembrokeshire in 1674. But he never received a promised pension before he died. His widow Anne was in dire financial straits in 1677. Poyer's widow was in even greater financial straits. In 1662 she unsuccessfully petitioned that her husband had lost £8,000 and she had lost her estate.

Today, almost 400 years since the Civil War, it requires some thought to understand why three patriots turned against their own side. Poyer, Laugharne and Powell, gave their all to the Parliamentary cause. They fought courageously and were not paid. They exhausted their own funds and borrowed to defend their strongholds and provide the arms and munitions necessary to fight. Their resulting poverty is shown as they were unable to provide for their wives after the war. They were strong and determined leaders. In contrast their numerous Royalist counterparts were only half hearted in their sincerity to their cause and would flee the battlefield at signs of resistance.

It must have been very galling to discover that while they were engaging the enemy on the battlefield, John Eliot and his friends were blackening their reputation in Parliament. The three officers clearly felt that Parliament was no longer supporting them. Poyer refused to surrender without payment of £1000 that he desperately needed as well as back pay for his troops. Without the support of Parliament after the first war, it looked as though they would be disbanded and left powerless and penniless. It seems that like Poyer, all three commanders considered that as long as they did not give up their strongholds of Tenby and Pembroke and retained their forces they were in a strong bargaining position to recover their losses. The three believed the County Committee was acting against them.

It is a great pity the Commons would not pay them what they were owed and thereby forced them into rebellion. It seems the three Parliamentary leaders misjudged the strength of their positions and possibly the damage done to their reputations in Parliament. The confiscation of their estates alone on June 5th ensured their poverty. Their rebellion was judged so serious that Oliver Cromwell and his Ironsides were ordered to ride across the country to defeat them. For further information the reader is referred to Howells (1987 cited below in Mathias, 1987a and b).

Suggested Further Reading

Bowen, L., 2020, John Poyer. *The Civil Wars in Pembrokeshire and the British Revolutions*: West Wales Press Ltd.,

John, T., 2008, *The Civil War in Pembrokeshire*: Logaston Press, 192 p.

Mathias, R., 1987a, Chapter VI. The First Civil War. In: Howells, B, (Ed.), 1987, *Pembrokeshire County History, Vol. III. Early Modern Pembrokeshire 1536-1815*: The Pembrokeshire Historical Society, National Library of Wales, Aberystwyth, p. 159 – 196.

Mathias, R., 1987b, Chapter VII. The second Civil War and Interregnum. In: Howells, B, (Ed.), 1987, *Pembrokeshire County History, Vol. III. Early Modern Pembrokeshire 1536-1815*: The Pembrokeshire Historical Society, National Library of Wales, Aberystwyth, p. 197 – 224.

30. SIR JOHN PERROT AND THE RUINS OF HIS MANOR

On the south side of Haverfordwest are the ruins of Haroldston Manor, once one of Pembrokeshire's finest. The NNW-facing manor was built by the Harold family around 1280 on slightly rising ground in the valley of a tributary of the Cleddau River at the highest navigable point for ships of the time. It was sold to the Perrot family around 1370 and remained in that family until the eighteenth century.

Sir John Perrot was born in Haroldston Manor in November 1528. He was the youngest of three children by Thomas Perrot and his wife Mary. At the time the family were the leading and largest landowners in Pembrokeshire. He became the most well known of the Perrot family and led a colourful life. He was a very large man with a larger than life manner, flamboyant and ambitious. He had great physical strength with a violent disposition and a reputation for brawling. He admitted that he was choleric by nature and would swear too much. He was noted for the 'majesty of his personage' and referred to as 'Good Sir John' by friends. He made a lot of friends and a lot of enemies.

His striking resemblance to King Henry VIII and similar personality gave rise to rumours that he was the illegitimate son of the King. This possibility is based on an account written by Sir Robert Nauton who married Sir John's grand-daughter Penelope. The basis seems to be Sir John's resemblance to King Henry VIII with a large strong physical form, a very strong personality and a bad temper. There is no possibility that his mother had a child by King Henry VIII but the subject was gossiped by his many enemies. There was however a strong similarity between the king and Sir John and in today's terminology they could be said to be 'clones'. At the time of writing in the American elections of 2020, Mr Joe Biden has said of President Trump that he and Mr. Boris Johnson, the Prime Minister of England, are clones. They are unrelated but both are bulky overweight persons with unruly blond hair, brash and with dominating personalities.

Sir John was schooled at St. Davids which then had a protestant bishop (William Barlow). Sir John became strongly protestant and learned several languages including French, Spanish and Italian. At the age of eighteen years he travelled to London and entered a three-year service as a page in the household of Sir William Paulet, Lord Treasurer of England and later the First Marquis of Winchester. From him he learned the social graces, manners and court etiquette and gained an introduction to King Henry VIII. Sir John had taken his first steps for the gentry along the path to wealth and fortune in the sixteenth century that required the favour of the sovereign. Nevertheless his apprenticeship was marked by brawling. King Henry offered him preferment but died before he could grant it. His successor King Edward VI regarded him as a valuable friend.

Sir John received his knighthood in 1547 at the coronation of King Edward VI. Because of his knightly skills at which he excelled, he was in June 1551 attached to the train of William Parr, First Marquis of Northampton to go to France to arrange the marriage of the teenage King to the infant princess Elizabeth of Valois, the daughter of King Henry II of France. Sir John made a friend of King Henry who was impressed with his skill in the hunt. Sir John was a reckless hunter and on one occasion saved the king's life in an encounter with a wounded boar. The king invited him to remain in France, and on Sir John's return to England, King Henry paid his debits. Back in England Sir John became a close friend of King Edward VI, who also paid off debits from Sir John's extravagant lifestyle. Sir John became a man of the king's bedchamber and in 1552 took up the post of High Sheriff of Pembrokeshire.

The arrival of Queen Mary I on the throne (reign 1553-1558) marked a difficult time for Sir John as he was a staunch protestant. Queen Mary reintroduced Roman Catholicism. Over 280 religious opponents were burned at the stake so that she became known as 'Bloody Mary'. Sir John, along with his uncle Robert (Edward VIII's Greek tutor) was accused of sheltering heretics at Haroldston Manor. Sir John was denounced for sheltering heretics by a neighbour Thomas Catherne of Prendergast and he served a short sentence in the Fleet prison. After this Sir John left the country to serve under the Earl of Pembroke in France. He was present at the capture of St. Quentin in 1557. He returned to England shortly before Queen Mary's death. Again he was in conflict with his neighbour Catherne, whom he took into custody after breaking into his house. Again Sir John spent some time in the Fleet prison for his action and was bound over to keep the peace.

On Mary's death, Sir John's fortunes improved. He was favoured by Queen Elizabeth (reign 1558-1603) who reintroduced the Protestant church. Sir John was chosen as one of four men to carry Elizabeth's Canopy of State at her coronation. Queen Elizabeth favoured Sir John with a string of lucrative appointments between 1559 and 1562. These included the stewardship of the manors of Carew, Coedrath and Narberth, the constableship of Narberth and Tenby castles and the jailership of Haverfordwest prison. Sir John was elected mayor of Haverfordwest on three occasions 1560-61, 1570-71 and 1575-76. In 1562 he was made Vice Admiral of the Seas around South Wales. The following year he was returned to parliament as a member for Pembrokeshire.

A commission in 1561 to discover concealed lands formerly belonging to the priory of Haverfordwest, led to legal battles over ownership. It enriched him as Sir John was allowed to keep any disputed land, but he made many enemies. Throughout the 1560s Sir John divided his time between the Royal Court and Pembrokeshire. He acquired a reputation for forceful and sharp business dealings and many envied his access to the Queen. He extensively remodelled Carew Castle, building the superb north range with its great mullioned windows. From Haroldston he is believed to have sponsored piracy and fisheries off Newfoundland. By 1570 Sir John was the most powerful man in Pembrokeshire.

But in 1570, Sir John reluctantly accepted the newly created post of Lord President of Munster in Ireland. The province was in the throws of the Desmond rebellions. These were led by the Earl of Desmond who was head of the FitzGerald dynasty and his followers - the Geraldines - against the extension of Elizabeth's government over the province. In 1571 Sir John landed in Waterford and reduced the province to peace in a violent campaign lasting two and a half years. As the rebel leader James FitzMaurice FitzGerald would not surrender, Sir John on one occasion cut off the heads of fifty rebels that had been slain in a battle and had them mounted on the market cross at Kilmallock. This act contributed to his reputation for rashness and did not meet with approval of all the government.

In 1572 after a second and successful siege of Castlemain – the Geraldine stronghold – FitzMaurice surrendered. Sir John authorised over 800 hangings. His actions were regarded as a success but his requests to be recalled were ignored. Sir John was dissatisfied with the support he was getting from England. He was also in trouble after he seized a Portugese ship the *Peter and Paul* laden with a rich cargo of spices. His actions in Ireland made him many enemies who would conspire against him. Sir John returned to Wales in summer 1573 without permission pleading ill health. On presenting himself in Court, he was permitted to resign his office.

Sir John returned to Haroldston Manor and occupied himself as Vice-Admiral of the Welsh Seas and was active on the Council of Marches. The latter was the regional administrative body for modern Wales and the English counties of Shropshire, Herefordshire, Worcestershire and Gloucestershire. In 1578, his Deputy Admiral accused him of tyranny, subversion of justice and dealing with pirates. Local merchants complained that as Vice-admiral of the Welsh Seas, Sir John was supposed to suppress piracy and smuggling but instead he was heavily involved in smuggling contraband. The tyranny charge was because he controlled local government to his own advantage. But Sir John retained the confidence of Queen Elizabeth 1st and became Commissioner for Piracy. In 1579 he was given command of a naval squadron of five ships and charged with cruising the coasts of Ireland and intercepting any Spanish ships there. The expedition was not very successful as they sighted and captured only one pirate ship.

This support for Sir John may not be too surprising as Queen Elizabeth I encouraged piracy against Spain and her great admirals Sir John Hawkins and his second cousin Sir Francis Drake were both involved in piracy and slavery. Indeed they both died on a joint treasure hunting expedition to the Caribbean that sailed in 1595. This English policy culminated in the Spanish Armada sailing in 1588 with the objective of overthrowing Queen Elizabeth, to protect the Spanish Netherlands and stop attacks by English pirates in the Atlantic and Pacific.

Queen Elizabeth thought highly of Sir John's work in Munster and asked his advice in 1581. She was impressed by his written reply advising on what should be done. In 1584, Sir John was appointed Lord Deputy of Ireland (the Queens representative and head of the Irish Executive) with the task of introducing the Plantation of the Province of Munster. This was a punishment for the Desmond rebellions. The Desmond dynasty had been annihilated and their estates confiscated. The plan was to settle the province with colonists from England and Wales. In addition to the Geraldine estates (in modern Limerick, Cork, Kerry and Tipperary), other lands in SW Cork and Kerry that had belonged to other supporters of the rebellion were to be resettled.

Sir John took with him to Ireland, as a sign of his wealth and power, thirt-four servants all wearing his livery with the family crest of a parrot with a spear in its claw. Before Sir John started work he learned of raids on the northern province of Ulster by Highland Clans. Sir John marched his army beyond the Pale into Ulster which stopped the raids. However Queen Elizabeth was very annoyed at his unadvised actions. In the south the Plantation work did not proceed smoothly as many were opposed to it. He became frustrated with the delays and in 1587 requested to be recalled. He had helped establish peace in Ireland but had at the same time continued to make many enemies. He was recalled in 1588.

Upon his return to England he was at first received with favour and appointed to the Privy Council. However in the political turbulence following the defeat of the Spanish Armada in 1588, his many enemies conspired against him. They were led by the Queen's principal secretary Sir William Cecil, first Baron Burghley. Sir John was accused of high treason: first for using contemptuous words about the queen; second for helping known traitors and Romanish priests; third for encouraging the rebellion in Ireland of Sir Brian O'Rourke; fourth for writing treasonable letters to the King of Spain, the Duke of Parma and the traitor Sir William Stanley. The last accusation was made by Dennis O'Rogham - a former priest and condemned prisoner. The evidence was signed correspondence by Sir John when he was Lord Deputy of Ireland, to King Phillip II of Spain and the Duke of Parma, in which treasonable promises and bargains were made concerning the future of England, Wales and Ireland. An inquiry revealed that O'Rogham was a forger of documents and Sir John was contemptuous about the forgeries.

Sir John's main trouble arose when his former secretary reported his frequent use in private conversation of violent language against the Queen. Sir John was confined to the Tower of London in 1592 and brought to trial on charges of high treason. The forged letters were reviewed and assessed, but it was the evidence of his remarks about Queen Elizabeth that caused the main problem. He was said to have called her 'a base bastard piskitchin woman' and questioned her legitimacy on numerous occasions. Sir Walter Raleigh commented that Sir John's main problem was in his 'words of distain'. Despite protesting his innocence Sir John was found guilty and sentenced to the death of traitors by being hung, drawn and quartered. Sentence was delayed for several months as Queen Elizabeth may have been reluctant to sign the death warrant for a possible half brother but was also reluctant to pardon him. During this interlude Sir John died in the tower of London in September 1592 and is buried in St. Peter's Church there. He was sixty-four years old when he died and had been a prisoner in the tower for eighteen months.

Sir John greatly liked the town of Haverfordwest and in 1580 he gave land and property to form a trust for the poor of Haverfordwest. This trust is still operating and today manages twenty-three properties as well as capital investments.

Sir John married twice. First to Anne Chayney of Kent who bore his heir Thomas, but died in childbirth. The second marriage was to Jane Pruet of Hartland, Devonshire who bore him a son William and two daughters, Anne (married Sir John Phillips) and Lettuce (who married Sir Arthur

Chichester). Sir John also fathered several illegitimate children. Best known was Sir James Perrot (1571-1637) who published a biography of his father (The life, deedes and death of Sir John Perrot, Knight). Less well known are a son, John Perrot, born in 1565 and a daughter Elizabeth.

During his lifetime Sir John remodelled both Carew and Laugharne castles and he also considerably expanded and developed the family home of Haroldston Manor. Two new halls were added, a squared gatehouse and a walled courtyard. In addition the gardens were developed to be the most expensive and beautiful in Tudor Wales as befitted a knight and high-status Elizabethan family. Long raised flower beds ran down to the stream, there was an ornamental pond with a fountain and long elegant vistas.

In the eighteenth century the manor was sold to the Pakington family after which it went into decline. There is a very fine etching of the three story Stewards Tower in the nineteenth century by H. Longueville showing the tower as occupied. This was the last part of the manor to be inhabited and it was abandoned later in the century. It has been in ruins since, with animals grazing and considerable robbing of stone.

Today Haroldston is approached through Merlin's Bridge. At the round-about take the Pembroke Road (signposted Burton, Llangwm, Hook, Freystrop) and pass under the railway bridge. Proceed to St. Issell's Avenue on the left and enter the Council Estate. Follow the road to the edge of the estate with St. Mark's school on the right. The road then becomes a narrow country lane. Follow this for about a kilometre until there is a junction with a cul-de-sac road on the right. At this point the ruins of the gatehouse at the main entrance to Haroldston Manor lie on the left hand side of the road. There are no signs but the ruins of the Steward's Tower and other stone walls can be seen through the gate. The gate is locked but the entrance for the public is a turnstyle a few hundred meters towards Merlin's Bridge.

There is a public footpath through the ruins and the remains of its extensive Elizabethan gardens that leads to a tributary of the River Cleddau. The latter can be crossed on a footbridge and the stream followed until it meets the asphalt road nearer Haverfordwest Priory. Regrettably with time the site has suffered with the railway line from Haverfordwest to Milford Haven crossing part of the gardens and the Haverfordwest sewage works being nearby, so that with some wind directions a visit can be spoiled. In December 2020 the site was despoiled by the presence of numerous beer cans and several old mattresses.

The ruins of Haroldston Manor include the remains of the Steward's Tower, an expansive courtyard and a vaulted range to the west. Haroldston has well preserved garden earthworks which include an 'L' shaped raised walkway just to the south of steward's tower, garden terraces and a sunken garden extending to the north. These gardens are believed to date back to the late sixteenth century. A new survey was made of the gardens by the Royal Commission in 2005/6. Of the manor little remains except a few feet of walls but well preserved are the cellars with a long arched roof. The site is the highest point on the river tributary to which Sir John could bring his small ships to unload.

Carew castle was granted to Sir John by the crown in 1558. There he was responsible for the last major phase of reconstruction. He rebuilt the north side into a series of rooms with vast mullioned windows overlooking the Carew River. It was a time when old fortresses were becoming fashionable residences. After the death of Sir John in the Tower of London in November 1592, the ownership of the castle changed hands several times. The castle played a prominent role in the Civil War. Since then it has gradually declined into a magnificent ruin. In 1983 the castle was leased to the Pembrokeshire Coast National Park for ninety-nine years and is now used for tourist events. Sir John was buried in the grounds of the Tower of London in the church of St. Peter Ad Vincula. It seems likely that the Queen might have pardoned Sir John, as after his death his widow was granted Carew Castle and his son, Sir Thomas, was restored to the family estates. For more information the reader is referred to Turvey (2005).

Suggested Further Reading
Turvey, R., 2005, *The Treason and Trial of Sir John Perrot*: Dinefwr Press, Lanadybie, Wales, 208p. ISBN 0-7083-1912-3.

31. THE PIRATE BLACK BART ROBERTS OF HAVERFORDWEST (1682-1722)

A summary of the early life of this notorious pirate who hailed from Pembrokeshire is given by Fenton (1811). His piratical activities are described by Captain Charles Johnson (1927) - the latter is a pseudonym for the writer Daniel Defoe and some may be fictional. Bartholomew Roberts was born John Roberts in the very small and poor village of Casnewydd Bach or Little New Castle on the river Sealy north of Haverfordwest in 1682. Significantly (in view of his later piratical career) Fenton described the village as 'a mean village consisting of a few straggling houses, and a church of the very meanest fashion'. Its name derives from a motte mound in the middle of the village that distinguishes it from an older earthwork, possibly from the Iron Age. Bartholomew's prospects as a landless peasant were not at all bright and he turned away from the poor village life. Like many in his position he escaped by taking to an adventurous seafaring life at the age of thirteen years.

Captured by a pirate.
Initially he did not choose to become a pirate and lived an honest and hard- working life until he was thirty-seven years old. Then in 1719, he sailed from London as second mate on board the *Princess* - a Guineaman - with Captain Plant. The ship was at Anamaboe, in Guinea, with two other ships (the *Hink* – Captain Hall and the *Morrice* – Captain Fin), trading for slaves, gold and ivory. The Welsh Pirate Howel Davies (Hywel Davis) aboard his recently captured ship renamed the *Rover* with thirty-two big guns and twenty-seven swivel guns arrived and captured them all. The next day Davies sailed south taking all four ships with him.

Roberts joins the pirates.
At first Roberts was reluctant to join the pirates but then he changed his mind. To mark the occasion he changed his name to Bartholomew. His

reasoning for changing is preserved in a statement attributed to him when at the height of his piratical success:

'In an honest service there is thin commons, low wages, and hard labour; in this plenty and satiety, pleasure and ease, liberty and power, and who would not balance creditor on this side, when all the hazard that is run for it, at worst, only a sour look or two at choking. No, a merry life and a short one shall be my motto.'

He would become a highly successful pirate with his own ship and crew capturing at least 470 vessels. He proved a strict and ruthless leader banning gambling and fighting amongst his crew. The name 'Black Bart' was used as the title of a poem written by twentieth century poet I.D. Hooson.

Pirating with Howel Davies.

Two days after leaving Anamaboe, Davies captured a rich Dutch prize. The Governor of Accra was aboard her with his effects, travelling to Holland. £15,000 in money was captured with other valuable merchandise. Davies retained thirty-five men to add to his crew including Roberts and then released the captured ships, their captains and the remainder of their crews. Davies then sailed to the Portugese island of Princes where he hoisted British colors and informed the governor that he was in quest of pirates. He was well received and came to anchor beneath the guns of the fort. The governor offered him anything he needed. Davies replied that the King of England would pay for the items.

Davies and crew spent some time at the island putting their ship in order. Davies then planned to capture the governor and some of his chief men by inviting them aboard ship for entertainment and then to hold them for £40,000 ransom. First he presented the governor with a dozen slaves as a present in return for civilities received. But a Portugese slave swam ashore that night and informed the governor of the plan. Next day Davies and his chief pirates went ashore to escort the governor and his party aboard ship. They were invited to the governor's house to take refreshments before boarding. They walked into an ambush and all except one were shot. Davies was shot through the bowels but arose, pulled out his pistols and fired them before falling dead. Only one man returned to the ship.

Elected leader of the pirates and the attack on Princes Island.

So only six weeks after Roberts was captured, Howel Davies was killed. At a meeting of the crew Roberts was elected as the new captain to replace Davies and the other senior positions were filled. He evidently had skills needed by the crew. He was a senior man with navigational skills and had shown courage in his new piratical career. He was ebullient and enjoyed drinking and music. He boldly persued his victims but was never known to force anyone to join his crew. He would devise his own pirate flag showing the skeleton of a man holding a flaming sword. When elected the crew was angry as Davies had been a popular and successful leader. They wanted immediate revenge.

A party of thirty men led by the bold and daring Mr. Kennedy, were landed and directly attacked the fort under the protective fire of the ships guns. The Portugese immediately abandoned the fort and retreated to the town. The pirates threw the guns of the fort into the sea and fired the fort before retreating back to their ship. But it was not enough. Bartholomew Roberts ordered an attack on the town. The pirates had seized a French ship in the harbour and they now lightened her and took her into the shallows close to the town and battered it with her twelve guns. Several houses were destroyed. Two Portugese ships in the harbour were set afire. The pirates then returned to their own ship and released the French ship and her crew before sailing away.

Bartholomew Roberts continued his success as a pirate when in the next few days he captured a Dutch Guinea Man that he plundered and then released. Two days later he took an English ship (the *Experiment*, Captain Cornet) at Cape Lopez. Her crew joined the pirates and the ship was burned. They then sailed for the Portugese island of St. Thomas, but finding nothing landed at Annabon Island for water and supplies. There they took a vote on whether to sail next for the East Indies or Brazil. The latter was decided upon. Twenty-eight days later they anchored at the uninhabited Brazilian island of Ferdinando where they watered and repaired their ship.

Pirates in Brazil.

The Brazil trip was not a success and after they had cruised the coast for about nine weeks without meeting any sail, they decided to head for the West Indies. But first they stood inshore where unexpectedly off the Bay of Los Todos Santos, they found a fleet of forty-two Portugese ships awaiting the protection of two men-of-war, each with seventy guns. Roberts, without identifying his ship, sailed in amongst the fleet, coming up alongside one of the deepest laden. He ordered the master to come aboard quietly or no quarter would be given. On arrival aboard the *Rover*, Roberts saluted the Master in a friendly fashion and told him they were gentlemen of fortune and required him to identify the richest ship in the fleet. If he directed them correctly he would be returned to his ship unmolested. The Portugese Master then pointed out a ship of fifty guns and a crew of 150 men – a greater force than the *Rover*. They then approached this ship and the captured Master was told to greet them and invite their master aboard the *Rover*. But the plan did not work and so Roberts ordered a broadside fired into the ship. She was then grappled and boarded. The fighting was short with many Portugese and two pirates killed. The alarm was raised in the fleet and Roberts prepared for battle, but the two men-of-war did not respond and the pirates with their captured ship sailed off.

The captured ship proved very rich with a cargo of sugar, skins and tobacco as well as 40,000 moidores of gold, valuable chains and trinkets, and a gold cross set it diamonds for the King of Portugal. The latter was later presented to the Governor of Guiana.

Pirates on the coast of Guiana.

Their next step was to find a safe haven where they might enjoy the pleasures of their ill-gotten gains. They sailed to Devil's Island in the River of Surinam on the coast of Guiana. There they were very well received and were able to make a considerable trade with their treasures and goods with the governor. It was also a place where they could enjoy drinking, dancing and especially the local women who vied for their attention because of the rich rewards made to them by the pirates. It was a great place to trade away their easily-gotten treasures, as well as trade the captured cargoes.

The pirates seized a sloop in the river and learned that a brigantine had sailed with her from Rhode Island laden with provisions for the coast. The pirates were in need of provisions and when the ship was sighted Roberts made a hasty decision that would cost him dear. He put forty men into the sloop and left immediately after the new arrival. But he took no provisions and water expecting a swift capture. He lost sight of her and eight days later found himself thirty leagues to leeward. With the wind and current against him he had no hope of beating back to the *Rover*. So Roberts anchored the sloop and sent her boat away to return to the *Rover* to bring her to the sloop. Meanwhile their need for food and water was dire. In desperation they tore up the floorboards of the cabin to make a raft to go ashore and collect water.

Deserted and the fate of the deserters.

After several days the boat returned with the most unwelcome news that in their absence, the bold Mr. Kennedy who had been left as lieutenant in charge of the *Rover*, had seized command as well as the prize ship and sailed off with them both. With Kennedy in charge most of the crew voted to give up piracy and return home privately as there was no amnesty available to pirates at the time. The captured Portugese ship, that was only half unloaded, was given to the Captain of the captured sloop along with his crew and four slaves. Captain Kennedy then sailed the *Rover* and her crew for Barbados.

Near Barbados they captured a ship from Virginia with Captain Knot who was a Quaker and carried no weapons aboard. Eight of the pirates decided to sail with Captain Knot for Virginia and they presented him with ten chests of sugar, ten rolls of Brazilian tobacco, thirty moidores and some gold dust to a value of about £250. They also gave presents to the crew. In return they travelled as passengers rather than working crew. Captain Knot was not happy that they carried their weapons with them everywhere. On arriving at the coast four of the pirates took a boat and made for Maryland, but were driven to an obscure place by a storm. But they were entertained by local planters. Meanwhile Captain Knot had arrived in North Carolina with the other four pirates. There he informed the Governor about the passengers he had been forced to bring with him. The Governor had all eight pirates arrested, tried and hanged. Captain Knot insisted that he and his crew hand over their gifts received from the pirates.

Meanwhile Captain Kennedy had captured a sloop carrying bread and flour to Boston. Kennedy and those pirates wanting to return home privately went aboard the sloop and departed. The residue who wanted to continue pirating were left aboard the *Rover*. Kennedy was illiterate and there was only one man aboard the sloop who thought he understood navigation. They set course for Ireland but arrived off the north-west coast of Scotland. Not knowing where they were, they abandoned the ship and finding a village claimed to be shipwrecked sailors. They split up and travelled for various destinations but their drunken behaviour and the way they threw their wealth about eventually led to their arrest and execution for piracy. Walter Kennedy was executed at Execution Dock on 19th July 1721. What became of the pirates left aboard the *Rover* is unknown, but they went ashore on one of the West Indian islands. Later the *Rover* was found drifting at sea with only nine slaves aboard. She was taken into St. Christopher. The fate of these men clearly illustrates the role of a capable pirate leader such as Bartholomew Roberts.

Pirates in the West Indies.

Meanwhile Captain Roberts with his forty men lacking provisions and water decided to head for the West Indies. Near Deseada Island they captured two sloops with provisions and other necessities. A few days later they took a brigantine from Rhode Island. They then headed for Barbados. Near the island they captured a Bristol ship with ten guns on her outward voyage. They pillaged her for three days taking clothes, money, twenty-five bales of goods, five barrels of gunpowder, a cable, a hawser, ten casks of oat meal, six casks of beef, several other goods and five men. They then released her and she made for Barbados to inform the Governor of their actions.

The Governor reacted immediately. Not having any men-of-war in Barbados at the time, he fitted out two ships to persue and capture the pirates. One was a Bristol galley with twenty guns and eighty men commanded by Captain Rogers of Bristol. The other was a sloop with ten guns and forty men commanded by Captain Graves of Barbados. Captain Rogers was appointed commodore. They sailed out of the harbour and two days later saw Bartholomew Robert's sloop. Roberts gave chase and the two government ships allowed him to catch up. Roberts, showing his pirate flag, fired a gun, expecting the two ships to haul to, but instead received a broadside. Roberts crowded on all sail and tried to escape. The galley kept up with him for a long time keeping up a constant fire at the pirates. In order to escape, Roberts was forced to lighten his ship by throwing overboard his guns and other heavy goods. From that time onwards he behaved very severely with any captured men from Barbados.

Roberts took the sloop to Dominica where he watered and bartered food for provisions from the local inhabitants. There he found thirteen Englishmen who had been put ashore by a French Guard de la Costa from Martinique. They had been taken out of two New England ships seized as prizes by the French vessel. The men were happy to join the pirates. Somehow word of their presence got back to Martinique where the governor equipped and manned two sloops to go after them. Roberts next took his men to the Grenadines to a bay on Carriacou where they spent a week cleaning the bottom of the ship. Roberts and his men then left suddenly in search of wine and women. They narrowly missed the two French sloops seeking them.

Pirates in Newfoundland.

They sailed for Newfoundland, arriving in June 1720. They entered the harbour of Trepassy with their black pirate colors flying, drums beating and trumpets sounding. There were twenty-two ships in the harbour and their crews immediately deserted them. The pirates had their celebration, but it turned into an orgy of destruction. All the ships were burned or sunk except for one – a Bristol galley. The fisheries and landing stages were also destroyed.

Roberts manned the Bristol galley that he captured in the harbour and fitted her with sixteen guns. He then sailed her out to the Grand Banks, where he found nine or ten French sailing ships. He sank them all except for one of twenty-six guns which he kept for his own use. The Frenchmen were released into the galley that was set free. Roberts christened his new ship The *Fortune*. Then in company with the sloop he set out on another cruise.

It was very successful and they captured five ships: *Richar* of Bideford, Captain Whitfield; the *Willing Maid* of Poole; the *Expectation* of Topsham; and the *Samuel*, Captain Cary of London. The *Samuel* was a very rich ship and was carrying several passengers, who were roughly handled to persuade them to hand over their valuables. The pirates opened the holds and entered them with axes and cutlasses and cut or broke open all the bales, cases and boxes they could find. Items brought onto the deck that were not wanted were thrown overboard. They carried off sails, guns, powder, cordage, £8,000 to £9,000 worth of goods. They were debating whether to burn or sink the *Samuel*, when they saw another ship on the horizon and set off in persuit. They caught her at midnight. She was a snow from Bristol bound for Boston, Captain Bowles. They treated the Captain barbarously because he came from Bristol – the same port as Captain Rogers who had attacked them off Barbados.

Two days later on 16th July, they captured a Virginian ship the *Little York*, Captain James Phillips, and the *Lo* of Liverpool, which they plundered and then released. The next day they captured a snow from Bristol, the *Phoenix*, Captain John Richards. Next was a brigantine, Captain Thomas and a sloop, the *Salisbury*. They took all the men out of the brigantine and sank her.

Return to the West Indies.

As provisions were growing short they left the Banks of Newfoundland and headed for the West Indies. They believed that around Deseada Island they might meet ships. They were out of luck and so headed for St. Christopher for water and provisions. Their requests were denied and so they fired on the town and burned two ships in the road. Next they called at St. Bartholomew. Here their reception was most cordial and they received a handsome treatment and refreshments from the governor. Here they were able to enjoy drinking and dancing and to barter for everything they wanted. They found the ladies of the island were competing to dress and behave attractively for them as the pirates rewarded them well.

Set out for Guinea.

Eventually satisfied with their pleasures and loaded with fresh provisions they voted to go next to Guinea. On route, at around latitude twenty-two degrees north, they met a French ship from Martinique that was richly laden. They thought her more suitable for their purposes and so exchanged ships. Their new ship was named the *Royal Fortune*. They continued their voyage in this ship to Guinea. On route Roberts proposed stopping at Brava, southernmost of the Cape Verde Islands to clean the bottom of the ship. But careless sailing took them too far to leeward to reach either Brava or the Guinea coast. So they decided to sail to the West Indies.

They chose to go to Surinam which was some 700 leagues distant, but where they knew they would be welcomed. But they had only one hogshead of water for the 124 men aboard. The decision caused much hardship. The men were limited to one mouthful of water per day. Some drank their urine or seawater and became hugely thirsty and died. Others pined and wasted away and also died. The crews became very weak. After two days with nothing to drink, they were surprised one night to find the ship in only seven fathoms of water and so anchored. Dawn revealed land from the mast head but very far away. A boat was immediately sent to collect water. It returned that night with a load of water and the information that they were off the mouth of the Marowinje or Maroni River on the coast of Surinam. The decided to water in Tobago.

Return to the West Indies.

They then steered for the latitude of Barbados, in the hope of finding a ship with provisions. Their luck held and they captured a brigantine, the *Greyhound*, of St Christopher's bound for Philadelphia. She provided them with a good supply of liquor and provisions. The mate of the *Greyhound* signed articles with the pirates and would eventually captain one of their ships. There they heard of the Governor of Martinique who had fitted out two ships to hunt them.

They decided to go to Martinique to punish the Governor. When they arrived Roberts hauled up the Jack indicating that he wished to trade. Twenty-one vessels came out to trade. Roberts captured them and ordered them to leave their money with him. He kept one vessel to take the trad-ers back to the shore and burned the rest. Roberts was very angry with the governors of Barbados and Martinique for trying to capture him. He then made a new flag for himself showing himself standing on two skulls with the letters ABH and AMH under them to signify a Barbadian's and a Martiniquan's head.

Roberts now sailed to Dominica where he met a Dutch ship with twen-ty-two guns and seventy-five men. There was a fight and when some of the Dutchmen were killed, they struck their colors. Next captured was a brig-antine from Rhode Island, Captain Norton. Taking the two captured ships with them, they proceeded to Guadeloupe. There they captured a sloop which they burned. They also captured a French flyboat laden with sugar.

Their next port of call was Mona Island in the passage between Hispaniola and Puerto Rico. They were planning to clean the bottom of their ship but found the seas too rough. So they sailed on to the north coast of Hispaniola. They stopped at Bennet's Key in the Gulf of Samana. There they cleaned the bottoms of their ship and the brigantine. While they were working two sloops arrived with Captains Porter and Tuckerman. Both claimed that they had heard of the fame of Roberts and came to learn from him the business of pirating. Roberts was delighted and spent some days and nights carousing with them. He then presented them with powder and arms and sent them off with his best wishes.

When the work on the vessels was finished, they set about carousing as they had captured an abundance of rum and sugar. But not everyone joined in the merriment. Harry Glasby who had been chosen as master of the *Royal Fortune* had at Mona departed with two others without making goodbyes. They were regarded as deserters and a detachment of men was sent to find them. All three were brought back the next day. It was decided to put them on trial. It was held in the steerage of the ship. A large bowl of rum punch, pipes and tobacco were provided. After the trial Glasby was released but the other two were tied to the mast and then shot. Next they manned Captain Norton's brigantine. Captain Norton and others were sent away in the captured Dutch ship.

They now had two additional ships, the *Royal Fortune* and the brigan-tine that they named the *Good Fortune*. They then sailed to the latitude of Deseada Island looking for ships to supplement their provisions that were again running low. They were fortunate to capture a richly-laden ship with Captain Hingstone bound for Jamaica. They took the ship to Barbuda where she was plundered.

Mutiny on route to Guinea.

Their next decision was to return to the coast of Guinea to purchase gold dust very cheaply. On route they captured many ships of all nations. They burned some and sank others, according to what they thought of the carriage and character of the ships captains.

They stopped at one of the islands and a party was sent ashore for water. On board Captain Roberts was insulted by a drunken crewman. He killed him on the spot. This angered some of the crew, in particular a Mr Jones, who had been absent in the watering party. On return he cursed Roberts, who ran him through with a sword. But Jones, despite his wound seized Roberts, threw him over a gun and beat him thoroughly. The dispute was settled by the quartermaster but there as a great resentment against Roberts by many of the crew. The unfortunate Jones, when he recovered from his wound was sentenced to two lashes from everyone aboard.

This event caused problems for Captain Roberts with an ill disciplined and drunken crew. He introduced stern measures and offered to go ashore with any man who disputed his orders, as he was not afraid of any of them and would settle any dispute by sword or pistol. When the two ships were about 400 leagues from the coast of Africa, on a dark night, the brigantine with about seventy men on board who disliked Roberts, slipped away and disappeared. Roberts decided to continue with the original plan.

Pirates on the African coast.

Roberts arrived at the Senegal River in late June 1721. It was a river with a major gum trade that was defended by two French cruisers, one with ten guns and sixty-five men and the other with sixteen guns and seventy-five men. On sighting Roberts the two French ships attacked. But when Roberts ran up the pirate flag, the two vessels surrendered immediately. The pirates took the two prizes into Sierra Leone. One prize became their consort and was renamed the *Ranger*, and the other became their store ship. The Sierra Leone River has a wide mouth with many sheltered bays on the north side suitable for wooding, watering and cleaning the bottoms of ships. Thirty Englishmen – former pirates – had settled in the bays as traders and made the pirates most welcome. One former pirate known as Crackers kept the best house in the place with three guns at his door to salute the arrival of pirates. Many trading ships from Bristol arrived here to trade beer, cider and liquor for slaves and ivory. The pirates remained here for six weeks repairing and cleaning their ships and carousing.

In early August they departed and made their way south along the coast to Jaquin. On route they captured and plundered many ships. From Jaquin they sailed on to Old Calabar arriving in October. It was a safe harbour and they cleaned the bottoms of the ships. They also divided up the spoils of their captures and drank heavily. While there they captured two or three Bristol ships. However the natives on learning that they were pirates refused to trade with them. So the pirates landed a party of forty men to attack. About 2,000 African men met them, but when the pirates fired their first shots the Africans retreated. The pirates burned the town. With no local trading, the pirates moved next to Cape Lopez and watered and then went on to Annabona for provisions. They then sailed out on what would be their last voyage.

The Last Voyage of Bartholomew Roberts.

In early January near Cape Lahou they captured two vessels of the Royal African Company. The *King Solomon* was captured by a boatload of twenty pirates. As the boat approached the ship her Captain Trahern fired a musket at them and they replied with a volley. The Captain called on his men to fight the pirates who were only half their number, but the boatswain, Mr. Philips, surrendered the crew. The ships were brought together and the *King Solomon* pillaged with much of her cargo thrown into the sea. The second ship captured that day was the *Flushing*, a Dutch ship. She was pillaged and robbed of her masts, yards and stores. The pirates then headed for Whydah, where the Portugese made their purchases with gold. On route they took several more ships.

At Whydah they found eleven sail in the road – English, French and Portugese. Three French ships each had crews of 100 men and thirty guns. But when they saw the pirate flag they all surrendered probably because most of their crews were ashore. Ten of the captured ships were each ransomed for eight pounds of gold dust. Some ships requested receipts for the payments and were given them by the pirates. One ship was not ransomed. She was the *Porcupine*, Captain Fletcher. She had almost completed loading her cargo of slaves. Her Captain refused to pay the ransom. So Roberts sent boats to unload the slaves before burning her. But the pirates in haste found the unshackling and moving the slaves a slow job, taking much labour. So they fired the ship with eighty slaves still chained, leaving them to either burn or jump into the sea where they were consumed by sharks.

In June 1721 Roberts learned that two men-of-war of fifty guns each – the *Swallow* and the *Weymouth* had left the Sierra Leone River on May 28th. They were seeking Bartholomew Roberts and his pirates to destroy them. The two ships spent from July 28th to September 20th at Port of Prince cleaning their bottoms. During their stay their crews were attacked by an illness and ten men died. The survivors were weak and sickly. *Weymouth* was in the worst condition and she was left on November 10th under the guns of Cape Corso with her crew unable to work ship. Captain Ogle in *Swallow* proceeded to sea, where the Trade Winds revived the sickly crew. She met ships that had seen Roberts and his pirates. They also received a letter informing them that the pirates were at Jaquin. They arrived there on the morning of January 16th but missed the pirates and continued searching the coast.

Finally on 5th February they found three ships anchored in Cape Lopez Bay. It was Roberts and his fleet. Roberts ordered *Ranger* to persue and capture *Swallow*, believing her to be a Portugese ship. The ships met and battle ensued. *Ranger* had thirty-two guns, and a crew of seventy-seven English men, sixteen French men and twenty African men. After two hours of fighting the main topmast of *Ranger* fell and with ten men killed and twenty wounded, *Ranger* surrendered. There were no casualties aboard the King's ship. As a boat from *Swallow* approached *Ranger* some of her crew attempted to blow her up by firing a pistol into barrels of gunpowder. But there was insufficient powder to destroy the ship although several pirates were badly burned in the explosion. It was found that *Ranger* was commanded by a Welshman - Mr. James Skyrm - who had lost a leg in the action.

Captain Ogle did not want large numbers of captured and wounded pirates aboard his ship. So he spent two days alongside the badly-damaged pirate ship making repairs. He then sent her with the prisoners in pinions and shackles with a crew of French men and four of his own men to Princes. He then set out in search of Rogers and the *Royal Fortune*. The two ships sighted each other on the morning of 10th February 1722. *Royal Fortune* was at anchor in a strait as *Swallow* approached. It was not a good meeting for Roberts as most of his crew were drunk and unfit for service. Roberts slipped his anchor. He determined to sail out close to *Swallow* and accept her broadside in order to escape the land. If he failed he would run his ship ashore, so the crew could escape on land.

Roberts was at the peak of his career as a pirate. He as a tall strong man of forty years age of proven courage and leadership, but a heavy drinker. On this, his last day, he was dressed in all his finery, a rich crimson damask waistcoat and breeches, with a red feather in his hat. Around his neck he wore a long gold chain with a diamond studded cross probably made for the King of Spain. He had his sword in hand and two pairs of pistols hanging on a silk sling hung over his shoulders. He was a colorful leader who gave his orders with boldness and spirit. He looked rather like one of the great Norman lords or earls who had seized the land in Wales and reduced the population to taxpaying landless peasants. He had escaped the poverty of his birth.

They passed *Swallow* but a change of wind or an error by the helmsman caused the pirate ship to be taken aback and her sails spilled the wind. *Swallow* was able to come about and overtake for a second broadside. Roberts was heavily hit in the throat by a piece of grapeshot. He sat down abruptly on the tackles of a gun. The helmsman ran to assist him, not realising he was wounded, but found him already dead. Some crew gathered and, as he had instructed them, they picked up his body and with all his fine clothing, jewellery and arms, they threw his body overboard. His merry pirate life had been a short one of only three years.

Without Roberts the crew lost the will to fight. The maintop of the *Royal Fortune* was shot away soon afterwards and the pirates surrendered. *Swallow* held off but sent her boat to collect prisoners, as it was feared the pirates might blow up the ship. *Royal Fortune* was found to have a crew of 157 men of which forty-five were Africans. Only three men were killed aboard the pirate ship and none aboard the King's ship. £2,000 in gold dust was found aboard her. The pirate flag showing the skeleton of a man holding a flaming sword in hand was recovered from the fallen mast.

Captain Ogle took the *Swallow* into Cape Lopez Bay, where he found the *Ranger* had been looted with £2000 in gold dust and other things taken as well. It was believed to have been taken by Captain Hill of the *Neptune* because the gold dust was later handed in at Barbados. The pirates were tried in Cape Corso Castle. Details of the trials and the names of the pirates are given by Johnson (1927). Seventy-four were aquitted. Fifty-two were executed outside the castle. Twenty prisoners were sentenced to seven years indentured service for the Royal African Company in all parts of Africa. Thirteen men had been killed in the two actions. Seventy-six captured African men serving aboard the two pirate ships were not tried, being regarded as unpaid slaves. Captain Chalenor Ogle of the *Swallow* was knighted for his services – the only man ever knighted for action against pirates.

Suggested Further Reading

Fenton, R., 1911, *A historical tour through Pembrokeshire*: Reprinted 2018, Herd Press, 818 p.

Johnson, C. Captain, (Daniel Defoe), 1927, *A General History of Pirates*: T. Warner, London, 180 p.

32. ADMIRAL LORD NELSON – A VISIT AND A BETRAYAL

The town of Milford Haven has an interesting connection with the Most Noble Lord Horatio Nelson, Viscount and Baron Nelson, of the Nile and Burnham Thorpe in the County of Norfolk, Baron Nelson of the Nile and of Hilborough in the said County, Knight of the Most Honourable Order of the Bath, Vice Admiral of the White Squadron of the Fleet, Commander in Chief of his Majesty's Ships and Vessels in the Mediterranean, Duke of Bronte in the Kingdom of Sicily, Knight Grand Cross of the Sicilian Order of St. Ferdinand and of Merit, Member of the Ottoman Order of the Crescent, and Knight Grand Commander of the Order of St. Joachim. He was also the hero of the American Revolutionary War Battle of Fort San Juan (1780) and the Fall of Grand Turk (1783), hero of the French Revolutionary Wars at the battles of Cape St. Vincent (1797), an attack on Cadiz (1797), Santa Cruz de Tenerife (1797), The Nile (1798), Copenhagen (1801) and the Raid on Boulogne (1801), and is best remembered for his heroic death during the Napoleonic Wars at the Battle of Trafalgar (1805). Two of many memorials to him are Nelson's Column in Trafalgar Square and the preservation in Portsmouth of HMS *Victory* – his flagship at the Battle of Trafalgar.

The link with Pembrokeshire came about because of his somewhat infamous relationship with Sir William Hamilton and his second wife Lady Emma Hamilton. Sir William had inherited land in Pembrokeshire including the site of the modern town of Milford Haven from his first wife Catherine Barlow of Slebech, who died in 1782. Sir William planned the development of the town of Milford Haven with its great natural harbour, today known as the Milford Haven Waterway. Sir William's agent in the area was his nephew Charles Francis Greville who brought the Nantuckett whalers as the first settlers to Milford Haven in the mid 1790s.

Lady Hamilton was born Amy Lyon in Cheshire and was the daughter of a blacksmith who died when she was two months old. She started work at the age of twelve years as a maid and became a model and dancer at the 'Temple of Health'. At the age of fifteen years she was hired for several months as a hostess and entertainer at Sir Harry Featherstonhaugh's country estate in the South Downs, where she became his mistress and conceived a child by him. Emma next became mistress to Charles Francis Greville (nephew to Sir William Hamilton) and at his request changed her name to Emma Hart. When Greville decided to marry for money, he sent Emma to Naples to his uncle Sir William where she became his mistress. It was a great shock to Greville when Sir William in 1791 at the age of sixty married her as she was twenty-six.

Lord Nelson's association with the Hamiltons really began in 1798, when at the age of forty years, Rear Admiral Lord Nelson of the Nile had what some people regard as a mid-life crisis. Others said that the wound he incurred to his forehead at the Battle of the Nile damaged the frontal lobes of his brain and created a psychological imbalance resulting in his loss of judgement and inhibitions. A more ordinary explanation is that in spite of being married, he fell head over heels in love with Lady Emma Hamilton, second wife of Sir William Hamilton, and this became the great romance that lasted for the rest of his life.

He had been at sea for six months and had sought the French fleet around the Mediterranean and found it in Aboukir Bay in Egypt and destroyed it between 1st and 3rd August 1798. During the battle he was struck on the forehead by a fragment of shot. A flap of skin and blood blinded his good eye and he thought he was dying and insisted on being remembered to his wife Fanny. He arrived in Naples intending only to get his battle damaged ship '*Vanguard*' repaired. The less damaged ships went further to Gibraltar. He had informed his Commander in Chief, John Jervis, Earl of St. Vincent that 'Nothing shall induce me to send the squadron to Naples, whilst our operations lie on the eastern side of Sicily; we should be ruined by affection and kindness'.

But in Naples he was received as a great hero, met by King Ferdinand of Naples and was hosted by Sir William Hamilton, the British Consul, and his second wife Lady Emma Hamilton. Lord Nelson was not in good health on his arrival having lost an arm, most of his teeth and suffered coughing spells. On meeting the hero, Lady Hamilton is reported to have flung herself on him and fainted. He was taken to the Hamilton home – the Palazzi Sessa – where Lady Hamilton nursed him.

The Hamiltons arranged a great party to celebrate his fortieth birthday, where his name and 'The Victory of the Nile' were picked out in three thousand lights. The entire dinner service was marked 'H.N. Glorious 1st August'. Eighty people dined, followed by seven hundred guests for supper and finally a ball with 1,740 guests. Nelson was accompanied by his stepson

Captain Josiah Nisbet (from an earlier marriage of his wife Fanny). Josiah became very drunk and was heard saying that Nelson was behaving towards Lady Emma as he should be behaving towards his mother.

Nelson then stayed on and moved in as a guest of the Hamiltons and accepted the position of military advisor to the court of Naples - an about face that did not contradict his orders to protect the coasts and island and prevent communication between France and Egypt. Nelson wrote praising Lady Hamilton to his increasingly estranged wife Lady Fanny Nelson. There followed two years of what was regarded as sheer folly. General Sir John Moore in summer 1800 wrote in his diary 'Sir William and Lady Hamilton were there attending the Queen of Naples. Lord Nelson was there, attending upon Lady Hamilton. He is covered with stars, ribbons and medals, more like a Prince of the Opera than the Conqueror of the Nile. It is really melancholy to see a brave and good man, who has deserved well of his country, cutting so pitiful a figure'. However Nelson and Lady Hamilton were in love and the aging Sir William Hamilton did not interfere and greatly admired Nelson whom he regarded as a friend.

Following turbulent times, Sir William Hamilton was recalled to England and Lord Nelson and the Hamiltons took the longest possible overland route back via Central Europe. They left on 13th July and arrived back in England on 6th November. They arrived in 1800 to a hero's welcome. It was at this time that Lord Nelson's wife Fanny Nelson met Lady Hamilton for the first time. Observers noted that Lord Nelson was cold and distant to his wife and paid much attention to Lady Hamilton (who was then pregnant with their child Horatia to be born 29th January 1801 at Sir William's rented home in London). Fanny Nelson gave her husband an ultimatum to choose between herself or Lady Hamilton. It was the end of their relationship.

Shortly afterwards Lord Nelson was back at sea and engaged in the Battle of Copenhagen in April 1801, to be followed by defence work in the English Channel. In October 1801 peace was signed with France and Lord Nelson retired to England in poor health to live as a guest with the Hamiltons. In summer 1802, the three set out on what became the Grand Tour travelling through Birmingham, Warwick, Gloucester, Swansea, Monmouth and on to William Hamilton's new town and port of Milford Haven.

In Autumn 1802 Nelson bought Merton Place – a house on the outskirts of modern day Wimbledon. There he lived openly with Emma, Sir William and Emma's mother in a 'ménage a trios' that fascinated and scandalised the British public. It was widely reported in the newspapers and became a very public affair and the biggest scandal of the age.

Charles Francis Greville invited Sir William Hamilton to inspect progress on Sir William's project on the former Barlow land of the then fledgling town and port of Milford Haven. The Hamiltons, Lord Nelson with Dr. Nelson (Lord Nelson's brother who was a doctor of Divinity) and his wife left Merton Place on 20th July 1802 to travel there. The party travelled first to Oxford where at the University Lord Nelson and his brother were awarded honoray L.L.D. degrees. The mayor presented Lord Nelson with a gold box containing the freedom of the city. The party then continued to Gloucester, Ross-on-Wye and Monmouth. Everywhere Lord Nelson was greeted by cheering crowds but sometimes things were spoiled for him by ribald remarks about his relationship with Lady Hamilton. At Monmouth the party approached from the north travelling by boat down the River Wye. There the corporation wanted them to stay longer so Nelson promisd to call again on the return trip.

Then it was on by coach to Brecon and another enthusiastic celebration. Nelson was taken to see the iron works at Merthyr Tydfil. Then on to more enthusiastic welcomes at Aberavon and Carmarthen. The party arrived in Pembrokeshire on July 31st, in time to celebrate the anniversary of the Battle of the Nile on 1st August.

The Hamilton party spent a week in Milford. The purpose of the visit was to publicise Sir William Hamilton's investment in the formation of the town and to attract investment. Charles Greville met the pary and hoped to gain further government money to invest in shipbuilding there. The party toured the new town of Milford, attended a fair, a cattle show and a regatta. Lord Nelson visited the Milford dockyard where three warships were under construction. The biggest one was the seventy-four-gun third rate HMS *Milford*

The party stayed at the New Inn in Milford Haven which had been completed in 1800. There Greville threw a banquet for the Hamilton party. The banquet was attended by local dignitaries including the Quaker whaling families who noted that Emma Hamilton cut up the meat for Lord Nelson. They disapproved of her unconcealed devotion to him in the presence of her husband who was in poor health. Lord Nelson gave a speech and it is possible today to go to the former New Inn, now the Lord Nelson Hotel, and order a meal and a drink and to mull over his banquet speech.

He began by praising Captain (later Admiral Sir) Tom Foley who was present. The captain was born in Narberth, Pembrokeshire. He had commanded HMS *Goliath* as the lead ship of Nelson's squadron at the Battle of the Nile. He had also captained HMS *Elephant* at the Battle of Copenhagen. Nelson would offer him the position of Captain of the Fleet prior to the Battle of Trafalger, but Captain Foley would turn it down because of ill health. Captain (later Vice Admiral Sir) Thomas Masterman Hardy took the position instead. The Hamilton party stayed at Foley House in Haverfordwest that was the home of Thomas's brother Richard.

Nelson went on to praise the advantages of the new town and its magnificent harbour. Its position on the west coast of Britain could cut as much as thirty hours off the sailing time to New York compared to London. Next he talked of the daily packets that sailed to Ireland and the importance of the new Customs House to this and other shipping trade. He reported how the Nantuckett Whalers, just settled in the new town, had already sent eight whaling ships to the Southern Ocean and had already established the port in this trade. He complimented the government decision to build ships at Milford on the waterway. He credited Monsieur Barrallier (the French engineer who was responsible for the ship building and whom he had previously met in the Mediterranean) for the quality of the ships. He expanded the idea that Milford was the best seaport for commerce on the west coast of Britain.

Finally Nelson concluded that the Milford Haven Waterway and that at Trincomalee in Ceylon were the two finest harbours that he had ever seen. At the request of Sir William Hamilton and Richard Greville, Nelson included a plea to the government for help with funding the dockyard project, that fell on deaf ears. A government dockyard at Milford was finally approved in 1809, but was moved to Pembroke in 1813.

Sir William Hamilton then presented the hotel with a portrait of Lord Nelson painted by Leonardo Guzzardi (it was later presented to Admiralty House in London by Sir Francis Greville). Lord Nelson then inscribed his name on one of the windows. The name of the inn was immediately changed to 'The Lord Nelson' and it remains intact and little changed on what was the Front Street of Milford Haven, that is now known as Hamilton Terrace.

There followed several days of touring Pembrokeshire and as on all the Grand Tour, the naval hero received great ovations. Greville also arranged a visit to a fair, a cattle show and a regatta for the Hamilton Party. On the 8th August the party toured Haverfordwest. The horses were taken away from their carriage that was drawn though the streets by a cheering population. They were led by the band of the Pembroke Militia and a troop of the Haverfordwest cavalry and the banners and flags of local companies and societies. They attended an open breakfast at Foley House (home of Richard, brother of Captain Tom Foley, who was a Haverfordwest Attorney). There the mayor of the town, Mr R.B. Prust and ten members of the corporation, presened Lord Nelson and Captain Tom Foley with the freedom of the ancient town and port. Lady Hamilton sang 'Rule Britannia' from an open window for the crowd. The party next visited Lord Kensington. They were then escorted out of the town by thousands of cheering spectators on their way to Picton Castle – the seat of Lord Milford.

The party also went as guests of Lord Cawdor at Stackpole Court. There Lord Nelson and Lord Cawdor talked for several hours about the French invasion at Fishguard some five years earlier. Jemima Nicholas who had rounded up French soldiers with her pitchfork was of interest.

The grand tour proved a strain for the ailing Sir William who died the following April (1803) and, as requested in his will, he was buried in Slebech in Pembrokeshire alongside his first wife. He left his wife Emma an annuity of £800. Soon afterwards Nelson returned to sea leaving Emma pregnant with their second child (a daughter who died a few weeks after her birth in 1804). Nelson was appointed commander-in-chief of the Mediterranean Fleet with HMS *Victory* as his flagship. He boarded her in Portsmouth and then joined the blockade of Toulon in January 1803, where he spent the next year and a half. On 23rd April 1804 he was promoted to Vice Admiral of the White while still at sea. He finally returned to Merton Place, Emma and Horatia in August 1805 but was recalled to sea only three weeks later. On 21st October 1805 Lord Nelson led the Mediterranean fleet of twenty-seven shps of the line to defeat a joint Franco-Spanish fleet at the Battle of Trafalgar.

Nelson had prepared his will before the battle. He had provided for his wife Fanny and his relatives. He had put £4000 in trust for Horatia. For Emma there was only Merton where she could not afford to live alone. Further, as she was not related nor married to him she would not benefit from any pensions, prize monies or awards if he was killed. He therefore added a Last Codicil to his will. He bequeathed Emma and Horatia 'as a legacy to my King and Country, that they will give her ample provision to maintain her rank in life'. He also requested that 'my adopted daughter, Horatia Nelson Thompson, would use only the name 'Nelson' in future'.

The letters of Lord Nelson, Sir William Hamilton, Lady Hamilton and Nelson's wife Lady Nelson have emerged over time and been published. In particular the work of Czisnick (2020) provides great insights into the relationships and infatuation of Nelson. This rare and expensive book is available on the internet though the Gutenberg Project. Nelson's affection for Lady Emma and their daughter Horatia is recorded in his last three letters to them written in September and October 1805, and found in his cabin after the battle of Trafalgar.

'To Lady Hamilton

Victory, September 25th 1802, off Lisbon

I am anxious to join the fleet for it would add to my grief if any other man was to give them the Nelson howl, which We say is warranted never to fail. I have read, my Emma, with much interest your letters which I got at Merton, but I must have many others afloat. I do feel by myself what you must have felt at not hearing from me from Jan 29 to after May 18th. I fancied that they had been stopped by Sir John's orders......I mention all the circumstances that my dearest Emma should not think that her Nelson neglects or forgets her for one moment. No, I can truly say, you are always present whereso ere I go. I have this letter ready in case I should fall in with anything from Lisbon homewards steering. May God bless you my best, my only beloved, & with my warmest affections to Horatia, be assured I am for ever your most faithful and affectionate.'

'To Lady Hamilton

Victory, October 19th, 1805, Noon, Cadiz, E.S.E., 16 leagues

My dearest beloved Emma, the dear friend of my bosom. The signal has been made that the Enemy's Combined Fleet are coming out of Port. We have very little wind, so that I have no hopes of seeing them before tomorrow. May the God of Battles crown my endeavours with success; at all events, I will take care that my name shall ever be dear to you and Horatia, both of whom I love as much as my own life. And as my last writing before the Battle will be to you, so I hope in God that I shall live to finish my letter after the Battle. May Heaven bless your prayers ......'

'To Miss Horatia Nelson Thompson

Victory, October 19th, 1805

My dearest Angel, I was made happy by the pleasure of receiving your letter of September 19th, and I rejoice to hear that you are so good a girl, and love my dear Lady Hamilton, who most dearly loves you. Give her a kiss for me. The Combined Fleets of the Enemy are now reported to be coming out of Cadiz; and therefore I answer your letter, my dearest Horatia, to mark to you that you are ever uppermost in my thoughts. I shall be sure of your prayers for my safety, conquest, and speedy return to dear Merton, and our dearest good Lady Hamilton.

Be a good girl, mind what Miss Connor says to you. Receive my dearest Horatia, the affectionate parental blessing of your Father,'

Lord Nelson was fatally wounded during the battle. He lived for about three hours before he died remaining coherent throughout. He died from blood loss into his chest cavity and a severed spine. The ships surgeon William Beatty had to tell him there was nothing anybody could do for him. Nelson enquired how the battle was going and was told by his Flag Captain (later Vice Admiral Sir) Thomas Masterman Hardy that fourteen or fifteen ships had surrendered. Nelson replied that he had expected twenty. He then told Hardy that he was dying but expected to live another half hour. He was in pain and unable to move. According to contemporary accounts his last words to Captain Hardy were 'Take care of my dear Lady Hamilton, Hardy, Take care of poor Lady Hamilton'. He paused and said faintly 'Kiss me Hardy'. Nelson then said 'Now I am satisfied. Thank God I have done my duty'. Hardy then left to go on deck. Nelson spoke once more to the ships chaplain the Reverend Alexander Scott 'Doctor I have not been a great sinner .... Remember, I leave Lady Hamilton and my daughter as a legacy to my country'. It was the first time he had referred to Horatia as his daughter. Shortly afterwards he quietly died.

The information of Nelson's final thoughts of Lady Hamilton and his daughter Horatia, were not desired in England as they did not fit the heroic image. Although Nelson had appointed the Reverend Alexander Scott to be his 'private confidential secretary' because of his skills with several languages, after Trafalgar the Admiralty gave Scott a cold shoulder. Captain Hardy did not release his information until two years after the death of Nelson.

Emma on learning the news was inconsolable. Despite the great jubilation of the British public at the great victory and the hundred years of peace it would bring, the British government did not respect Nelson's will nor his dying wishes regarding a pension of public monies for his mistress Emma and his illegitimate daughter Horatia. They received nothing. Nor was Emma permitted to attend his funeral. But the government did shower considerable wealth on Nelson's family. Nelson's sisters were granted £15,000 each, his wife Fanny was given a pension of £2,000 annually. Nelson's brother William was given an annual pension of £5,000 plus £99,000 to purchase a suitable estate and other honors. Because Lord Nelson died apparently without legitimate issue, his viscountcy and his barony created in 1798 both 'of the Nile' and of 'Burnham Thorpe in the County of Norfolk' became extinct upon his death. But the barony created in 1801 'of the Nile and of Hilborough in the County of Norfolk', passed to Lord Nelson's brother, the Reverend William Nelson. The latter was also created Earl Nelson, and Viscount Merton of Trafalgar and Merton in the County of Surry in recognition of his brothers services, and he also inherited the Dukedom of Bronte.

Without any male protector, Lady Hamilton was losing her looks and had become fat. By 1812 she had sold Merton and was very heavily in debit. In 1812 and 1813 she was arrested for her debits. From prison she wrote to the Prince Regent for help, knowing he was a supporter of Nelson. Most unfortunately at that critical time her letters from Lord Nelson were stolen and published. Nelson had indiscreetly written in them his fears for Emma of the lecherous attentions of the Prince Regent. For example he wrote that the Prince Regent was 'dotingly fond of such women as yourself, and is without a spark of honor in these respects'. The letters were widely read and some believed Emma had sold them for money. Any royal help vanished.

On release from King's Bench Prison, with help she fled from her creditors to Calais with Horatia, where she died in poverty in January 1815 a few months before her fiftieth birthday. Lloyd's agent in Calais paid for her funeral and whisked the thirteen-year-old Horatia back to England, before she could be held for her mother's debits. There Horatia lived with Lord Nelson's sisters. At twenty-one she married her neighbour, the Reverend Philip Ward, and they had eight children. The daughter of Britain's two greatest eighteenth century celebrities lived out her life as a quiet clergyman's wife in rural Norfolk

A check with the Lord Nelson hotel in Milford Haven today revealed that the glass with Nelsons signature, and some letters of Lady Hamilton, had long ago been stolen. Another check revealed that Lord Nelson's nephew had presented St. Katherine's Church in Milford Haven with the truck of the mainmast (a large circular disc of wood that capped the mainmast) of *L'Orient* – the vast French ship that blew up at Aboukir Bay in the Battle of the Nile. The truck was described there by Richard Fenton (1811). However it was later deemed as not appropriate for a church and was passed on to Admiralty Offices in Whitehall.

Suggested Further Reading
Anonymous, 1865, Article on the Nelson visit to Pembrokeshire: *The Welsman*, 24th March 1865, p.3 (Archives, National Library of Wales).

Anonymous, 1896, Note on Nelon's visit to Haverfrdwest: *South Wales Echo*, 22nd October 1896, p.3 (Archives, National Library Wales).

Anonymous. 1904, Article on Nelson and Lady Hamilton, *Evening Express,* p. 3 (Archives, National Library of Wales).

Czisnick, M. (Ed.), 2020, *Nelson's Letters to Lady Hamilton and Related Documents*: Navy Records Society Publications, 660 p. (Available through the Gutenberg Project).

Hibbert, C., 1994, *Nelson – A Personal History*: Viking Penguin Books, London, 472 p.

Knight, R., 2005, *The Pursuit of Victory: the Life and Achievements of Horatio Nelson*: Penguin Books Ltd., The Strand, London, 874 p. ISBN 0-713-99619-0

McKay, K.D., 1989, *A Vision of Greatness – The History of Milford Haven 1790–1990*: Bruce Harvan Associates, Haverfordwest, Dyfed, 397 p.

33. THE NANTUCKETT WHALERS OF MILFORD HAVEN

A colony of American Quakers came with their whaling ships from Nantuckett Island in the USA in 1792 to Milford Haven. They founded a Southern Ocean whaling industry in south-west Wales to provide oil for the street lights of London. This was the result of a surprising chain of events. It began in 1536 during the dissolution of the monasteries by King Henry VIII when brothers Richard and Thomas Barlow (brothers of Richard Barlow appointed Protestant Bishop of St David's) purchased from King Henry VIII the Hospitallier Commandery of Slebech, Pill Priory and Haverfordwest priory with their extensive lands. The lands of Pill Priory, including the future site of Milford Haven, were inherited by Sir William Hamilton on the death of his first wife Catherine Barlow of Slebech in 1782.

The next step was a critical visit in 1784 when Sir William as lord of the manors of Hubberston and Pill, and proprietor of several large farms near Hubberston met on site with his nephew the Right Hon. Charles Greville. Sir William first realized the potential of the lands of Pill Priory on the north shores of the sheltered Milford Haven Waterway as a site suitable for trading with Ireland (only 80 miles away across the Irish Sea) and America. An application was made to parliament to set up a commercial town that might also support the Royal Navy. In 1790 an act was passed enabling Sir William Hamilton and his heirs to build quays, docks, roads and establish markets and set up a mail service between Milford Haven and Waterford in Ireland. The appointment of Sir William as 'Envoy extraordinary to the Court of Naples' kept him away from Wales, so the management and development were placed entirely in the hands of Richard Greville who acted as his agent.

Greville needed hard-working, enterprising people capable of developing commerce and industry to establish the new town and port. One of his initiatives was to invite a group of American whalers to operate from the new town. These people were Quakers whose ancestors had emigrated to America a century before and settled on the island of Nantuckett where they established a successful whaling industry based on the Southern Ocean. Following the American War of Independence (in which Nantuckett remained neutral) there was poverty in Nantuckett and high import taxes placed on whale oil and spermacetti candles by the British government.

Greville invited American Quaker families to establish a whaling fleet at Milford Haven and government permission was obtained to establish twenty-five families, thirteen ships and 182 sailors. The first fifty settlers arrived in 1792 in five whaling ships from Nantuckett. The first whalers who arrived with their families were Samuel Starbuck, Daniel Starbuck, Samuel Starbuck Junior, Timothy Folger, Timothy Folger Junior, Samuel Barnabus Swain, Peter May, David Grieve, Benjamin F. Folger, David Coleman, Johnathen Paddock, Nathanial Macy, Uriel Bunker, Frederick Coffin, and James Gwinn. Another key person was Benjamin Rotch who arrived in 1794 from Dunkirk. They were all Quakers and soon built large homes and established a Southern Ocean whaling trade with twenty ships making voyages to Africa, America, Australia, the South Atlantic, the South Seas, New Zealand and the Galapagos Islands. There was a good market for whale oil in London for the street lighting, lamps and candle making.

In addition to their whaling achievements, the American families established other businesses in Milford Haven. Daniel Starbuck opened a shop while his son Gayer managed a brewery at Priory Lodge. Benjamin Rotch's son Francis together with Samuel Starbuck Junior and John Phillips of Haverfordwest founded the first bank in Milford Haven. Samuel Starbuck Junior also became a miller and baker and introduced American corn bread into Wales. The most influential of these families in their UK roles were the Starbucks, the Folgers, the Coffins and the Rotches. Many of their names are preserved in Milford Haven today as street names.

The family names are famous in the annals of whaling in North America and one name is recorded in one of the most dramatic tragedies of the whaling industry. In 1819 the whaleship *Essex* (Captain George Pollard Junior) left Nantuckett and sailed into the Pacific. When in a remote area of sea west of the Galapagos Islands on November 20th 1820 the *Essex* was rammed by a whale and sank. The crew of twenty spent three months at sea in three whaleboats and most died. A few were rescued months later. The few survivors had resorted to cannibalism. At one point the starving men held a lottery to choose a man to be eaten. It fell to teenager Owen Coffin who was a nephew to George Pollard. The captain offered to take his place but Coffin refused. He was shot and eaten. Back in Nantucket Coffins mother would never speak to George Pollard again as she stated that he had taken his nephew to sea to train him but had ended up eating him. It was the fate of the *Essex* that inspired Herman Melville to write his famous book 'Moby Dick', first published in 1851.

In 1801 the first of the original Quakers died (Abigail Starbuck wife of Samuel Starbuck) and she was buried in a plot of land designated for a Quaker Meeting house and burial ground. The Meeting House was built in 1811 and continues to operate today. It is surrounded by a small walled area that is the burial ground for these first settlers. Inside are the graves of many famous Nantuckett whaling families marked by low stones with only their initials (SS for Samual Starbuck, DS for Daniel Starbuck and TF for Timothy Folger).

A description of Milford Haven in 1809 is given by Fenton (1811 reprinted 1994). This was shortly after the visit of Lord Nelson and the Hamiltons in 1802. His description is enthusiastic and reports progress along the lines outlined by Lord Nelson in his speech during his visit. Fenton describes how St. Catherine's church stood at the head of three streets mainly empty but with buildings under construction. A customs house had been constructed and five ships conducted regular sailings to and from Ireland. A mail coach arrived daily. A dockyard below the town had been constructed after a French engineer Mr. Louis Barallier had been brought to the town site in 1797 by Greville to oversee the building of a naval yard and construction of ships within it. Barallier had previously held the post of Assistant to the Inspector General of Naval Construction in London.

At the time of Fenton's visit, two king's ships – the *Nautilus* and the *Lavinia* had been completed and a third – a seventy-four gun warship - was under construction. On the west side of Priory Pill was the town of Hakin. Fenton reports that The Observatory above Hakin had been built and furnished with expensive instruments. A mathematical school had been established alongside. A Mr. Firminger had been appointed astronomer. The shell of the observatory building still stands but is now tightly embedded in a modern housing estate.

Of the Nantucket whalers, Fenton wrote:

'They are an industrious well-disposed people, with the dignified simplicity of manners and strong understanding that their set is generally distinguished for.'

The principal of the American settlers was Mr. Rotch who first established himself and his family in the town of Milford Haven, building an impressive residence. But before it was completed he purchased Castle Hall above Prix or Castle Pill on the east side of the new town. The whaling ships were probably kept in Prix or Castle Pill below Mr. Rotch's home as the crew may have lived in 'The whalers cottages' still standing on Cellar Hill on the east side of the town. The crew would have lived near the ships that required attention and supervision when in port.

Today in Milford Haven the Friends Meeting House is still in use and has recently produced a pamphlet 'A Quaker Walk around Milford Haven', available at the Tourist Office of Milford Haven. The walk reveals that the houses of the leading whaling families are some of the most substantial buildings in the town and rival the Lord Nelson Hotel. Indeed some of them are so big that today they are used as pubs and hotels. It must have been quite a boost to the development of the new town to build such large homes. This was not an accident but rather because Charles Greville in order to encourage the American whalers to emigrate to Milford Haven provided a number of inducements for them. These were:

1. Free use of Hubberston and Castle pills for their ships.

2. The granting of favourable leases and the transfer of the value of their American possessions on condition that they built in Wales to the same value on Sir William Hamilton's land.

3. Provision of a site for a Meeting House and burial ground.

4. Favourable rates for leasing land.

The whaling industry provided work for many people. A store was built. Oil was transferred into casks and shipped to London is small trading schooners. Ships were refitted and victualled for very long voyages. Sadly after such a good start, the whale oil business declined. Initially this was due to the fact that after the death of Richard Greville in 1809, government support for the industry was withdrawn and finally the demand for whale oil for the street lights of London ceased, when gas lighting was introduced.

Suggested Further Reading
Griffiths, S., *A History of Quakers in Pembrokeshire*. The Meeting House, Society of Friends, MilfordeHaven, 46 p.

McKay, K.D., 1989, *A Vision of Greatness – The History of Milford Haven 1790 – 1990*: Btuce Harvatt Associates, Haverfordwest, Dyfed, 379 p.

Website: www.quakers-in-Pembrokeshire.org.uk

34. THE FORTS OF SOUTH PEMBROKESHIRE

Walkers of the South Pembrokeshire Coast Path will notice that there are rather a lot of abandoned military forts around the coastline. This reflects the historic role played by the prominent peninsula of Pembrokeshire jutting out into the Irish Sea. Since the Norman invasion of Pembrokshire (Roger de Montgomery in 1093 and Martin de Turribus in 1094), there have been several invasions. In 1405 Owen Glendwr with an invasion force of French troops landed in the Milford Haven Waterway. In 1485 Henry Twdwr (Tudor) did a similar thing and went on to the Battle of Bosworth Fields and set up the Tudor dynasty. In 1797 following the French Revolution a French invasion force landed in the north of the county near Fishguard.

In the half century following the Battle of Waterloo in 1815, the strength of the French Navy and a possible invasion was a political concern. In the early nineteenth century Britain had the strongest navy in the world but concerns were raised in parliament by the Duke of Wellington in 1844 and Sir John Fox Burgoyne in 1846. They felt the need for permanent coastal defences to protect naval dockyards, ports and harbours used by merchant vessels. In 1860 a Royal Commission for the Defence of the United Kingdom recommended the building of many new forts to defend the ports and naval establishments. The fear was of wooden sailing ships armed with cannon using black powder. The proposals were strongly supported by the then Prime Minister Lord Palmerston, who initiated one of the greatest episodes of fort building ever undertaken for the British Isles. They proved to be the most expensive and extensive system of fixed defences ever undertaken in the British Isles. The result in Pembrokeshire was that in addition to existing forts, another ten massive grey limestone forts were built to defend the Royal Naval dockyard at Pembroke Dock and the Milford Haven Waterway. These forts still still stand intact today.

On the north side of Piccadilly in London, almost opposite the Ritz Hotel, there is an old three story town house (no.94, Cambridge House) that is dwarfed by the surrounding higher more modern buildings. A blue plaque on the wall identifies it as the London residence of Lord Palmerston who was Prime Minister from 1855. It was the the site of many splendid social and political gatherings. After the death of Viscount Palmerston the house was purchased as the Naval and Military club in 1865 when it became known as the 'In and Out Club' due to prominent signs on the entrances.' It was used until 1996. It then fell into disrepair until purchased in 2011. Happily it is now undergoing a £166 million conversion into a modern luxurious hotel.

Lord Palmerston (1784 - 1865) was born Henry John Temple, son of the Irish peer Viscount Palmerston. He succeeded on his father's death in April 1802 to the Viscountcy. He entered Parliament at the age of twenty-two years. At the age of twenty-five he was offered the post of Chancellor of the Exchequer which he declined, accepting instead the post of Secretary of War. He held this post for twenty years serving five Prime Ministers. Between 1832 and 1852 he served both Whig and Tory governments. He believed that the government's foreign policy should be to increase Britain's power in the world. He supported 'gun-boat diplomacy'. He was disliked by Queen Victoria. In 1855 Lord Palmerston at the age of seventy years became the oldest ever elected British Prime Minister and held the position until his death in 1865. He held this position throughout the American Civil War and his sympathies were with the Southern Confederacy.

Perhaps unfairly the forts became known as 'Palmerston's Follies' because on their completion the threat had passed mainly as a result of the Franco-Prussian war of 1870, also because of advances in technology. The Palmerston forts were built as a deterrent and as such they succeeded and there was no French invasion. The Royal Commission forts were designed with iron-clad warships and rifled artillery in mind. The Commission included experts on both. HMS *Warrior*, the first Royal Navy armoured battleship was laid down in 1859 and completed two years later. She completely outclassed every other battleship then afloat showing how the Royal Navy was very aware of the impact of new technology. It was not the development of ironclad warships that rendered these later forts obsolete, so much as the subsequent rapid improvement in armour and rifled artillery. The move away from 'black powder' to more modern propellants such as lyddite much enhanced the range and power of guns.

There were older forts already in Pembrokeshire before the Palmerston forts. These are: 1) Paterchurch Battery; 2) Two gun or Martello Towers at the dockyard in Pembroke; 3) The large Defensible Barracks overlooking the dockyard; 4) Dale Fort. The forts completed in 1858 were a direct response to the ascent of Emperor Napoleon III in France in 1851. Work had started on some forts that were then included in the recommendations of the Royal Commission. The list of Palmerton forts built around the Milford Haven Waterway and the south part of Pembrokeshire is considerable: 5) The West Blockhouse and Battery; 6) Fort Hubberston; 7) Popton Fort; 8) Scoveston Fort; 9) South Hook Fort; 10) Stack Rock Fort; 11) Thorne Island Fort; 12) St. Catherine's Fort (Tenby); 13) Chapel Bay Fort; 14) East Blockhouse Fort and Battery. Today most of these fortifications are listed buildings and can be closely seen from the Pembrokeshire Coast Path. The forts are next described separately.

1) THE PATERCHURCH BATTERY (1759)

The artillery battery was built in the mid 1810's on the bank of the River Cleddau on land purchased in 1759 to protect the waterway. An expansion of the dockyard in 1844 resulted in the battery being inside the dockyard walls.

2) TWO GUN OR MARTELLO TOWERS (1849-1857)

Two gun or Martello Towers were built of local limestone blocks to protect the Pembroke Dockyard. Pembroke Dock North East was built in 1851 and Pembroke Dock West between 1848 and 1851, They were manned in the eighteenth century until they were decomissioned in 1882. Pembroke Dock West was manned by one officer and thirty-three men. The roof housed several guns and three twelve pound brass howitzers. Today one is a private dwelling and the other a local museum.

3) THE DEFENCIBLE BARRACKS (1842 – 1845)

These were built on the Barrack Hill overlooking the town and dockyard of Pembroke Dock between 1842 and 45. The Royal Naval Dockyard operated from 1840 to 1926 and at its peak employed 3,000 men. The barracks housed the Royal Marines who defended the dockyard. Built of large limestone blocks, the fort is diamond shaped with a dry moat guarded by corner bastions. A drawbridge led over the moat, through an entrance arch into the gate house. Inside the fort the square barrack block comprises four double story terraces. Accomodation was for one officer of field rank, eight commissioned officers, seven NCOs and 240 other ranks. Originally there were sixteen twenty-four pounder cannon and there are rifle loops for 663 muskets. Rain water was collected into an 87,000 gallon underground tank. From 1885, gas was supplied from the Admiralty Gasworks nearby.

During World War II, Arthur Lowe of 'Dad's Army' fame, was stationed in the Defencible Barracks. Today the barracks are not used.

4) DALE FORT (Completed 1858)

The fort was completed in 1856 on the small narrow peninsula of Dale Point on the north side of the Milford Haven Waterway very near the village of Dale. It had a garrison of sixty men and an armament of one eighty-pound Millar's Pattern shell gun, seven sixty-eight-pound guns and two thirty-two pound guns. It became obsolete in 1871 but was reoccupied in 1892 and altered for the installation of a Zalinski dynamite gun. This was a new coastal defence weapon that fired a fifteen inch shell weighing 966 pounds over 4,500 yards using compressed air. However the gun became obsolete almost immediately when a new explosive called lyddite was invented. The fort was decommissioned in 1902 when it became a private house. During World War I it was used as a signal station. The fort was reused again in World War II as a Degaussing Range to measure the magnetic signature of ships to prevent them from triggering magnetic mines dropped by the German Luftwaffe around the waterway. If the signature was incorrect then the ship would be sent into Milford Docks for correction. Today the fort is used by the Field Studies Council as the Dale Fort Field Centre offering training courses to schools, families and individuals.

5) THE WEST BLOCKHOUSE AND BATTERY (Completed 1858)

This was completed in 1858 situated on the cliffs at the west side of the entrance to the Milford Haven Waterway, about a mile from St. Ann's Head. It comprised a battery of six sixty-eight-pounder cannon with defensible barracks behind to give protection from landward attack. The fort had accommodation for forty-one men and one officer. The rooms on the first floor were lined with pine planks for insulation and with coal fires burning were comfortable from the boisterous outside elements in this exposed site. The fort has a dry moat and is entered by means of a wooden bridge. The fort was remodelled in 1901 to take four five inch guns as well as two quick firing guns on the roof. In 1904-05 concrete gun emplacements were built on the cliff top above the fort and equipped with two 9.2 inch guns and three six-inch guns. During World War I the West Blockhouse was garrisoned by the Royal Artillery. It was brought back into use during World War II also garrisoned by the Royal Artillery. During World War II, an anti-submarine boom extended between the West and East blockhouses, that was attended by two defence boom tugs. The fort was long abandoned but has now been restored by the Landmark Trust and accommodation is available for visitors. The fort lies adjacent to the Pembrokeshire Coast Path.

6) FORT HUBBERSTON (1863 to 1865)

Very visible today is the fort that lies at the east end of Gelliswick Beach, Milford Haven. The fort was built between 1863 and 1865. Together with Popton Fort on the opposite of the waterway, the two forts provided an interlocking field of fire. It had a large battery which had eleven guns and a large barracks for 250 men at the rear. It was manned by the Royal Pembrokeshire Artillery and the 24th Regiment of Foot. The fort was abandoned after World War I. It was reused in World War II as an air raid shelter and army camp for American military personnel. Today the fort is owned by the Milford Haven Port Authority and remains derelict. In 2011 it was designated the fifth most endangered archaeological site in the UK. The fort is closed to the public as there have been a number of non-fatal accidents there.

7) POPTON FORT (Completed 1865)

The fort was built on the south shore of the Milford Haven Waterway opposite Stack Rock Fort, South Hook Fort and Fort Hubberston. It lies on Popton Point on the east side of Angle Bay. Work was completed in 1865. It had two batteries, the Moncrieff Battery on the west side and the Open Battery on the north. Accommodation was for ten officers, five staff sergeants, 158 NCOs and privates in the barracks, as well as eighty-six NCOs and privates in the casemates and six married men. The casemates contained eleven nine-inch twelve-ton rifled muzzle-loading guns with ten six-inch Montcrieff guns in pits above the casemates. There was also an open battery with a ten-inch eighteen-ton rifled muzzle-loading gun with nine nine-inch twelve-ton rifled muzzle loading guns and a separate battery of two seven-inch rifled breech-loading guns. The fort was abandoned in the early twentieth century and fell into decay. It was put back into use during World War II. In 1957 it was purchased by the British Petroleum Oil company and became part of their oil pumping station, when it was fully refurbished and the hexagonal barracks used for offices and stores. The complex was sold to Texaco to become a part of Texaco's Angle Bay refinery. It has recently been sold on to the Valero Oil Company. It is not open to the public but the Pembrokeshire Coast Path passes alongside it

8) SCOVESTON FORT (1861 to 1864)

This was built on high ground on the north side of the Milford Haven waterway between the towns of Milford Haven and Neyland. It was sited to protect the dockyards at Milford Haven, Neyland and Pembroke Dock. Construction began in 1861 and finished in 1864. It is a hexagonal fort in plan and is surrounded by a thirty-six foot wide moat. The fort was designed for a garrison of 128 men with thirty-two guns. It was never garrisoned but used only as a training camp for volunteers and militia. There was increased activity at the fort during World War I, when a series of trenches were dug in the surrounding land, extending from Waterston to Llangwm, to protect the fort from land attack. During World War II, the fort was used as an air raid shelter by the residents of Neyland and later as a warehouse to store munitions for use on D-Day. Today the fort is long abandoned and almost entirely overgrown by thick vegetation and is not accessible to the public nor near the coast path. It is best seen on Google Earth where the hexagonal plan is still distinct.

9) SOUTH HOOK FORT (1859 to 1865)

The fort was built on the north side of the Milford Haven Waterway near Stack Rock Fort between 1859 and 65. It consists of two horseshoe shaped barrack blocks behind a twenty gun battery facing out to sea. In 1890 the western fifteen gun battery was rebuilt to take two ten-inch breech loading and three ten-inch rifled muzzle loading guns but only one ten-inch breech-loading gun was mounted. Between 1901 and 04, the batteries were replaced by three six-inch breech-loading and three ten-inch rifled muzzle- loading guns. Two twelve pounder quick-firing guns were set up at the west end. The guns were removed in 1935 and the fort sold in 1936. It was requisitioned for World War II and became HMS *Skirmisher* and was operated by WRENs controlling all the naval movements on the Milford Haven Waterway. In the 1950s the site was purchased by the Esso Oil Company and became a part of their refinery there. The fort was used for offices. Today the site is part of the South Hook Liquid Natural Gas Terminal and the fort is inside the perimeter fence. However the battery is just outside the fence adjacent to the Pembrokeshire Coast Path.

10) STACK ROCK FORT (1859 to 1871)

Most visible today the fort (Plate 23) was built on the Stack Rocks within the Milford Haven Waterway opposite the village of Herbrandston and easily visible from many vantage points around the waterway. The fort is located just to the west of the LNG terminal jetty of South Hook. The fort was built between 1859 and 1871 with sixteen ten inch and seven nine inch rifled muzzle loading guns. These were upgraded to four twelve pounder quick firing guns in 1902. The fort was disarmed in 1929. It is now privately owned but unoccupied.

11) THORN ISLAND FORT (1852 to 1859)

Equally visible is Thorn Island Fort. This was built between 1852 and 1859 on a two acre island near the south side of the entrance to the Milford Haven Waterway in the community of Angle. Originally it had a battery of nine sixty-eight pounder smooth-bore muzzle loading guns and a garrison of one hundred men. During World War I a defence electric light emplacement was built on the island. During World War I the fort formed one end of a boom defence across the entrance to the Milford Haven waterway, the other end being at the other side of the entrance at Dale Point. Lately the fort became a privately-owned hotel – the Thorn Island Hotel – but is today closed down.

12) ST. CATHERINE'S FORT (Completed 1867)

This fort was built on a small tidal island lying between Tenby's popular sandy North and South Beaches on the south coast of Pembrokeshire. The island is linked by a beach at low tide to the mainland. The fort was planned as one of a chain along the south shores of Pembrokeshire to prevent a landing and overland attack on the facilities and Naval establishments of the Milford Haven Waterway. The other proposed forts on Caldy Island and at Lydstep, Freshwater East and Freshwater West were never built.

The small rectangular fort was built in 1867. The guns and iron protective shields did not arrive until the 1880s. The fort comprises gun casements facing north to cover Tenby harbour and the beach towards Saundersfoot and south towards Penally and Manorbier. Each face had three seven-inch rifled muzzle-loading guns firing through iron shields. Two small rifle galleries protected the west face and entrance to the fort which has a drawbridge. At the east end of the basement level is the powder magazine and two shell stores. On the roof are three gun platforms for nine-inch rifled muzzle-loading guns facing south east, one of which can be traversed through 360 degrees.

The fort was garrisoned from 1873 to 1910, again from 1914 to 1918 and finally 1939-1945. Many detachments were there including the Royal Marines, the 4th Defence Battalion R.A., elements of the Belgian Army, the Home Guard and an RAF detachment. The fort was released by the military at the end of World War II. In 1959 it was sold and converted into a private residence called Gun Fort House. It was next used as a small zoo. Today the fort is being converted into a museum.

13) CHAPEL BAY FORT (Completed 1891)

CHAPEL BAY FORT was completed in 1891 and is one of the earliest forts in the world to be built of mass concrete, i.e. concrete without reinforcing. The main fort is surrounded by a moat thirty feet deep. It had three ten-inch rifled muzzle loading guns. In 1901 these were replaced by three six-inch breech loading guns. Inside there is barrack accommodation for 100 men, along with a Master Gunner's house, an Officers Mess, toilet blocks, kitchens and magazines. In World War I the fort was used for ships suspected of carrying contraband that were moored under the forts guns. During World War II the fort controlled some of the anti-aircraft guns that defended the Milford Haven Waterway. After the war the fort was derelict for many years. The fort is now privately owned and is undergoing extensive renovation.

14) EAST BLOCKHOUSE FORT AND BATTERY (Completed 1904)

The blockhouse was completed in 1580 for King Henry VIII. Today little of it remains. In 1903 a Coastal Defence Battery was competed nearby with brick buildings for gun crews, officers and a cookhouse. The battery had three six-inch guns. The six inch guns were withdrawn in 1914 along with one of the 9.2 inch guns in 1917. Two six-inch guns from the Chapel Bay Battery were added in 1918. In 1929 a 9.2-inch gun replaced those removed earlier. A practice battery of quick firing guns was built on the flank of the 9.2-inch battery. In 1925 two twelve-pounder guns from South Hook Fort were mounted there but removed in 1938. The two six-inch guns were removed in 1941 and were replaced by two twelve-pounder guns for a few months only. A few days later another twelve-pounder gun arrived. In 1944 the battery was disarmed. The ammunition did not leave until 1947. Today the concrete mounts for the 9.2-inch guns and a twelve-pounder gun can be seen, but the six-inch positions have been buried. The underground magazines, shelters and engine room have also been buried. The structures are of concrete and today the small fort has been modified by infilling the windows and doors, leaving only small circular entrances. The building is now a refuge for bats and swallows. The Pembrokeshire Coast Path passes these structures.

Suggested Further Reading

Phillips, B.A., 2013, *Pembrokeshire's Forts and Military Airfields 1535 – 2010*: Logaston Press, Herefordshire 105 p., ISBN 978 1 906663 73 5.

PLANED (Pembrokeshire Local Action Network for Enterprise and Development). Undated. *A Guide to the Military Heritage of Pembrokeshire*: Civil War to Cold War.

35. THE GREAT NAVAL DOCKYARD AT PEMBROKE

A Naval Dockyard operated at Milford Haven in Hubberston Pill (the site of the present docks) from 1802 to 1814. The Navy Board paid an annual rental of £250 for the land. The Frenchman Jean Louis Barrallier was employed by the British Government as Superintendent of the Yard. He also worked as town architect for Charles Francis Greville. The yard used local labour. Timber from the Forest of Dean and iron from the Penydarran Ironworks near Newport were shipped in by coastal vessels. During its life the Dockyard produced seven ships, some of which were:

Milford launched 1809

Portsmouth 317 tons launched 1811

Surprise fifth rate forty-six guns 1072 tons launched1811

Myrmidon sloop twenty guns 509 tons launched 1813

Rochfort second rate eighty guns 2082 tons launched 1814

The Navy Board tried to buy the dockyard and a price of £4,445 was agreed with Charles Francis Greville. Unfortunately he died and his brother Robert Fulke Greville, who succeeded him as a life tenant of the estate, refused to accept that price. For the town of Milford the decision was a major setback as an opportunity for employment and wealth was missed. So the Milford Dockyard was abandoned and the Navy Yard moved to a shoreside farming area known as Paterchurch which became the present town of Pembroke Dock. The new facility became known as Paterchurch Dockyard. There were advantages in moving as the water at Paterchurch was deeper and to remain at Milford would have required costly dredging. The first workers moved there from Milford Haven in February1814. Their first task was to fence off the land and build cottages for the workforce. The name of the dockyard changed to Pembroke Dockyard in 1817 at the request of the mayor of Pembroke.

The dockyard would operate for over a century from 1814 to 1926 and 250 warships including five Royal yachts, were built there. At its peak the dockyard employed 3,000 men. A brief history of the dockyard and an excellent catalogue of every ship built at Pembroke with a photograph or drawing and description of most is given by Phillips (2014).

The great need for skilled workers resulted in shipwrights from as far afield as Plymouth arriving. In addition because of the need for buildings, slipways and a boundary wall, many stone masons were employed. There was not enough accommodation for the workforce. So in July 1813 the old sixth-rate frigate HMS *Lapwing* was brought around from Plymouth to be run ashore to act as an office and accommodation for clerks. She was broken up in 1828. In 1832 HMS *Dragon* was beached on the waterfront to act as a barracks for a Royal Marine detachment to guard the new dockyard. She was broken up in 1850. In 1860 the Metropolitan Police took over the security of the dockyard.

There was still not enough accommodation for the growing workforce and their families. The old town of Pembroke underwent a great boom with all rooms occupied and rents high. Many workmen travelled daily more than eight miles to work from surrounding towns and villages including Milford Haven. Many arrived daily by rowing boat but most walked. For the senior staff renting a home nearby incurred exorbitant costs. In 1846, a defensible barracks was completed on a hill above the dockyard to accommodate 400 men. The barracks were manned by the Royal Marines who had been living aboard the beached hulk of HMS *Dragon*. A railway line connected to the dockyard in 1864.

The dockyard grew to reach a total of thirteen building slips for ships, making it one of Britain's main Naval shipyards for over a century. However by the early years of the twentieth century the facilities proved inadequate for the construction of larger warships. At this stage larger warships could not be armed at Pembroke Dock but went to other Naval Dockyards to complete their fitting out. No examples of the largest dreadnaught type of battleship were built at Pembroke Dock as the yard could not accommodate such large vessels. From the first launching of two small sister frigates HMS *Ariadne* and *Valorous* in 1816 to the last a fleet oil tanker *Oleander* in 1922, a total of 250 ships was built in 106 years.

The life of the dockyard spanned from the Napoleonic Wars to after the First World War. This was a time of great change in warship construction from wood to iron and then to steel and from sail to steam. The first forty-five years saw the construction of nineteen first and second rate ships representing the culmination of the art of wooden ship construction. In October 1829 the vast line-of-battleship HMS *Howe* was launched. She was a great three decker built for the Royal Navy and was twice the size of

Nelson's *Victory*, displacing 6,577 tons – a vast wooden steam battleship. The *Tartarus* launched in 1834 was the first of a series of paddle-wheel steam vessels. In 1831 HMS *Valorous* was launched. She was the last paddle frigate built for the Royal Navy. The 1850's saw the dockyard build and launch the last of the Royal Navy's great wooden battleships. The three decker HMS *Duke of Wellington* was launched in September 1852. She was originally named *Windsor Castle* but this was changed on the death of the Duke earlier in 1852.

The shipbuilding at Pembroke Dock can be divided into two eras. First was the era of 'the Wooden Walls' – wooden ships with broadside armament where the only protection was oak. This was followed by the era of the ironclad. The latter began with the launch of the iron-built ironclad HMS *Warrior* on the Thames in 1860. At Pembroke Dock it began with the launch in June 1862 of the wooden-hulled iron plated frigate HMS *Prince Consort*. She had been started as a wooden screw two decker but was completed as a wooden ironclad with plates 4.5 and three inches thick. There followed thirty years of advancement. The first iron ship built there was HMS *Penelope* launched in 1857. The last two decades of the nineteenth century saw the dockyard produce a series of major capital ships. The first of these was the turret ship HMS *Edinburgh* in 1882, followed by such famous ships as *Collingwood*, *Howe*, *Anson*, *Nile*, *Empress of India* and *Repulse*. The heaviest battleship built at Pembroke was HMS *Hannibal* of 14,000 tons launched in 1896. There followed ten years of production of armoured cruisers of increasing size. HMS *Duke* launched in 1901 was at 533 feet and six inches the longest ship ever built at Pembroke.

The five Royal Yachts built at Pembroke Dock were: HM Yacht *Victoria and Albert* (paddle yacht) launched 1843; HM Yacht *Victoria and Albert* (paddle yacht) launched 1855; HM Yacht *Alberta* (a paddle passage boat) launched 1863; HM Yacht *Osborne* (paddle yacht launched 1870) and HM Yacht *Victoria and Albert* (screw yacht) launched 1899.

A little known fragment of history and unrelated to the Pembroke dockyard was the building and launching of a corvette for the fledgling Japanese navy. She was the *Hiei* built by the private Milford Haven Shipbuilding and Engineering Company at Pennar and launched in 1877.

After the First World War there were huge reductions to be made in the naval fleet. There was not enough work for all the Naval dockyards. The end of the Pembroke Dockyard was sealed by a disastrous fire in 1922 when the mold loft burned down. In 1926 the dockyard was closed and the site offered for lease. The dockyard covered eighty acres with a dry dock, eight shipbuilding slips. four slipways with cradles operating on three, a deep water jetty, buildings including residences, offices, workshops, store-houses, electric light and power facilities. It was a calamity for the town of Pembroke Dock that overnight became a town of unemployed workers and pensioners. A quarter of the population left the area.

On 31st March 1930 the former Naval Dockyard was transferred from the Admiralty to the Air Ministry and became an air station. This lasted for twenty-three years until 31st March 1959 when the station closed. The air station expanded steadily until the Second World War. Many of the old workshops and stores were knocked down to make space for new aircraft hangers and slipways were constructed to bring the seaplanes out of the sea. Flying boats moored off the former dockyard were a daily sight. The station was operational throughout the six years of the war. Its main wartime role was convoy protection during the Battle for the Atlantic. The post-war era was one of a peacetime role for the Sunderland aircraft that continued to fly until the station was closed.

By the Second World War, the town of Pembroke Dock had grown and there was much of military interest that resulted in the town being badly bombed by long-range German aircraft particularly between summers of 1940 and 1941. The targets were an Admiralty Oil Tank farm with seven-teen tanks at Llanreath, the Llanion barracks, the dockyard with naval facilities, the Sunderland flying base (then the largest in the world), a communicarions centre and the military airfield nearby at Carew Cheriton. Eleven oil tanks burned for eighteen days at Llanreath in August 1940 after being bombed by three German Junkers eighty-eight aircraft. 600 firemen attended, five died and there were 1,148 casualties.

As a schoolboy visiting Pembroke Dock in the 1950's by crossing the waterway on a paddle steamer, my memories are still of the streets where sections of houses were still missing after the bombing. My uncle and aunt lived in a large house on the Barrack Hill that showed repairs to all the floors and ceilings, where a bomb had fallen through the house but failed to explode. Today Pembroke Dock is a rather strange fossil town rich in old Admiralty buildings but with high unemployment. The main daily event is the arrival and departure of the Irish Ferry from Cork. This involves a slow passage along the Milford Haven Waterway, now busy with the oil and Liquid Natural Gas industries. The dockyard survives as an industrial tourist site and includes a Sunderland aircraft museum.

Today, almost a century has passed since the dockyard closed and the ships are long gone. However the wreck of one of the ships built and launched at Pembroke Dockyard is today making headlines. She is HMS *Erebus* a 105 foot long wooden bomb vessel launched in June 1826 (Palin,

2019). She was built with enormous strength to be used as a mortar ship, but was soon obsolete. In 1839 she and another bomb vessel HMS *Terror* were assigned to a major Antarctic exploration voyage led by Captain Sir James Clark Ross. *Erebus* as flagship was commanded by Ross and *Terror* by his friend and second in command Captain Francis R. C. Crozier. The ships were based in Hobart, Van Diemens Land where the two officers became guests of the Lieutenant Governor Sir John Franklin and his wife Lady Jane.

For three Antarctic summers the two ships explored around the unknown continent. In January 1841 they sighted and named the 12,400 foot high active volcano Mt. Erebus. A lesser volcano nearby was named Mt Terror. On finally departing Van Diemens Land, the two officers hosted a great ball aboard the two ships for their many friends there. The ships returned to Woolwich where they were immediately prepared for another polar expedition.

This expedition was commanded by Sir John Franklin aboard *Erebus* with *Terror* again commanded by Captain Crozier. The purpose was to complete the mapping of the North-West Passage and if possible to sail through it, returning home via the Pacific Ocean. The ships departed the Thames on 19th May 1845. The two ships with 129 men aboard were all lost without any survivors. They wintered on Beechey Island but became trapped in the ice in September 1846. Sir John Franklin died on 11th June 1847 and Captain Crozier took over command of the expedition. Lieutenant Commander James Fitzjames of *Erebus* took over command of *Erebus*. The ships were abandoned in April 1848 and the survivors set out on foot for Hudson's Bay outposts some 1200 miles away. None survived.

The ships were lost for the next 166 years when the wreck of *Erebus* was discovered in 2014 with her main deck only in ten feet of water by a Canadian Government consortium seeking the wrecks. *Terror* was discovered in deeper water in 2016. The wreck sites have been protected by the Canadian Government working with the local Nunavut Government and Parks Canada. The latter is carrying out archaeological investigations of the wrecks trying to learn what happened to the lost expedition. The wrecks are accessible for only a short time each summer when the sea is ice free. Underwater video films of the wrecks and of their interiors, the latter made by remotely operated underwater cameras, are now available on the internet. The contents of the cabins are remarkably preserved by the very cold waters. Excavations are likely to continue for some years. The mystery has been discussed recently by Roobol (2019).

Suggested Further Reading

Palin M., 2019, *Erebus: The story of a Ship*: Arrow Books, 354 p.

Phillips, L., 2014, *Pembroke Dockyard and the Old Navy – A Bicentennial History*. The History Press, Malta. 352p., ISBN 978 0 7509 5214 9

Roobol, M.J., 2019, *Franklin's Fate*: Conrad Press, Canterbury, 368p.

36. GULF STREAM TREASURES ON PEMBROKESHIRE BEACHES.

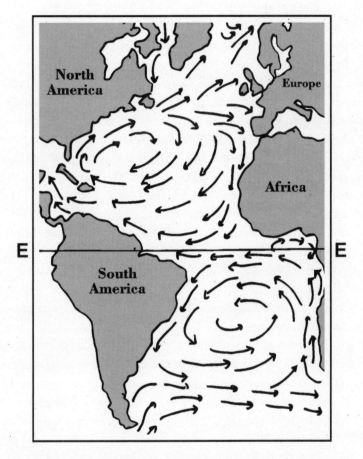

Figure 11. Currents of the North and South Atlantic Ocean

Pembrokesire's golden sand beaches are a major summer holiday destination for families. Children play happily all day in the sand, rock
pools and sea. But there is an art in finding a warm and sheltered spot.
First some local knowledge helps. Google Earth is a wonderful new tool
that can be freely downloaded into ones computer and with it the sandy
beaches of Pembrokeshire can be identified and studied before arriving
for the holiday. It is not necessary to make long daily drives to the tourist
centres of Tenby and Saundersfoot, as there are many other sheltered local
beaches around the coast. Nor is it a good idea on a cool windy day to

put a family on open beaches such as Newgale and Broad Haven, unless surfing. Yet many visitors do this and carry poles and shelters and even tents to the beach to get out of the wind. A little knowledge of wind and tides can make a big difference.

Above the cliffs of the Pembrokeshire coast, the land is generally flat as it is a raised marine platform carved by the sea long ago. The land rises in series of these platforms towards the Preseli Mountains in the north of the county. To get the best out of a day on the peninsula it is necessary to know both the state of the tide and the wind direction, so that snug sheltered sandy coves can be selected. State of the tide is important as there are places where with an incoming tide one can be cut off. Such places are the south end of Marloes Bay and especially Musselwick beach. It is also important to know the state of the tide as on some of the sandy beaches their vast expanses of sand can disappear around high tide and very little beach is left. Most Pembrokeshire beaches have high cliffs. So by selecting a beach on the sheltered side of the peninsula, it is possible as early as April to have a tropically warm day on the beach with the family. The Pembrokeshire beaches face in every direction including east (Mill Bay, Watwick Bay and Dale). By selecting a beach where the wind is blowing offshore a suntrap beneath the cliffs can be found. Rising tides advance over sun-warmed sands to create warm shallows ideal for small children. Rock pools can also provide warm swimming.

The dominant wind direction on the Pembrokeshire peninsula is from the south west. On such days the north facing beaches of Musselwick, St. Brides, Little Haven, Abereiddy, Aber Mawr and Aberbach are sheltered. However other beaches such as south facing Lindsway Bay with coves and cliffs provide shelter from north winds, and the west side of this beach is sheltered from westerly winds. Marloes Sands with high cliffs provides shelter from easterly winds. On days of northerly winds the south-facing beaches of the St. Davids Peninsula (Portharaw, Solva, Poinz Castle), and those of the Dale Peninsula (Watwick, Lindsway, Sandy Haven) as well as those of the Castlemartin Peninsula (all the south coast beaches to Tenby and Saundersfoot) are warmest.

Having found a beach for a day, there are many interesting things to look for. One of these is the great variety of rocks found as pebbles on the beaches. These show a remarkable variety. Most are derived from the ancient Paleozoic rocks that make up the county. But quite a few of the rocks, flints, basalt, and granite do not originate in Pembrokeshire. They were carried to Pembrokeshire in the great Irish Sea glacier in the Ice Age. These strange rocks are known as erratics and have sources in the Scottish islands, northern Ireland and north Wales. A guide to birds and flowers can be helpful because of the wide varieties of each that can be seen in the hedges near the beaches and on the sea cliffs.

When visiting a Pembrokeshire beach, it is interesting to know that there are two great circular currents or gyres in the North and South Atlantic oceans. They rotate in opposite directions – clockwise in the North Atlantic and counter clockwise in the South Atlantic (Figure 11). The great conveyor belt of current in the North Atlantic arises near the Caribbean Islands and moves north-west across the North Atlantic to arrive off the coasts of the British Isles where one arm continues on towards Spitzbergen, while another continues to rotate south and then across the equator. The current running from the Caribbean to the UK is the 'Gulf Stream' or 'The North Atlantic Drift'. All British schoolboys are told how this stream of relatively warm water prevents Britain from being covered in ice during the winter months. In contrast Newfoundland in Canada at the same latitude as Britain, is ice bound in a frozen sea for the winter months and has the very cold Labrador Current flowing south along its coastline.

The Gulf Stream acts as a great conveyor belt carrying things that float and swim from the tropics into Pembrokeshire water. So the beaches of Pembrokeshire, like those of Devon and Cornwall and the southern and western coasts of Ireland will have things washed ashore from distant parts. Objects wash ashore on Pembrokeshire beaches that originate in South America, the Caribbean and the east Coast of the USA. In addition these same waters also carry leatherback turtles, tuna, crayfish, sharks and trigger fish to the British coasts and they can be seen from boats or washed ashore. One should bear this in mind when walking the Pembrokeshire beaches.

Large objects that have travelled across the North Atlantic for months grow coatings of large goose barnacles. When the object (tree, buoy, boat) washes ashore and is stranded above the water, the many large barnacles will writhe about. According to Gerald the Welshman these barnacles were not classified as food and could therefore be eaten at times of religious fasting. In January 2023 a large palm tree trunk heavily coated in goose barnacles washed up on Broadhaven beach. The south-westerly winds drifted it north along the coast and onto Newgale beach (Plate 24). The tree measured five meters and seventeen centimeters long and was fifty centimeters wide at the base and twenty-seven centimeters at he top. It was not a coconut palm as the trunk was smooth. It had travelled around 5000 miles from the Caribbean. When I visited it it was snowng lightly and a very bleak wind as blowing in from the sea. I was delighted to find a reminder of the balmy climate of the tropics so far north in our cold winter weather.

The palm trunk did not arrive alone as on the beach with it were several battered mahagony tree trunks.

Tropical seeds also arrive on the Pembrokeshire beaches. (Plate 25) shows two hard black seeds collected by the author from Lindsway Bay and Freshwater West beaches. They are called 'sea beans'. The smaller one originates in the Amazon River. It is not uncommonly found on the beaches of the Caribbean islands where they are collected to make necklaces. The second is a large flat reddish heart-shaped seed. This is common on the Caribbean beaches as it grows on trees and bushes nearby. Coconuts in their husks and usually battered by waves against the rocks of Pembrokeshire, are also rarely found on the Welsh beaches. Their source is the Caribbean islands, where they abound on the beaches that are fringed with coconut palms.

Water-rounded scoria and pumice fragments can be found along the high water mark of Pembrokshire beaches. These floating stones also originate on the beaches of the volcanoes of the Caribbean Islands. Eruptions there sometimes release vast amounts of pumice down the island rivers and into the sea, where the larger fragments can float for months. Interestingly if hot pumice lands in the sea, then the volcanic glass will crack and the pumice will become waterlogged and sink. Small pumice fragments float for only a few days before becoming waterlogged and sinking. Care must be taken not to confuse rounded blocks of foam concrete (insulation blocks) with pumice. The artificially uniform size of the bubbles in the uniformly grey material of water rounded fragments of a foam block give the man-made origin away.

Water rounded bright-orange pieces of mahogany bark are not uncommon along the high tide mark on Welsh beaches. These come from the rivers on the Caribbean Islands (e.g. Dominica) where mahogany plantations exist and where the trees are grown and felled commercially.

In the Caribbean and Florida, mahogany tree trunks sink in the shallow coastal waters where they can be recovered commercially. It is therefore surprising to find whole mahagany tree trunks washed up on Welsh beaches. Examination will show that these trees are usually bored by teredo worm tubes to a sponge-like interior that much lightens the tree and helps it float.

American utility poles are larger than British poles and have their date of cutting, wood type and chemical treatment burned into the trunk. The British poles have their information deeply cut into the wood. Both types of pole arrive fairly frequently on the Welsh beaches where they can be cut up to make gate posts.

The Gulf Stream also carries tropical life to the shores of Pembrokeshire.

A large leatherback turtle that arrived is hanging on the farmhouse wall on Skomer Island. Sharks are not uncommon and a sport shark fishery once existed off Cornwall. In 2016, a thirteen foot (four meters) long blue Marlin washed up on Freshwater West beach. It was only the third ever found in the UK. Its condition was excellent and it was taken to the Natural History Museum in London, where it is now on display in a glass tank of glycol. The fishermen of Pembrokeshire are catching Caribbean crayfish and trigger fish that have taken up residence in Pembrokeshire waters. A surprise visitor in 2021 was a walrus from Baffin Bay (between Baffin Island and Greenland) that must have travelled south-east with the Labrador Current past Newfoundland to the vicinity of Nova Scotia and then been picked up by the Gulf Stream / North Atlantic Drift and carried across the Atlantic. It was reported first in Ireland and then on the south coast of Pembrokeshire.

This collection of Pembrokeshire histories will finish now with a last story that might surprise people. It concerns the Age of Saints in the fifth and sixth centuries in Pembrokeshire. This was an unusual time because many Celtic Saints arrived in Pembrokshire and built their religeous houses close to the sea. They travelled by boat around Britanny, Cornwall, south Wales and Ireland. Examples were St. Patrick, St. David , Saints Aidan, Ishmael, Teilo and Padarn. On the south coast at Castlemartin there is St Govans chapel and well where St Govern is reputed to have been shipwrecked. There is also St.Twynnells and St.Petrox. Lamphey near Pembroke records Saints Tyfai and Teilo. At Llanstadwell there is St. Tudwal's Church. On the Dale peninsula there is St Ishmaels village, Saint Botolph's estate and St. Bride's chapel. On the south side and end of the St. David's Peninsula there is Saint Elvis farm, Saint David's cathedral, Saint Non's chapel, Saint Justinian's chapel and Saint John Point. Inland in Pembrokeshire there is St. Leonard's well at Crundale, and St. Michael's church near St Clears. Along the north shores of Pembrokeshire there is the village of St. Nicholas, St. Hywel Church at Llanhowell and St. Brynach's church in Nevern.

It was only when taking a holiday with my family on the Dingle Pennsula of County Kerry that I learned of Skellig Michael. This is a twin peaked rock of fifty-two acres rising to 218 meters above sea level some 11.5 kilometers offshore on the south-west coast of Ireland. The magnificent scenery of the island became famous after its use in some of the Star Wars films. Today it has a population of gannets, puffins, razorbills and about fifty grey seals. Near the top is an abandoned but well-preserved Celtic monastery. It is one of nine monasteries on the rugged headlands and rocks of this coastal stretch of County Kerry. Monks at that time shunned society and chose instead to live in isolation in prayer and personal communication with God. They found their spirituality in the isolation amid the jagged rocks particularly on the south-west coast of Ireland. The abundance of blocks of rock on the cliffs provided them with their building material, in particular for the beehive dry-stone huts or cells that abound there. On Skellig Michael there are small plaforms high on the peaks that look out onto vast expanses of the ocean with its many moods and colours. There are dramatic sunsets and spectacular night skies. It is never silent with the calls of the sea birds, the roar of the surf and the moaning of the wind on the rocks. The spirituality of these places is enormous. Visitors to Pembrokeshire might visit the isolated Grassholm Island thirteen kilometers (six miles) west of Pembrokeshire with its great gannet colony, to get some idea.

On Skellig Michael flights of stone steps lead up to the early sixth to eighth century Christian monastery at 180 m. The monastery comprises two dry-stone oratories, six magnificent beehive cells, and a monks cemetery. There is a tenth to eleventh century church where the stones are mortared together. The monks cemetery is of particular interest. It is situated alongside the beehive huts and the similarly-constructed oratories. The graves are marked by stone slabs, some with crosses carved onto them and crude stone crosses. They are reminiscent of the Dark Age memorial stones of Pembrokshire. The monastery had only one abbot and about twelve monks. The monastery was a site of pilgrimage during the sixteenth century. In 833 AD the monastery was plundered by Viking raiders who carried off the Abbot Eitgal who died of starvation while a prisoner. The island was again raided by the Vikings in 838 AD.

History tells us that after a suitable periods in the monasteries, a monk might be called upon to go out and spread the Christian word. This was probably done using curroughs. These are wooden frame boats with a hull of skins or leather that are typical of the south-west coast of Ireland. They were made famous by the 1977 voyage by Tim Severin who sailed a leather currough to American, following the legend of St. Brenden. What is very interesting here is that monks cast themselves adrift in boats from monasteries of the Skellig Michael area at the mercy of wind and tide or from the religeos point of view, in the hands of God. But they were also in the Gulf Stream or North Atlantc Drift along with the Caribbean debris. So many Celtic saints in boats originating in the monasteries of south-west Kerry, would have been carried by the dominant south-westerly winds and the Gulf Stream to make landfall on the shores of westen and southern Pembrokeshire. There they could give thanks and set up their churches that remain there today. It is suggested that this might be a factor in explainng the unusually high number of Celtic saints who arrived on the coast of Pembrokeshire.

Suggested Further Reading

Bourke, E., Hayden, A.R., and Lynch, A., 2011, *Skellig Michael, Co. Kerry: the monastery and South Park*: Archaeological stratigraphy report of excavations 1986 – 2010: Dept. pf Arts, Heritage and the Gaeltacht, Govt. of Ireland, 32 p.

Severin, T., 1978, *The Brendan Voyage: sailing to America in a leather boat to prove the legend of the Irish sailing saints*: Reprinted 2000, Modern Library., 304 p.

Somerville, B.T., Rear Admiral, 1950, *Ocean Passages of the World*, Second Edition, Hydrographic Department, Admiralty, 368p. Also: Third Edition, 1973.

APPENDIX 1. SOME HIGHLIGHTS OF PEMBROKESHIRE HISTORY

The name Pembrokeshire is the anglicised version of the Welsh or ancient British Penfro (latter Pen for "promontory" or "head" and Bro meaning "region" or "land"). Although situated in the remote west of the UK, the area known today as Pembrokeshire has played some major roles in British history in the past. Some of the highlights are listed here.

c. 450,000 BP. First men arrive in Britain

c. 250,000 BP. Oldest known archaeological remains of man in Wales.

c. 32,000 BP. Neanderthal people die out leaving only Homo sapiens.

c. 38,000 to 27,000 BP. Early Upper Palaeolithic Homo sapiens in caves of South Pembrokeshire and Gower hunting woolly mammoths and other animals

c. 14,000 to 10,000 BP. Late Upper Paleozoic people returns to the caves of South Wales.

c 10,000 to 6,000 BP. Mesolithic (Middle Stone Age) people in Wales: The Wogan cave, Nab Head near St. Brides.

c. 7,000 to around 4,500 BP. The sunken forests around the coast of Pembrokeshire were growing and can now be seen at low tide at Newgale, Marros, Aber Mawr and other beaches after storms have moved the sand.

6,000 to 4,000 BP. The Neolithic with the first Neolithic farmers. Neolithic burial chambers of Pentre Ifan (near Newport), Carreg Coetan Arthur (in Newport), Trellys (St. Nicholas), Carreg Samson (Mathry), Garn Llidi (St. Davids), St. Elvis (Solva), Garn Turne (Letterston), Hanging Stone (Rosemarket), Devil's Quoit (Angle), Kings Quoit (Manorbier).

c. 4,500 B.P. to 2,700 BP. Bronze Age, Celtic people arrive. Beaker people, Bronze Age cairns on tops of Preseli Mountains.

c. 2,700 B.P. to AD 1000. Iron Age people arrive. Numerous fortified farms, hill forts and promontory forts built and occupied e.g. Foel Drygarn,

Foel Ayr, and Foel Eryr in the Preseli Mountains and Castell Henllys near Newport.

AD 43. Emperor Claudius invaded Britain. By AD 78, the Roman conquest of Wales was complete.

AD 140. Ptolemy, in his GEOGRAPHIA (c. AD 140) referred to the inhabitants of the south-west peninsula of Wales as the Demetae, and to their land as Demetia.

AD 410. Roman legions depart Britain.

Late fourth century – early fifth century. The Irish tribe the Deisi arrive in Dyfed from Deece in Co. Meath and establish the Royal line of Dyfed. They were led by Eochaid Allmuir. A descendant, Aircol Lawhir had a court at Lis Castell (Lydstep near modern Milford Haven). Another descendant Voteporix or Gwrthefyr 'the tyrant of the Demetae' who died in 540 is commemorated by an inscribed memorial stone now in Carmarthen Museum bearing the Ogham inscription VOTECORIGAS and the Latin inscription MEMORIA VOTEPORIGIS PROTICTORIS. The dynasty lasted until 814.

7th Century. England defined and occupied by invading peoples dominated by Anglo-Saxons. The remaining Ancient Britons or Celts gather in Wales to rebuild their successor state to that of Western Rome.

850. First Viking raids in Wales.

AD 877. Hubba the Viking with 2000 men in twenty-three ships wintered at Milford Haven.

AD 873. Asser Menevensis, believed to have been born in Trefasser in Llanwnda parish, was made bishop of St. Davids (Roman Menevia) in 873. He was a famous scholar and King Alfred made him his tutor and advisor. He sought the Kings protection against Hyfaidd ap Bledri, King of Dyfed (who died in AD 892). He wrote LIFE OF ALFRED but it was not finished. He was appointed Bishop of Sherborne and died in AD 909.

907. First Viking raid on St. Davids.

AD 904. Hywel Dda (Howel the Good) made King of Dyfed. He married Ellen, daughter of Llywarch ap Hyfaidd (died 904). From 942 until his death in 950 became King of most of Wales (except the south east).

909. Bishop Morganau of St. Davids murdered by Viking raiders.

920. Hywal Dda merges Dyfed and Sessyllwg to form the kingdom of Deheubarth.

1080. Bishop Abraham of St. Davids murdered by Viking raiders.

1093. Prince Rhys ap Tewdwr and one of his sons killed in battle with the Normans near Brecon. He was the last ruler of South Wales or the Kingdom of Deheubarth.

12th Century. The Commandery of Knights of St. John of Jerusalem was established at Slebech early in the twelfth century. It was granted lands in several parts of Pembrokeshire

1100. St.Davids church founded in Hubberston.

1100. Princess Nest married to Gerald de Windsor on orders of King Henry I.

1106 and 1116. King Henry I sends Flemish refugees from flooding to Rhos (the Dale Peninsula of Pembrokeshire).

1109. Princess Nest abducted by Owain ap Cadwgan

1138. Gilbert de Clare became the first Earl of Pembroke, created by King Steven in 1138. He was known as STRONGBOW for his prowess as an archer. The term was inherited by his son, Richard, Earl of Pembroke.

1056. Gruffydd ap Llywelyn becomes first King of all Wales.

1170. Richard de Clare, Earl of Pembroke assembled a fleet of knights and archers and sailed from the Milford Haven Waterway to invade Ireland and became King of Leinster. He did this against the wishes of King Henry II.

1170. Adam de Roche founded the Benedictine Priory in Lower Priory, Milford Haven.

1171. King Henry II sailed to Ireland with a fleet of 400 ships and army of 500 mounted knights, 4000 men at arms and many archers to prevent Ireland becoming a Norman state.

1185 and 1210. John (son of King Henry II) sailed from Milford Haven Waterway to Ireland.

1324. Earliest reference to coal mining in Pembrokeshire (inquisitor post mortem of Aymer de Valence, Earl of Pembroke).

1337. Princess Gwenllian executed by Normans.

1349. The Black Death ravages Wales.

1394 and 1399. King Richard II sailed from the Milford Haven Waterway to Ireland.

1405. A French squadron of ships landed troops in the Milford Haven

Waterway in support of Owain Glyndwr and his army of 8000 men. They then unsuccessfully lay siege to Haverfordwest Castle, but destroyed the town and then marched across South Wales to invade England. Their meeting with the Kings army was a standoff and starvation drove them back to Wales.

1479. The status of county was conferred on Haverfordwest with a charter of incorporation in 1479 and was confirmed under the Acts of Union in 1542/3. In 1761 it was granted its own Lord Lieutenant. It ceased to be a parliamentary constituency in 1885.

1485. Henry Tudor (born Pembroke Castle in 1457) landed at Mill Bay near Dale after fourteen years exile with an army of 2000 French mercenaries. He was joined by Sir Rhys ap Thomas with his army and the two marched together to the Battle of Bosworth field where King Richard III was defeated and the House or Tudor established with Henry crowned as King Henry VII.

1505. Sir Rhys ap Thomas held a great tournament at Carew Castle to celebrate his being made a Knight of the Garter by King Henry VII.

1535 and 1542. King Henry VIII ends the Marcher Lordships with the Laws of Wales Act and forms the shires including Pembrokeshire.

1536 to 1541. Dissolution of the monasteries, priories, convents and friaries in England, Wales and Ireland by Parliamentary Acts under King Henry VIII.

16th Century. William Camden (1551-1623) in his BRITANNIA referred to the Flemings in Pembrokeshire and stated 'their little territory is called by the Britains ANGLIA TRANSWALLIA'.

1642. Start of the Civil War. Only Pembroke and Tenby declare for Parliament.

1644. Royalist forces under Lord Carbery lay siege to Pembroke Castle. But the Parliamentary fleet arrived by sea to lift the siege and attack Royalists at the Battle of Colby Moor.

1648. Siege of Pembroke Castle by Oliver Cromwell and Parliamentarian troops against rebellious Parliamentarian troops in the castle.

1651-53. A second plague of Black Death rages in Pembrokeshire.

1758. Sir William Hamilton marries Catherine Barlow of Slebech who owned much property in Pembrokeshire including the lordship of Hubberston and Pill.

1782. Sir William Hamilton inherits Hubberston and Pill.

1790. An Act of Parliament received royal assent for Sir William Hamilton and his heirs to build quays, docks, piers and a market in the Lordship of Hubberston and Pill in the County of Pembroke.

1791. Sir William Hamilton marries Emma Hart who becomes Lady Emma Hamilton.

1792. First whaling ship with America whalers from Nantuckett arrives in the Milford Haven waterway to settle and set up a whaling industry to sell oil for the street lamps of London. The industry operated out of Milford until around 1820.

1796. The Navy Board starts building ships at Hubberston Pill.

1797. Last Invasion of Britain. Four ships carrying a French expeditionary force led by an American arrive and land near Fishguard but soon surrendered shortly afterwards after a spree of drunken looting.

1797. A whale oil warehouse is built at Milford Haven.

1802. Lord Nelson, Sir William and Lady Hamilton arrive in Pembrokeshire on their famous tour and the new town's first hotel is renamed 'The Lord Nelson Hotel' which still operates today on the Front Street renamed Hamilton Terrace.

1809. Work abandoned on the Greville Observatory, Milford Haven.

1810. Many Quakers return to America because whale oil demand falls as gas lamps appear.

1814. Workers move from Milford Haven to form a new dockyard at Paterchurch. It was named Pembroke Dockyard by the mayor of Pembroke in 1817. The Naval Dockyard at Pembroke Dock operated as a ship building center throughout the nineteenth century and became the finest shipbuilding yard in the world. It completed 250 naval vessels and five royal yachts and employed up to 3000 people.

1856. Isambard Kingdom Brunel's South Wales Railway line completed to Neyland and the Great Western Hotel was built on the waterfront.

1860 – 63. Hubberston Fort is built.

1875. The *Great Eastern* arrives in Milford Haven to refit after laying Trans-Atlantic Cables, and remains there until 1880.

1888. The first ship enters the completed Milford Docks. She was *the Sybil* a 127 ton steam trawler. She marked the beginning of the fishing era that lasted until 1959.

1914. Belgian fishermen arrive as refugees in Milford Haven.

1930. Former Naval Dockyard at Pembroke Dock was transferred to the Air Ministry for use as the main Atlantic flying boat and seaplane base for both the RAF and Royal Navy. It operated for twenty-three years and was closed in 1959.

1940. German Navy starts dropping mines in the Milford Haven waterway.

1944. Seebees (American Naval Construction Unit) build a temporary hospital near Hubberston Fort anticipating D-Day casualties.

1959. End of the fishing industry at Milford Haven when Iceland extends her fishing limits further offshore. A last ditch attempt to find new fishing grounds off the coast of Africa fails.

1960. H.R.H. the Duke of Edinburgh opens the first oil refinery (Esso) at Herbrandston on the Milford Haven Waterway.

1964. Texaco Oil Refinery opened by the Queen.

1968. Opening of Gulf Oil Refinery by Royal Family.

1983. Esso Oil Refinery closes.

1989. Royal Armament Depot closed.

2009. Opening of first Liquid Natural Gas terminal at South Hook, Milford Haven by HM The Queen, Prince Phillip, Prince Andrew and the Emir of Qatar

2009. Opening of the Dragon Liquid Natural Gas terminal at Waterston, Milford Haven.

APPENDIX 2. HISTORIC PLACES TO VISIT IN PEMBROKESHIRE.

North Pembrokeshire.
1. A drive through the Preseli Mountains with a stop at the Foel Eryr lookout. www.howwetravel.co.uk/foel-eryr/

2. The Neolothic burial chamber of Pentre Ifan (signposted on the north side of the Preselies) and Carreg Coetan Arthur burial chamber in Newport.
    https://cadw.gov.wales/visit/places-to-visit/pentre-ifan-burial-chamber
    https://cadw.gov.wales/visit/places-to-visit/
    carreg-coetan-arthur-burial-chamber

3. Gors Fawr Stone Circle near Maenclochog Dde.
    www.stone-circles.org.uk/stone/gorsfawr.htm

4. Foel Drygarn near Maenclochog Dde.
    www.babyroutes.co.uk/walking-routes/pembrokeshire-walks/
    foel-drygarn-hill-fort-walk/

5. The reconstructed Iron Age village of Castell Henllys.
    www.castellhenllys.com

6. Bird, whale and dolphin watching from Strumble Head.
    www.andrewswalks.co.uk/strumble-head.html

7. A visit to St Davids cathedral www.stdavidscathedral.org.uk

8. A boat trip to Ramsay Island www.ramsayislandcruises.co.uk

South Pembrokeshire.
1. The Quaker walk in Milford Haven
    (see: www.milfordhavenquakers.org/blank-page)

2. A visit to Pembroke Castle www.pembrokecastle.co.uk and the medieval town (see: www.pembroketownguide.org.uk and click on 'Visit Pembroke Town Gide' that has a map of the walk).

3. Carew Castle and medieval cross. www.carewcastle.com

4. Manorbier Castle www.manorbiercastle.co.uk

5. Mullock Bridge www.dyfedarchaeology.org.uk/HCL/milford/area/316.htm

6. St. Mary's church and effigies in Carew Cheriton village. www.stmaryscarew.com

7. Upton Castle, church, effigies and garden www.visitpembrokeshire.com/attraction-listing/upton-castle-gardens

8. Haverfordwest Priory (ruins) www.coflein.gov.uk/en/site/94103/

9. The Priory (ruins), Milford Haven www.pillpriory.co.uk

10. The Admiral Nelson Hotel, Milford Haven www.historypoints.org/index.php?page=the-lord-nelson-hotel

11. Pembroke Dockyard and The Sunderland Museum. www.sunderlandtrust.org.uk

12. A day trip to Skomer Island to see the puffins and blue bell carpets. www.pembrokeshire-islands.co.uk

13. Hoyle's Mouth Cave near Tenby Golf course, Penally. www.ancientmonuments.uk/129995-hoyle-mouth-cave-penally

14. The sunken forest at Marros www.thebeachguide.co.uk/south-wales/carmarthenshire/marros-sands.htm

15. A visit to Bosherton's lily ponds www.nationaltrust.org.uk/stackpole/trails/bosherston-lily-ponds-freshwater-magic-walk

APPENDIX 3. SOME INFORMATIVE WEBSITES.

Milford Haven Quakers www.quakers-in-Pembrokeshire.org.uk

British National Parks www.nationalparks.gov.uk

Castell Henllys Iron Age Fort www.castellhenllys.com

Pembrokeshire coast path national trail www.nt.pcnpa.org.uk

Pembrokeshire Coast National Park www.pembrokeshirecoast.org.uk

The Pembrokeshire Bookshop (with a good selection of books on Pembrokeshire) www.pembrokebooks.co.uk

The Pembrokeshire Walking Trail – Accessible trails for walking, cycling and horse-riding www.walkingpembrokeshire.co.uk

The Coast Path of Wales www.walescoastpath.gov.uk

Flying Boat Centre Pembroke Dock www.sunderlandtrust.org.uk

Visit Skomer, Skolkholm, Grassholm islands www.pembrokeshire-islands.co.uk

Visit Skomer. Skolkholm, Grassholm www.boatrides.co.uk

Ramsay Island Cruises www.ramsayislandcruises.co.uk

Carew Castle www.carewcastle.com

Pembroke Castle www.pembrokecastle.co.uk

Manorbier Castle www.manorbiercastle.co.uk

Other Castles www.cadw.wales.gov.uk

Solva Woolen Mill www.solvawoolenmill.co.uk

Tenby Museum and Art Gallery www.tenbymuseum.org.uk

ACKNOWLEDGEMENTS

This volume came about because I lived for thirty years as a geologist in Saudi Arabia. The television was not worth watching and the internet was banned for most of the time. There were no cinemas, nightclubs, bars nor churches. So I used to carry out a pile of books and read widely. The histories were written mainly using my own library. However the manuscript was greatly improved by two peer reviewers - Mr David Norris and Mr Edward Perkins of the Pembrokeshire Historical Society. They not only provided me with information but identified publications of which I was unaware. Some of these books are large and rare and not found in many libraries. Here Project Gutenberg helped, also the newspaper archives of the National Library of Wales. I am indebited to Dr Sandra Coates-Smith, Secretary to The Pembrokeshire Historical Society for persauding members Mr David Norris ad Mr. Edward Perkins to peer review the manuscript. The chapter on Paleolithic hunters was much improved by an excellent online lecture by Dr. Rick Peterson on two of the Pembrokeshire caves organised by the Royal Society of Biology. Wikipedia provided valuable checks on name spellings and dates.

My thanks also go to my family with whom I enjoyed a lifetime of summer holidays in Pembrokeshire. Special thanks to Mr Michael Webb of Milford Haven who accompanied me on some of the exploration, including a two day summer search in dense undergrowth and fallen trees to find Hoyle's Mouth Cave. To Tenby Golf Club for permission to visit the caves. To Mr Roland Edwards, Warden of St. Mary's Church at Carew Cheriton village for opening the church during a Covid lockdown to allow me to photograph the effigies. The staff and curator of Milford Haven Museum are thanked for permission to photograph the mammoth tusk. My gratitude to Charlotte Mouncey for her hard and dedicated work in producing this book, to Emma Lockley for the indexing and to artist Maria Priestley for turning my rough sketches into some of the figures. Plate 8 is published under license to the Royal Commission on the Ancient and Historical Monuments of Wales. I thank my wife Dr Anne Roobol for reading through the proofs.

INDEX

Note: Biographies of most people named here are today readily available on the internet and Wikipedia.

D

H